Ecclesianarchy

Ecclesianarchy

Adaptive Ministry for a Post-Church Society

John Williams

scm press

Published in 2020 by SCM Press
Editorial office
3rd Floor, Invicta House
108–114 Golden Lane,
London EC1Y 0TG, UK
www.scmpress.co.uk

SCM Press is an imprint of Hymns Ancient & Modern Ltd
(a registered charity)

Hymns Ancient & Modern® is a registered trademark of
Hymns Ancient & Modern Ltd
13A Hellesdon Park Road, Norwich,
Norfolk NR6 5DR, UK

British Library Cataloguing in Publication data
A catalogue record for this book is available
from the British Library

978-0-334-05980-6

Typeset by Regent Typesetting
Printed and bound by
CPI Group (UK) Ltd

Contents

Preface

This book has been a long time in gestation. A few years ago, after over 40 years of active participation in the Church of England, 30 of them in ordained ministry, I came to a troubling conclusion: a surplus of ecclesiology and ministerial theology is impeding the prospect of the Church renewing its connection with contemporary people, culture and society.

As a newly practising Christian in the 1970s, I was introduced to shared, collaborative, 'every-member' models of ministry. From my time at theological college in the 1980s, my commitment to these became intentional and strategic. I strove to develop these practices in parochial ministry in the 1990s, and worked to help other parishes do the same in a diocesan post in the early 2000s. I also tried to attend to my own development as a practical theologian, completing a doctoral thesis in 1986, and contributing to diocesan ministry strategies, writing discussion papers and publishing articles in ministry practitioner-related journals.

From 2008 until my retirement in 2017, I held a senior lecturer post in theology and ministry, teaching students in training for both lay and ordained ministries at diocesan schools of ministry. During this time, I continued to research and publish in the field of evolving patterns of ministry in the Church of England and other mainstream denominational churches. Towards the end of this period, I developed an interest in the emerging independent churches, together with the growth of chaplaincy as a fascinating but under-reported alternative ministry model. The more I reflected on my experience as a practitioner and theological educator, scrutinized ministerial strategies being pioneered within my own church communion and learned more about the approaches being taken within the new churches, the more the troubling conclusion referred to above was borne in upon me.

This book is my attempt to work through the unsettling position I have reached, to locate it in a wider historical and contemporary socio-cultural context, to analyse and assess its implications and conduct a thought experiment. Supposing the churches could suspend ecclesiological constructs and reimagine ministerial order without restraint, in response to present-day needs, what might the resulting expressions of ecclesiality look like? I have coined the term *ecclesianarchy* to capture this, because – although critics might accuse me of wanting to unleash chaos – I believe a case can be made for treating anarchy as a valid, if challenging, conceptuality for the character of 'church'.

I want to make two points for the avoidance of misunderstanding. My approach is sometimes provocative, but there is absolutely no intention to disparage or belittle the challenges faced and sacrifices made by thousands of ministers, lay and ordained, who have to work within the inherited ecclesial structures. The second point is that this is not a manifesto for any particular form of alternative, experimental or radical form of church and ministry. My argument is that all models can be burdened by an excess of ecclesiology, wherever requirements for the proper structuring of the life of the Church and the ordering of its ministry are regarded as warranted by fundamental theological tradition. I have concluded that there should be many expressions of church that do things in startlingly different ways; but not that any one of them can justifiably lay claim to be the *correct* way, in the sense of *God-given*.

I am grateful to all those who have encouraged me over the years to pursue my thinking about ministry and to commit some of those thoughts to writing. Among them I must pay tribute to two now departed this life, Bishop Geoffrey Paul, who when Bishop of Hull first stimulated my appetite for theology in the late 1970s, and Professor, later Bishop, Stephen Sykes, who encouraged me to undertake doctoral studies in Durham in the 1980s. Other mentors and supporters have included colleagues and advocates of shared ministry in the Diocese of Wakefield between 1993 and 2008, among them Canon Margaret Bradnum, Canon Dr John Lawson and the Revd Janet Sargent; and Bishop Stephen Platten, who gave me a positive steer towards developing my academic interests and publishing my work. Among colleagues at York St John University from 2008 to 2017, Louise Redshaw, Professor Andrew Village and Dr Ann Christie have been friends and supporters on my theological pilgrimage towards this book. Professor Jeff Astley gave me valuable guidance about publishers and proposals. Thanks are also due to those who commented helpfully on drafts of some chapters of the book: my colleagues Andy Village and Chris Maunder, fellow advocates for collaborative ministry Malcolm Grundy and Joanna Cox, and two of my students, Jonathan Foster and Rachel Shackleton. Last, I need to thank my wife Ann-Marie, who has understood my need for times of seclusion, sometimes away from home, in order to write.

Introduction

Post-church society and radical ecclesiology

The doctoral thesis I completed before ordination (Williams, 1986) opened my mind to two key issues I have grappled with ever since. The first concerns the evolving patterns of presence and influence of the churches under the impact of social, cultural and religious change, and hence the crucial relevance to ecclesiology of the sociology of religion. The second is the search for new expressions of ecclesiality: springing from a desire in the 1980s to respond to secularization, but today more often to 'postmodernity'. I use this term with a caveat: it is too soon to be certain whether it is a new era or a convulsion within the history of modernity, and therefore some may prefer to speak of 'late' or 'advanced' modernity, to avoid giving the impression that modernity is over and has been superseded by something else. The first part of this Introduction explains the terms used in the title of the book.

In the subtitle, the present context is designated a 'post-church society', defined by Mobsby and Berry (2014, pp. 1–2) as one in which 'the majority of the population do not attend church and no longer see the Church as a major feature of life'. Clearly this does not mean that church is no longer present; there are churches aplenty, and new ones are constantly being started. But in a 'post-church' society, the churches are most obviously characterized by what they are *no longer*. Across the societies of Western Europe that were the cradle, not of Christianity, but of Christendom, the churches no longer occupy the position or play the role that Christendom allocated to them. These societies, including Britain, in varying degrees no longer live under the 'sacred canopy' (Berger, 1967) of the Church: it no longer dominates day-to-day life; it is no longer obeyed, or even heeded, as the principal moral authority; its gospel is no longer heralded as the one and only saving truth. It no longer constitutes the spiritual or religious arm of government, except in certain vestigial or ceremonial ways. Churchgoing is no longer a social obligation, nor a badge of respectability; Sundays are no longer set aside for rest and worship. The churches are no longer the customary recourse at times of birth or marriage, and the same seems likely to happen in due course at times of death, as the last generation to have grown up as churchgoers dies out.

Attention to Christianity and its legacies continues to be manifested across a wide range of looser, less formal intimations and activities that no longer constitute 'church' in any substantive sense; *dis*organized religion prevails over the organized variety, and 'commitment' is no longer regarded as for the many, or even for a significant minority, but for the pious few. The ecclesial landscape is now one in which fresh expressions, pioneer ministries, new monasticisms, alternative worship communities, emergent collectives and more are jostling for prominence in a tide of ecclesial experimentation and innovation. Such an environment looks like anarchy by comparison with the stately, reassuring and familiar presence of inherited Church, an object of affection as well as the home of much undemonstrative piety.

In this book I am setting out to envisage how a historical institution like the Church of England might 'reimagine ministry' in a way more in tune with the fluidity and hybridity of cultural practices and social realities in the post-Christendom environment of advanced modernity. Such a project requires willingness to set aside a burdensome surplus of 'orthodox' ecclesiology and ministerial ordering, in order to travel light and gain a much swifter, more nimble responsiveness to changing circumstances. In recent years, many books have contributed to a reimagining of Christian ministry, drawing attention to a range of essential qualities for an effective ministry in the contemporary world. Robertson (2007) insists that ministry should be collaborative; Sadgrove (2008) urges the need for wisdom; Heywood (2011) commends a reimagining in line with a theology of mission; Starkey (2011) wants to rediscover creativity; Allain-Chapman (2012) and Smith (2014) emphasize resilience; Oliver (2012) counsels sanity; Thompson and Thompson (2012) recommend mindfulness. Each of these identifies a valuable necessity for twenty-first-century ministry: and I want to add another, that ministry is always and everywhere *adaptive*.

The quality of adaptivity, when applied to an organization or institution, signifies an inherent capacity for evolutionary variation in response to changing contexts. It lies beyond the scope of this work to delve further into organizational theory, but the following definition expresses how the term 'adaptive' captures what the Church needs to be:

'Situationally Adaptive Organizations' ('SAOs') are *adaptable, multi-structured hybrids that provide an organizational tool chest, rather than a single tool* [emphasis mine], so that the most appropriate organizational structure and resource can be optimally applied in response to rapidly changing and varied situations. (Chasan, 2014)

The best evidence we have from the earliest centuries of Christianity points to an attitude of adaptivity in the spirit of this definition: churches responding to circumstances as they evolved, 'making it up as they went along', trying things out ad hoc and adopting what seemed to work. The concept has been employed by Ann Morisy (2004, chapter 1), who argues that the contemporary Church is in an 'adaptive zone', which demands radical 'outside the box' thinking about ministry and mission. David Heywood has developed Morisy's ideas in relation to the Church as a learning community, where 'adaptive change' will be 'non-hierarchical' and entails a grass-roots movement of addressing 'outdated and inauthentic ways of working' in favour of innovation and experimentation (Heywood, 2017, pp. 3–4).

In advancing a case for an adaptive approach to ecclesiology and ministry appropriate to this post-church environment, this book proposes the term 'ecclesianarchy' to capture the character of the churches emerging in response to contemporary social and cultural change. The suffix '-archy' derives from the Greek *archē* (αρχή), originally conceived by Aristotle as the 'beginning' or 'efficient cause' that propels an idea into reality. For example, in the socio-political world the idea of a 'society', manifesting order and stability, requires a form of *archē* to create and sustain it, a foundation of rule and governance such as 'monarchy', literally 'rule by "one"' – that is, a named individual, or 'hierarchy', 'rule by a sacred authority', such as a priesthood. This range of meaning, from 'origin' to 'rule', is mirrored in the New Testament, where *archē* sometimes denotes 'beginning' or 'origin' (e.g. Mark 1.1; John 1.1; Acts 11.15; Phil. 4.15), and in other places 'ruler' or 'principality' (e.g. Luke 12.11; Rom. 8.38; Titus 3.1). The root meaning of 'anarchy' is therefore the *absence* of such an ordering structure.

The idea of 'ecclesianarchy' is therefore plainly paradoxical for the Church, which has historically modelled an ultimate *archē* through a hierarchical representation of the divine governance of this world, its political institutions, people and communities. It has been shaped and formed in such a way that innovations can only be contemplated as permitted deviations within a basically centralized hierarchical structure that functions as the guardian of historical continuity. Nowadays, such a Church increasingly appears remote, oppressive and uncongenial; church as ecclesianarchy is more like an organism, flourishing, waxing and waning in multiple adaptations and mutations over time and place. It is characterized by creative energy flowing among and between persons, by distribution and difference, and often by a bracing unpredictability. It is identified by fundamental ecclesial 'family resemblances', such as 'the apostles' teaching and fellowship, the breaking of bread and the prayers' (Acts 2.42).

These are the commitments that drive the enquiry conducted in this book. For the most part, I work within the discipline of a practical ecclesiology, drawing on over 40 years' experience of ministry, teaching, reflection and writing. I do not write as a researcher into primary sources, but as a theological educator striving to make the work of others available to a church public beyond the academic guilds to which it is too often restricted. In consequence my approach is eclectic, bringing together material from a wide range of sources to develop and amplify my arguments. In the academic world this may seem an overly ambitious strategy, but since nowadays I have neither a career to advance nor a reputation to protect, it is a risk I am willing to take. The bibliography indicates the scope of my reading from both theological and sociological perspectives in the literature of historical and contemporary Church, ministry and mission. The next section goes on to say a little more about the present context.

Twenty-first-century developments

Mission-shaped Church

For more than 15 years, the Church of England has been committed to a process of reimagining Christian ministry in response to social and cultural change. The *Mission-shaped Church* report (Archbishops' Council of the Church of England, 2004) recommended that every diocese should have 'a strategy for the encouragement of ... fresh expressions of church, reflecting the network and neighbourhood reality of society and of mission opportunity' (p. 145). Addressing the General Synod in November 2010, the Archbishop of Canterbury, Rowan Williams, endorsed the 'quinquennium goals' for the Church, the second of which was 'to re-shape or reimagine the Church's ministry for the century coming, so as to make sure that there is a growing and sustainable Christian witness in every local community'. Out of this came an ongoing initiative of 'reimagining ministry', headed up by the Church's Ministry Division (General Synod of the Church of England, 2012).

On becoming Archbishop of Canterbury, Justin Welby commended these initiatives in his address to Synod in July 2013, stating that the goals 'force us to look afresh at all our structures, to reimagine ministry, whether it be the ministry of General Synod, or the parish church, or a great cathedral, or anything between all of those three' (Ministry Division of the Church of England, 2013). Subsequently, the Church of England launched a more wide-ranging programme entitled 'Renewal and Reform', which produced a suite of reports and recommendations covering all aspects of the Church's life from ministerial training to laws concerning churchyards. The report *Developing Discipleship* (2015) offered 'Ten Marks of a Diocese Committed to Developing Disciples', one of which was that 'innovation and experiment are encouraged in mission, ministry and discipleship'.

Since the *Mission-shaped Church* report, much strategic thinking about ministry and mission in the Church of England (and elsewhere) has been influenced by what I have called a 'popular postmodernity' (Williams, 2011) which selects certain elements of a postmodern analysis of twenty-first-century cultures and societies, and seeks to shape a church response to them. These responses, typified by the growth of 'fresh expressions of church', have tended to focus on the challenges of communication and presentation: how can 'church' be made more culturally accessible? How might it achieve a closer fit with the cultural attitudes of the post-baby-boomer generations who have become progressively more alienated from conventional organized religion? Innovations have rarely been allowed to penetrate the ecclesiological foundations of inherited patterns of ordained ministry, resulting in rising tensions in some new church contexts, as previously unchurched people raise awkward questions about the degree of conformity to 'traditional church' that can be required of them. These challenges lead to doubts about whether the 'Mission-shaped Church' formula can be enough, and so the final part of this introductory discussion turns to one example of a more radical option.

Post-Christendom church

The notion of the post-Christendom church as the only viable future is exemplified in the work of Stuart Murray (2004, second edition 2018), who analyses the culture of Christendom as the condition in which Christianity became 'normative religion' in the Western world from the time of Constantine onwards. Society is treated as having been Christian-ized, key social institutions are uncritically seen as founded on Christian principles, and the population are regarded as Christian by default unless they explicitly opt out (for a useful summary, see pp. 82–7). Murray argues that this dominant paradigm has bequeathed to the Church a legacy of deeply ingrained inherited patterns of thinking and practice that have now become profoundly problematic.

Murray identifies four ways in which what he calls a 'Christendom mindset' has been operative in the churches. First, there is a misuse of the Bible, as selected Old Testament texts and concepts are treated as on a par with the life and teaching of Jesus as a source for both ecclesiology and social and political teaching (pp. 120–1). Among the examples he considers are the defence of sacral monarchy (p. 191), the Sabbatarianism of the 'keep Sunday special' campaign (p. 197), and the rejection of pacifism in favour of 'just war' theory (pp. 116 ff., 204). Second, as a means of religious social control, Christendom privileges doctrinal and ritual conformity over authentic Christian lifestyle based on the Gospels, as the touchstone of a living faith (pp. 121–4). Third, by its co-option of entire populations into the Christian religion, Christendom creates and sustains a 'two-tier Christianity': hence the clergy–laity divide and the distinction between 'committed' and 'nominal' believers (pp. 125–8). Fourth, Christendom supports coercive practices in evangelism and regards the maintenance of social *order*, forcibly if necessary, as a greater value than the promotion of social *justice* (pp. 130–2).

Although these Christendom characteristics might be expected to be found most often among traditional defenders of the established churches, Murray also sees the Christendom mindset at work among evangelicals committed to new strategies for mission. This is evident whenever approaches to evangelism continue to trade on assumptions about a continuing unfocused 'goodwill' towards the Church; when experimental forms of worship continue within the paradigm of 'performance', presentation and monologue; and when moral causes are taken up that collude with conventional notions of social order, rather than promoting social justice through the practice of radical discipleship (pp. 200 ff.). In essence, Murray wants to see little companies of disciples of Jesus, formed around a multiplicity of needs and opportunities, often acting as communities of resistance, peacemakers and reconcilers, breaking bread informally around the common table, listening and conversing across the boundaries of faiths and unbelief. It is an Anabaptist vision containing much for the so-called mainstream churches to ponder.

All of the issues raised briefly in this Introduction will be treated at greater length in the chapters that follow; here is an aid to navigation.

Outline of chapters

Chapter 1 contextualizes the study within a broad, selective analysis of the impact of contemporary sociological and cultural change on religion, church and ministry, sufficient to set out the major points of challenge. Chapter 2 attempts to provide a wider contextualization of my argument by way of a historical reading of ecclesiology and ministerial theology and practice as essentially contested. Readers who are less interested in the longer historical context of debates about ministry may choose to omit this chapter. Chapters 3 and 4 focus on two crucial areas of unresolved debate: the historical and contemporary expression of Christian ministry in the threefold order of bishops, priests and deacons, and the underlying theologies, and inherent problems, of ordination. Chapters 5 to 8 survey adaptations of ministry developed over the last few decades in response to the pressures of social and cultural change: varieties of shared, lay and collaborative ministry, the impact of Pentecostal and charismatic traditions, the particular case of chaplaincy, and the Fresh Expressions initiative. Chapters 9 and 10 employ a 'deconstructive' approach to respond to the climate of postmodernity, remodelling the social role of Christian faith in terms of the practice of the 'impossible', and envisaging the deconstructed church as an 'ecclesianarchy' with an adaptive, decentralized ministry. Chapters 11 and 12 address some practical implications for the theological education and personal support of ministers, focusing on the tensions between role and person. The Conclusion reprises the argument of the book as a whole and suggests some ways forward.

I

Liquid Modernity: Hallmarks of the Post-Church Society

The condition of postmodernity

This chapter offers an overview of features of the contemporary cultural environment in the post-Christendom West that challenge the churches to reimagine their ministry and mission. The first task is to establish what is meant by describing the context as 'postmodern'.

At the beginning of his seminal work *The Postmodern Condition*, Jean-François Lyotard announced: 'Our working hypothesis is that the status of knowledge is altered as societies enter what is known as the post-industrial age and cultures enter what is known as the postmodern age' (1984, p. 3). In particular, this altered status of knowledge manifests in an 'incredulity towards metanarratives', or 'big stories' (*grands récits*) that purport to provide a unified overarching framework of explanatory power, within which all other fields of knowledge achieve their proper interpretation. As Tim Woods puts it, 'there is a disillusionment with ambitious "total explanations" of reality such as those offered by science, or religion, or political programmes like Communism' (2009, p. 20). Two crucial points stand out at once. First, the thesis of postmodernity is of enormous relevance for theology and the Church, which have historically relied heavily upon precisely the kind of 'grand narrative' now called into question. Second, whereas at the height of modernity, empiricists argued that science has rendered religion untenable as a source of true knowledge, the postmodern temper problematizes both science and religion insofar as they make these totalizing claims.

It is important to note that Lyotard refers to the postmodern *condition*. This is significant for theologians, because it leaves open the possibility of recognizing the cultural styles and attitudes we classify as 'postmodern' (the 'condition'), to which the churches need to respond, while retaining a critical distance with regard to the philosophy. This distinction is observed by Graham Ward, who uses the term postmodern*ism* for the more theoretical philosophical framework, and postmodern*ity* to refer to the experienced cultural situation (Ward (ed.), 2005, p. xiv). It would be a denial of the postmodern mindset itself to embrace 'postmodernism' as an *'ism'*, turning it into some kind of grand narrative in its own right. The churches, therefore, have tended to engage with the indicators of 'postmodernity', the cultural condition of our time, rather than with 'postmodernism' and its philosophers.

Stanley Grenz writes of the erosion of confidence in a series of 'myths' of modernity: that progress is inevitable, that 'truth is certain and hence purely rational', and that 'knowledge is [wholly] objective' (1996, p. 7). In abandoning 'the quest for a unified grasp of objective reality', the postmodern mood calls into question the idea of a *'univ*erse', in the face of the irreducible plurality and unending 'flow' of knowledge that resists being gathered and demystified into a single field. As David Harvey puts it, faced with 'ephemerality, fragmentation, discontinuity and the chaotic', the postmodern mind 'swims, even wallows, in the fragmentary and chaotic currents of change as if that is all there is' (1990, p. 44). From an evangelical Christian perspective, Kieran Beville depicts the postmodern person as 'intimately fractured', struggling to find a connected, relational identity, manifesting fluidity of personality and worldview, with a rejection of dogmatism and a desire for experience, a longing for community, and an openness to the supernatural (2016, pp. 95–118).

These features of the condition of postmodernity are manifested in the popular phenomenon of the quest for 'spirituality'. In 2005, Channel 4 ran a series called *Spirituality Shopper* in which non-religious young people were given a variety of 'taster experiences' of spiritual practices to discover whether they would find some personal benefit in them. An entertaining review appeared in the *Daily Mirror*:

> In the first of three programmes, triple-jumping Christian Jonathan Edwards performs a mystical makeover on 29-year-old Michaela Newton-Wright, whose great job in advertising leaves her feeling strangely shallow and unfulfilled. Explaining that it's not necessary for her to actually believe in any of the religions, Jonathan introduces Michaela to an array of God-bothering options for her to mix and match. She gets lessons in Buddhist meditation, cooks a meal for friends on the Jewish Sabbath, gives Sufi dancing a whirl, visits one rather surprised old lady and is even persuaded to give up hair straighteners for an imaginary Lent. It's easy to scoff at the idea that spiritual enlightenment can be achieved in four weeks without believing in anything at all ... But amazingly after one month the transformation in Michaela is astonishing – her hair really is much, much curlier. (Jane Simon, 'Today's TV', *Daily Mirror*, 6 June 2005; cit. Voas and Bruce, 2007, p. 52)

Despite the typically sceptical and humorous journalistic tone, this does capture several familiar elements in the culture of popular postmodernity. Michaela is entirely alienated from any kind of conventional religion or church life. She is attracted by the notion of not having to *believe* anything but just to experience it, the idea of an entirely eclectic approach to giving things a try, and the expectation that the objective is some sort of personal therapeutic or cosmetic benefit. Today's churches have to operate in an environment where Michaela's attitudes and responses are commonplace, and the cultural landscape is critical for the expressions of both church and mission that will or will not connect with someone like her. A somewhat ironic addendum to this story is that within a couple of years of hosting this programme, Edwards himself publicly announced the loss of his Christian faith when he abruptly pulled out of his role as a presenter of BBC's *Songs of Praise* in February 2007. The encounter with the condition of postmodernity at its most prolifically relativistic can indeed be corrosive of conventional religious convictions.

Church responses: accommodation or resistance

Within the world of organized religion, the responses to the postmodern temper have tended to be expressed as a binary choice between accommodation and resistance. As Hannah Steele asks in her exposition of the theology of the 'emerging church' movement, 'is the church subject to the whims of cultural change, forced to compromise and change or risk inevitable extinction? Or is the church to function as a prophetic voice to be followed?' (2017, p. 155). Steele herself strongly favours the latter option, but put in these binary terms this is a false choice. A degree of accommodation is always inevitable, as the Church cannot help but be part of the culture; but it is from *within* that compromised position that the gospel handed on *through* culture continues to harbour the subversive alternatives that can break out afresh when the time is opportune (see Martin, 1980).

The binary choice of accommodation or resistance was prevalent in the 1960s in relation to the response of the churches, not yet to postmodernity, but to secularization. Some more progressive theologians sought to respond in terms of a moderate adaptation of church and mission to cultural change (Richardson, 1966; Barry, 1969), whereas others of more conservative views judged them to have capitulated to the spirit of the age, and urged a more robust affirmation of orthodox essentials (Mascall, 1965; Holloway, 1972). Yet at just this time, a major debate about the 'secularization thesis' was beginning within the sociology of religion (Wilson, 1966; Martin, 1967). Bryan Wilson defined secularization as 'the process whereby religious thinking, practice and institutions lose social significance' (1966, p. 14), an inevitable and irreversible consequence of the advance of modernity. David Martin on the other hand demanded a much more complex analysis of what was happening to religion under the conditions of modernity: 'far from being secular, our culture wobbles between a partially absorbed Christianity, biased towards comfort and the need for confidence, and beliefs in fate, luck and moral governance incongruously joined together' (1967, p. 76).

A defining moment in the de-churching of society that made significant advances in the 1960s (Brown, 2001) was the 'ferment' that came to its most prominent public focus in the events surrounding the publication of John Robinson's *Honest to God* (1963), in which the 'accommodation versus resistance' debate was central. The next section will take this as a case study, not so much considering the contents of Robinson's book as the lessons to be learned from the controversy it precipitated.

Honesty to God in the swinging sixties

In post-war Britain, religion (and especially Church of England religion) remained a powerful mainstay of inherited moral attitudes. Brown and Lynch cite the case of Margaret Knight, a lecturer in psychology, who in 1955 presented two talks on the BBC making the case for humanism, and urging that religious education should encourage a non-dogmatic attitude towards diverse faith traditions. One newspaper warned: 'Don't let this woman fool you. She looks – doesn't she? – just like a typical housewife: cool, comfortable, harmless. But Mrs Margaret Knight is a menace. A dangerous woman. Make no mistake about that' (cit. Brown and Lynch, 2012, p. 332). Had today's technology been available then, she would no doubt have been subjected to a torrent of abuse on Twitter.

Within a decade, the 'menace' of Mrs Knight's views steadily became normal public ethical discourse; 'religiously-legitimated moral principles' were now 'the preserve of committed minorities, rather than being part of the taken-for-granted assumptions of the majority of the population' (McLeod, 1995, p. 4). The fallout from this was noteworthy, focused nowhere better than in the publication of *Honest to God*, a slim paperback by the Bishop of Woolwich, John Robinson, a former Cambridge biblical scholar, proposing an overhaul in the Church's thinking about the fundamentals of theology and morality (for the *Honest to God* debate, see Clements, 1988, chapter 7; Bowden (ed.), 1993; Williams, 1986 and 2015). As a bishop, Robinson had scandalized the media by giving evidence in favour of the publication of *Lady Chatterley's Lover* at the obscenity trial of October 1960. His remark that 'what Lawrence is trying to do is to portray the sex relationship as something essentially sacred … as in a real sense an act of holy communion' (cit. James, 1987, p. 95) was a piece of 'modern theology' far beyond what most of those who heard of it could take (Williams, 1986, p. 159).

Robinson's prior notoriety, combined with some high-profile efforts by the churches in the early 1960s to respond to the onset of a sharp decline in attendances by various strategies of modernization, often through the medium of popular culture, were critical factors in extending the reach of *Honest to God* to a wider audience. Debates about updating the Church were already under way: for example, at Salisbury Cathedral a 'Pop Evensong' was held, which produced the response from one critic: 'it does not speak very highly for the standard of preaching nowadays if the only method of drawing people to Church is to pander to their worst instincts' (*Church Times*, 6 April 1962). John Robinson went on ITV's youthful religious magazine *Sunday Break* to be quizzed by a group of sceptical teenagers; and the Archbishop of York, Donald Coggan, discussed God, sex and the younger generation with the pop singer Adam Faith on the BBC. (Coggan said, 'Religion is so jolly relevant to this life.')

On 4 November 1962, the BBC's flagship religious discussion programme, *Meeting Point*, featured the Cambridge theologian Alec Vidler in conversation with the agnostic journalist Paul Ferris, who was a keen commentator on the affairs of the Church of England (Ferris, 1964). The ensuing controversy was not caused by anything critical about the Church said by Ferris, the self-confessed outsider, but the remarks of the insider Vidler, who signally failed to assume the role of the Church's defender. Among the opinions he advanced were that the Church ought not to concentrate so much on 'religion', that open discussion should replace the sermon, and that he was 'bored with parsons' and thought the 'clerical caste' ought to be abolished. In response to the *Church Times* report under the headline 'Cambridge Priest's Attack on Church', one woman wrote: 'Those of us who are struggling to teach the young and uphold our Churchmanship in a materialist world are not helped when her ordained ministers themselves deny all that we have received and learnt to hold most dear.' Put crudely, the BBC was now living in the 1960s, while this woman remained lodged firmly in the 1950s.

Honest to God thus became the rallying point for those on either side of the debate about the future of the churches and the vitality of faith in a context of secularization, towards either a more far-reaching adaptation to the 'modern world' on the one hand, or a more vehement confrontation of it on the other. Within the overall 'accommodation versus resistance' question, key issues in Robinson's writings included whether conventional organized religion continued to have value as a vehicle for conveying the reality of God to contemporary men and women, and whether faithful church membership was compatible with a spirit of critical, open enquiry towards the dogmatic and moral teachings of the Church. All of these issues are present with still greater urgency in the situation facing the churches more than half a century later and are relevant to how they approach the need to reimagine ministry.

What is different is that in the early years of the twenty-first century, the favoured sociological framework for thinking about church renewal has shifted from secularization to 'postmodernity' (Archbishops' Council of the Church of England, 2004), but it remains the case that either 'selling out' to the culture, or railing 'prophetically' against it, is a false dichotomy. The Church cannot speak 'into' the culture from some hypothetical neutral space beyond it, but must tackle head-on the ways in which the culture is both forming and challenging it as an institution, and the faith it proclaims. Only if this takes place might some kind of 'prophetic' outcome be envisaged; but this happens only on the far side of the movement of deconstruction, to be explored in Chapters 9 and 10. Before proceeding any further with an analysis of the contemporary cultural landscape, however, it will be helpful to sketch the contours of the journey by which we got to where we are.

Narratives of decline

In historical perspective, there is actually much to celebrate in the state of the churches in the third millennium: church buildings have never been better kept; clergy have never been more thoroughly trained; congregations have never been more actively involved in sharing ministry; worship has never been better led, on the whole, than today. But *churchgoing* has largely ceased to be a regular habit. The *Church Health Check*, published in a four-part series in the *Church Times* under the oversight of Linda Woodhead, is forthright about the statistics:

> The Church's greatest failure in our lifetime has been its refusal to take decline seriously. The situation is now so grave that it is no longer enough simply to focus on making parts grow again. The whole structure needs to be reviewed from top to toe, and creative and courageous decisions need to be made. (31 January 2014)

The narrative of decline is traced typically from a high point somewhere in the late nineteenth century. This choice of timescale makes it easy to attribute declining churchgoing to an advancing process of secularization beginning with the Enlightenment and the Industrial Revolution, and accelerating throughout the last century. Callum Brown draws on a range of oral testimony to record numerous examples of the drift away from regular churchgoing among the generations born towards the end of the nineteenth century and early in the twentieth:

> 'Mum and dad were not churchgoers, but we were made to go to Sunday School always' ... 'hundred per cent Christians but not church-goers', teetotallers who never gambled and who made their children say prayers at night ... parents who only went to church to christen their children, but ... [son] went to a massive range of religious organ-isations, including Sunday School, Band of Hope and the Church of England where he was a choirboy ... parents ... not churchgoers in the 1900s, but they kept a strict Sabbath with no games, play or work, and clean and special clothes to be worn ... (2001, pp. 142–3)

The generational change that initially saw parents abandoning church-going in adult life, but still favouring some kind of church affiliation on the part of their children, through Sunday schools and various youth organizations, has led further down the line to a progressive alienation. Adults whose only active involvement with the Church was being sent by their parents to children's activities have not opted to do the same for their own children on becoming parents themselves, leading in due course to a generation where neither parents nor children have ever had any experience of church at all, except possibly for the occasional christening, wedding or funeral. David Voas has concluded on the statistical evidence from a Europe-wide survey that 'each generation in every country is less religious than the last' (Voas, cit. Moynagh, 2017, p. 121).

Steve Bruce, a sociologist who continues the tradition represented by Bryan Wilson, regards this failure to pass on the habit of churchgoing to the next generation as a key critical factor in what he expects to be an irre-versible trend: 'Churches decline because they lose members – by death or defection – faster than they recruit ... we have enough information to sug-gest that the main problem is declining success in socializing the offspring of members' (Bruce, 2011, p. 69). Grace Davie, whose sociological work on the other hand owes much to David Martin, is more sanguine, accept-ing the 'statistics of decline' but offering a more positive evaluation than Bruce of the continuing substratum of Christian influence and presence within British society that will help to keep the churches ticking over:

> The centre of British society is gradually drifting away from Christianity, but remains deeply coloured by it ... engaged Christians are likely to become one minority amongst others, but will have the weight of history on their side – an advantage that brings with it considerable responsibility. (Davie, 2015, pp. 223–4)

However, the measurement of decline by looking at churchgoing figures starting from a Victorian high point begs the question whether there was previously a golden era of Christian piety, devotion and commitment and, if so, when it was. This is by no means easy to establish, because in an era of Christendom, when the Church occupies a dominant position in society and a conventional religious outlook and practices are all-pervasive, there can be a cultural settlement in which 'virtuoso religion' is performed by the clergy and religious orders, while the laity are held to a lower standard. For example, the eleventh-century abbot William of Malmesbury 'complained that the aristocracy rarely attended Mass, and even the more pious heard it at home, but in their bedchambers, lying in the arms of their wives' (cit. Percy, 2001, p. 87). Scarisbrick in his *The Reformation and the English People* argues that 'most medieval people seldom went to church, and when they did, probably arrived only for the elevation of the host' (Percy, 2001, p. 89). The historian Keith Thomas concludes that in the late sixteenth century 'a substantial proportion of the population regarded organized religion with an attitude which varied from cold indifference to frank hostility' (1971, p. 26).

The laxity and lukewarm character of religious observance in the eighteenth century, notwithstanding the Wesleyan and Evangelical revivals, is well known. For example, Parson Woodforde records in his classic *Diaries* that on Sunday 17 October 1758 only four people attended church; on 5 September 1759 – another Sunday – he took the afternoon off to go 'to the Bear-baiting in Ansford'; and on 5 October 1766 he forgot that it was St Luke's Day and didn't turn up to take a service at one of his churches (cit. Percy, 2001, pp. 88–9). While the nineteenth century is imagined to be a more vibrant time for religious fervour, evidence to the contrary is not hard to find. One amusing example must suffice:

> The interior of the church was quite as cheerless to my mind as the exterior – bare, and cold, and dreary ... The worshippers were few, and the worship cold. The priest delivered his part in a tone of apathy, and the replies of the people were faint and languid; the reading of the clergyman was not good, that of the poor clerk barbarous. (Joseph Leech, mid-nineteenth-century report, cit. Francis (ed.), 1989, p. 106)

The purpose of these historical snapshots is to suggest that whatever is happening to the churches today, it is not a *simple* matter of inexorable religious decline in modernity, proven by dwindling churchgoing figures. What makes the contemporary situation different from all those examples of religious indifference and laxity of practice from across the centuries is captured astutely by the journalist Ysenda Maxtone Graham: it is not that 'people don't go to church because they don't want to', as a retired clergyman told her; rather, 'people don't go to church because it doesn't even occur to them that they might' (1993, pp. 123, 124–5). In this post-church environment, Linda Woodhead's challenge about 'reviewing the whole structure from top to toe' means addressing a more profound and far-reaching crisis in which 'church' no longer has resonance for a generation born into late modernity in places like Britain where the heritage of Christendom casts the longest shadow. This will entail not just developing 'growth strategies' and practical tools, but engaging honestly with questions of ecclesiology, ministerial theology and sociology, which the remainder of this chapter will begin to do.

The end of religious conformity

The 'post-church society' is the product of drastic cultural change, as Maxtone Graham's observation about it not even occurring to people that they might go to church illustrates. Culture is an inescapable product of active meaning-making by humans, both individually and collectively, as Brown and Lynch emphasize: 'we never simply experience the world "as it is", but filtered through the cultural frames and meanings available to us in our particular situation' (2012, p. 329). In this process, 'cultural structures make society possible by providing the meaningful "inside" of social life' (p. 330). In contributing to this 'meaningful inside', religious faith and practice have often operated as a significant 'thickener' or enricher of culture, but for most secular westerners today, 'church' plays little or no role in this process. This is seen in Michaela's job leaving her 'feeling strangely shallow and unfulfilled' – there is something culturally 'thin' about it that she is aware of, but no longer knows how to address.

Brown and Lynch argue that there has been a progressive dissolution of a type of social conformity in which the Christian religion played a key role. In the post-war years of the forties and fifties, British children were schooled in 'conservative and respectable ordinariness':

... made through the rhetoric of the 'juvenile delinquent' to fear the establishment's terror of deviancy, the young were trained in the benevolent greyness of short trousers and school uniforms to savour the special treat of rationed sweets and to expect little more. (p. 332)

Girls in particular had cultural expectations laid upon them of 'being a nice girl', observing a code of manners, a 'please-and-thank-you'd politeness', for whom in the villages and small towns 'the competitions in the annual Produce Association show provided one of the most exciting occasions of the year' (Valerie Walkerdine, cit. Brown and Lynch, 2012, p. 332). Such domestic, everyday niceties underpinned by conventional religious practice fit well with the state of affairs described by historian Hugh McLeod:

> Christianity provided a common language that served in many different areas of life and was ... to a large extent taken for granted, by the majority of the population ... a certain minimum of Christian doctrine, ethics and ritual observance had become a normal part of life ... for anyone who had not made a conscious decision to reject them. (1995, p. 7)

The following sections explore some outcomes of the end of this kind of religious conformity: the increasingly voluntaristic, pluralistic nature of religion; the alternative routes into either no religion at all, highly conservative or sectarian forms of religion, or popular cultural expressions of 'banal' religion; and the concept of religious liquidity.

Voluntarism and pluralism

Grace Davie develops a mixed picture of religion in Britain today which amounts neither to a single-track descent into oblivion nor a trumpet blast of revival (2015, pp. 3–4). A key element in her analysis is the shift from a 'model of obligation or duty' to one of choice (p. 4). As the historical churches have been foundational in shaping British culture for a very long time, it is unsurprising that they retain a certain traction at critical life-transitions, or on emotionally charged public occasions. However, this does not mean that most people generally look to them in any profound way for fundamental guidance about belief or morals. This is because the expectation of religious conformity has almost entirely eroded away, so that the committed religious minority are self-consciously *choosing* this way of life. An irony of the situation is that when clergy of the Church of England opt to exercise their ministry according to this voluntaristic model, typically in rejecting so-called 'folk religion', they come into conflict with those who retain vestiges of the earlier type of occasional conformity; over requests for infant baptism, for example, or popular sentimental inscriptions on gravestones. As a result, as Brown and Woodhead wryly observe, there is a risk that the Church is seen as 'the only organization for which the customer is always wrong' (2016, p. 191).

As a second element, Davie identifies religious pluralism as one of the counter-trends that hold out the possibility of a different kind of religious future. Of particular significance is the impact of migration into the UK that introduces large practising religious communities, both Christian (for example, the 'Windrush generation') and other faiths, especially Islam (Davie, 2015, pp. 9–10). These raise vital critical questions for the churches about inclusion, hospitality and diversity within their own life, and the place of religious faith in the public arena. Davie points out that Britain's 'secular elites' often react with discomfort to the renewed intrusions of religion into public life, seeing them as challenging the religious neutrality of the state, and Christians as well as Muslims increasingly find themselves caught up in debates about this (pp. 10–11). Immigration also throws a spotlight on the wider world, where the public salience and popular practice of religion is very different from in Europe, which is now 'an exceptional case' where religion is concerned (Davie, 2002).

Both voluntarism and pluralism by their nature modify or slow down the secularizing trend, but there are also critical mutations of religious perception and practice that contribute to the creation of a problematic climate for the churches.

'No religion', conservative religion and 'banal' religion

Brown and Lynch propose that 'in the wake of the decline of a *dominant* Christian culture, a new cultural context has emerged involving … cultural forms of "non-religion", the consolidation of new religious subcultures and the circulation of new cultural constructions of "religion"' (2012, p. 331). This is a more nuanced approach than an unreconstructed secularization theory that simply treats increasing modernity and declining religiosity as a zero-sum game. Rather, as David Voas has put it, 'people stop being religious more quickly than they start being wholly secular' (cit. Brown and Lynch, 2012, p. 340): there are 'transitional spaces' where people can temporarily reside on a journey, not just from a religious to a secular identity, but something more complex.

The first such space is the bay marked 'no religion', in the sense that it becomes culturally acceptable to tick the 'none of the above' box in a questionnaire that enquires into a respondent's religious affiliation. Those who declare they have no religion are not necessarily hostile to religion; indeed, many simply care little or nothing for it as something that scarcely registers on their life's radar. Steve Bruce, a stout defender of the 'strong' version of secularization theory, compares this intermediate 'no religion' phase with a neglected garden: 'without constant pruning, selective breeding, and weeding, the garden loses its distinctive character, as it is overtaken by the greater variety of plant species in the surrounding wilderness' (2011, p. 19). Such no-religionists may well contrast religion unfavourably with 'spirituality', the position broadly assumed by the Channel 4 programme above.

A second bay in which some will find a parking place along the journey away from conventional religious observance stands in stark contrast with 'no religion', in forms of conservative (sometimes referred to as fundamentalist) religion, sustained by a cohesive and culturally all-embracing subculture. The third is what Danish scholar Stig Hjarvard has called 'banal religion', defined as 'the circulation of images of religious symbols and practices in ways that form a backdrop for everyday life without necessarily forming an important part of people's identities or their understanding of the world' (Brown and Lynch, 2012, p. 344; see also Ward, 2011). These constitute diametrically opposed responses to the dissolution of religious conformity as well as to the encroachment of non-religion. Conservative religion demands tight social cohesion to bolster belief, strong commitment and doctrinal rigour; banal religion is individualistic, loosely aligned to belief and resistant to systematization and organizational structure. Together, they represent an ongoing process of renegotiation of the cultural patterning of religion in the absence of a single tradition of 'normative' Christianity.

Religious liquidity

These religious cultural changes form part of what the sociologist Zygmunt Bauman (2001) termed 'liquid modernity'. In modernity, social identities formerly established by unchanging 'estates' inherited by birth (aristocracy, peasantry and so on) gradually gave way to status derived from 'class', based on educational and occupational rather than inherited criteria. With this change the possibility of social mobility arose, which in turn created a 'solvent' effect on traditionally fixed social institutions. Along with many others, religious institutions, beliefs and identities are progressively 'dissolved' as modernity evolves. However, Bauman acknowledges that in other areas the legacy of modernity has not been 'liquidity' but a sense of inexorable givenness, notably in the economic domain in which global free market capitalism is deemed to be the system to which there is no alternative. Hence, 'as modernity has solidified around social structures based on capitalism and the global free market, so the liquefying effects of modernity are now felt more powerfully at the level of individuals' sense of identity and meaning' (Lynch, 2002, p. 29).

Allied to the notion of 'liquidity', Pete Ward uses the concept of 'flow' as an umbrella term for the ways in which the Christianity represented by the churches overflows the banks of a channelled 'church' practice and culture into a more fluid environment (2008, p. 168). He notes that this constitutes a 'mixed blessing' (p. 176): despite its adaptability, such liquid religion may seem equally as impenetrable to those completely outside it as conventional 'church' does; hence the need to go on to enquire how the religious and theological flow, having escaped its churchly confines, can go on to have purchase in the wider unbelieving world. As an example he uses a recording of Gospel songs by the American country singer/songwriter Iris DeMent: in appropriating these songs, it is important to DeMent to affirm the authenticity of her use of them by saying that, for her, they are 'not about religion' but 'about something bigger'. The same example is used by Helen Morris (2019, p. 30) to illustrate the 'recontextualizing' of church. For Ward, such initiatives represent 'flow' as 'a missiological challenge': it moves the Christian content outside the Church's 'control', and opens up the potential for people to be influenced by it in hitherto unknown and unpredictable ways (p. 180).

Religious and spiritual capital

These ideas about 'no religion', religious mutation, liquidity and flow under the conditions of advanced (or post-) modernity, can be gathered into a potentially more positive prospect for the churches by deploying the concept of religious and spiritual capital. The concept of capital draws on the work of Marx, who uses the term specifically in the economic field to denote that which accrues and embodies material value. In capitalism, capital becomes more than just a concrete entity (a certain quantity of material asset in someone's possession) and takes on a more abstract form as a medium of social relations. On this basis, later thinkers such as Pierre Bourdieu have been able to redeploy the concept of capital from the economic sphere into different contexts, hence 'social capital', 'political capital', 'religious capital' and so on. All of these refer to the resources in circulation with accrued value that can be drawn upon to mobilize action and command authority in their particular field: for example, governments that run out of political capital are liable to be kicked out by the electorate.

Mathew Guest (2007) cites the judgement of James Beckford that the religion that has 'come adrift from its former points of anchorage' nevertheless retains the capacity to function as a vehicle of change (or of resistance to it). However, 'it is likely to be mobilized in unexpected places and in ways which may be in tension with "establishment" practices and public policy' (Beckford, 1989, p. 170). Guest sees this deregulated religion as a continuing positive benefit when seen as 'spiritual capital', which could come to expression in three ways: through 'a collection of the knowledge, tastes and other resources an individual amasses through-out their experience', or 'inculcated through education', or by a 'process of unconscious socialization' (2007, p. 191). This type of spiritual capital may be quite difficult to 'realize', as in at least the first and third of Guest's ways it may be accrued largely unawares by those who possess it. This makes 'inculcation through education', or a process of cultivating religious and spiritual literacy, all the more essential in today's society.

Guest believes that even institutions deeply rooted in tradition can be the bearers of an original 'charism' that retains the capacity to break forth afresh in new ways:

> The emerging 'spiritual capital' ... is a liquid flow of ideas and values that, while uprooted from their original institutional context, are never-theless shaped by the traditions out of which they emerged, traditions that still steer their course, mould their practical expression and infuse the language in which they are affirmed, silenced or challenged. (2007, p. 198)

The image of religion 'cut adrift' (Beckford) or 'uprooted' (Guest) captures well the situation that David Lyon (2000) summarizes by saying that religion has become 'deregulated'. It is a phenomenon familiar to clergy: for example, Jessica Martin tells of a widower who was hugely grateful to her for the way she handled his wife's funeral but joked afterwards, 'I hope I don't see you again for years.' Another mourner thanked her for the prayers at the service, remarking that they were 'just the same' as the rituals of healing by crystals she and her mother regularly under-took (Martin and Coakley (eds), 2016, pp. xv–xvi). Martin is honest enough to admit that she had underestimated how hard it would be to get people to come to church, as distinct from generating positive good-will towards her ministry in the community. A revealing and extravagant case of 'deregulated religion' occurred in the funeral of reality TV star Jade Goody in 2010, depicted by the journalist Cole Moreton (2010, pp. 24–5). He notes that at points where the service touched base with more conventional funeral liturgy, the congregation 'switched on their mobile phones and rang their friends'.

In this state of flux, the concept of a culturally carried 'spiritual capital' might become a fruitful instrument of retrieval and renewal for the churches. Chris Baker characterizes the social and cultural space that will be most favourable to the flow of spiritual capital as hybrid: 'hybridity, the fusion of two or more identities into a new identity, is … the cultural norm that informs all our identities as individuals and urban dwellers, and the spatial and political realities that shape our daily existence' (2009, p. 26). The hybrid space is identified neither with the public institutions of society nor the enclosure of private (family) life, but is located where the diverse and the disparate, the fluid and transient, can enter some kind of creative cohabitation in search of a way of being no longer defined by the 'narratives of modernity based on colonialism, class and patriarchy' (p. 16).

Baker's work is a stimulating example of the more nuanced approach to the prospects of the churches in the contemporary cultural environment argued for in this chapter. Secularization theory cannot be corralled into either a narrative of inevitable decline, or a premature celebration of the 'post-secularity' that favours the new 'spirituality' over the old 'religion'. Nor should a simplistic diagnosis of the fall in churchgoing numbers be allowed to rest on the assumption of a golden age of piety climaxing in the Victorian era. There are lessons to be learned from the earlier uncritical deployment of the secularization model by the churches to guide their strategic planning. The popular postmodernity analysis must not be allowed to fall into the same trap, as if once we have defined the cultural context as 'postmodern', we can determine a 'plan' of what the Church ought to do, as though somehow capable of acting from *outside* that context. The reality is that a culture that gives expression to hybridity, liquidity, mutability and flow challenges those more solid institutional forms of hierarchy, continuity and order that have characterized many inherited traditions of ecclesiology.

Chapter 2 will develop a historical reading of ecclesial order and ministry as essentially contested, in which a number of fault-lines repeatedly provoke further disputes and tensions that disturb the seeming equilibrium of supposedly settled models, revealing them to be always and everywhere provisional and questionable.

2

Unfinished Business: The Historical Contestation of Ministry

A note about references: throughout this chapter, except where otherwise shown, references to pre-modern historical sources are drawn variously from Stevenson, revised Frend (1987); Bettenson and Maunder, eds (1999); McGrath, ed. (2007). To avoid overloading the text with more detail than necessary, individual citations and page references are not given.

This book interrogates ministry strategies for today in the context of the churches' efforts to respond to the culture of postmodernity. A critical element of this is the deconstructive approach that treats seemingly settled and permanent institutions as provisional and contingent. This chapter offers a historical reading of ecclesiology and ministerial order in this light: ministry is seen as a perpetually contested area within ecclesial discourse and practice, with all inherited orders and structures for ministry arising as responses to social and cultural context. There is no incontrovertible, permanent expression of ministry around which all churches can unite. The first part of the chapter presents the overall case for this reading.

The subsequent sections explore the unfinished business of ministry and ministerial orders within the Church under four heads. The first considers the tradition of the 'threefold ordering of ministry' as an overarching framework. The following sections address three related ecclesiological issues that have a critical bearing upon how ministry is understood: the validation of ministry through either charismatic endowment or institutional authorization, the setting of ministry within a 'bottom-up' grassroots movement or 'top-down' hierarchy, and the missional objective of ministry as either a 'Christianized society' or a religiously and ethically distinctive community. In respect of each of the four themes in turn, soundings are taken from different periods of Church history, in particular the early centuries up to the collapse of the Roman Empire, the late medieval period leading to the Reformation and its aftermath, and modernity since the nineteenth century.

Contestation and contingency in ministry

'Ministry is contested, and the very thing that we depend upon to unite the Church becomes one of the things that divides it' (Hoyle, 2016, p. x). Diarmaid MacCulloch points out the irony in this: early Christianity sought to bolster its 'rhetoric of unity' by (among other things) 'embodying authority in ministers set aside for the purpose', and yet ministry 'has in fact proved one of the major forces to divide Christianity' (2010, pp. 127–8). Catholic scholar John Burkhard comments that 'full communion ... continues to evade us because issues of ministry are so divisive', despite the fact that for the primitive Church, 'ecclesiology and ministry were secondary issues' (2004, pp. 23–4). For Richard Holloway, the problem is the tendency for Christianity to see its institutional arrangements 'not as the best way of getting things done, but as divinely decreed and intrinsically significant' (1997, p. xiv), leading inexorably to 'feuds between different expressions of Christianity, usually focused on their organizational systems'.

If, then, ministry is so vexatious a source of division, its contested nature should perhaps be reframed as a positive benefit rather than an intractable problem. The Catholic historian Adrian Hastings has argued that in matters of ministry, it is not a justifiable argument against any proposed change that it challenges or contradicts inherited ecclesiology: 'ecclesiologically it is not wrong because it has not been done before' (Hastings, cit. Melinsky, 1992, p. 174). As Melinsky puts it, 'the Church has power to construct and reconstruct its ministry ... because it has always been doing so since apostolic times'. This opens up the possibility that for ministry 'no foundations are evident, no structure is legitimated, because ... God does not intend such things for the church' (Mason, 2002, p. 24). To believe otherwise becomes a hindrance: commenting on Charles Gore's *The Church and the Ministry* (1919), Hoyle notes that despite the more progressive elements in Gore's thinking, his certainty that all the structures and orders of ministry were ordained by God from the beginning meant that 'he could not ... quite imagine what ministry might need to become' (2016, p. 70).

Reflecting on the movement for women's ordination in the 1980s, Rowan Williams acknowledged elements of indeterminacy in the way that patterns of ministry were evolving:

There are quite a few who would say that, at the moment, a theology of [ordained] ministry is neither possible, nor desirable: we have inherited a jumble of rather irrational structures and practices which we are slowly – and *pragmatically* – learning to adjust and rationalize or even modernize; and in this sort of situation we are inevitably going to treat all theological perspectives on the ministry as provisional. (1984, p. 11)

The immediate context shows that Williams, while acknowledging this situation, did not personally share the view that all theological perspectives on ministry are provisional. Nevertheless, it is an interesting pointer to the future archbishop who would 20 years later be credited with originating the phrase 'a mixed economy church', encouraging the unleashing of experimentation that resulted in the flourishing of 'fresh expressions of church'.

An approach to orders and structures for ministry that treats them as contested and contingent can be seen as stemming naturally from the nature of the Church as both a theological creation and a socio-historical reality. Hastings avers that 'for better or worse, the world sets the Church's agenda', and 'the diversity and changeableness that are such characteristics of Christian history are the best proof that it is so' (1992, p. 19). Writing from a feminist perspective and drawing on the work of Rosemary Ruether, Natalie Watson observes that 'the church always finds itself in a dialectical tension between being an established historical institution and a spirit-filled community which works on its constant renewal' (2002, p. 70). Ruether herself goes further, maintaining that 'all patterns of church polity are relative and historically developed, patterned after political and social patterns in the culture' (cit. Watson, 2002, p. 70). The consequence of this relativity, according to the philosopher-theologian John Caputo, whose work will feature later in the book, is that 'the church is a provisional construction', and therefore all churches need to engage in 'a process of incessant self-renewal or auto-deconstruction' (2007, p. 35). It is in this spirit that the investigations in this chapter are carried out.

Ministry as threefold order

The early centuries

The preface to the rites of ordination in the 1662 Anglican Book of Common Prayer states: 'It is evident unto all men diligently reading holy Scripture and ancient Authors, that from the Apostles' time there have been these Orders of Ministry in Christ's Church: Bishops, Priests and Deacons'. One might be inclined to respond, 'but not as evident as all that'. The road from what is 'evident' in the New Testament to what we have in the 'three orders' today is at the very least a long and winding one. This section traces some important staging points on that historical journey; the contemporary situation is explored in more detail in the next chapter.

As far as the picture drawn from the New Testament is concerned, something along the following lines seems reasonably certain (for useful summaries, see Rorem, 1990; Melinsky, 1992, chapters 1 and 3; my view of the emerging patterns of ministry in the New Testament mostly follows Dunn, 2006, chapter 6). Jesus called and, in some way, commissioned a group of followers to carry his message and his works beyond his earthly lifetime, and these became known as 'apostles', those who are 'sent'. This was clearly a coveted badge of honour, as St Paul had to fight his corner for the right to apply this title to himself despite never having known Jesus in the flesh. The apostles founded the first Christian communities, and in due course so-called 'elders' or presbyters were appointed from among them to preside over their ongoing life, though it remains unclear whether or not Paul did this. Probably an alternative name for the presbyters in the first instance was 'overseers' (*episkopoi*), translated as 'bishops'. As a result of some controversy in the early Jerusalem church, some individuals were set aside to take care of the practicalities of social welfare in the community. Church tradition came to refer to these as 'deacons', though St Luke doesn't explicitly use this term for them; some, as the stories of Stephen and Philip show, went out preaching and evangelizing.

Summing up the evidence, Donald Senior (1990) concludes that 'the nature and form of ordained ministry ... are subject to ongoing development' (p. 13). The New Testament and early Church exhibit 'considerable diversity' of ministerial structures; different patterns existed in different places at the same time. Both the presbyter and *episkopos* roles probably derived from the synagogue, continued in the Jerusalem-based Jewish Christian community presided over, according to Acts and Paul, by James, the brother of Jesus. This presbyter/bishop model subsumed within it several former ministerial roles such as those set out in the lists in Paul's letters, including pastors, teachers and leaders. The term 'priest' (Greek *hiereus*) is used in a Christian context only in relation to the high priesthood of Jesus and the collective priesthood of the whole Church, never as a distinct order of ministry; this will however be treated more fully in the two following chapters.

The twofold pattern of presbyters/overseers and deacons, with some variation about the roles of the latter (and some ambiguity about the ongoing role of 'apostles'), is about as far as the New Testament takes us. Writing from Rome to the Corinthians close to the end of the first century, Clement refers to a ministry of 'bishops [*episkopoi*] and deacons', the first of which he seems to refer to interchangeably as 'elders' (*presbuteroi*).

The Didache (probably roughly contemporary) also refers to bishops and deacons, explaining that these are to 'minister to you the ministry of the prophets and teachers', which suggests awareness of a broader spectrum of recognized ministries in line with the Pauline letters.

Early in the second century, the writings of Ignatius of Antioch appear to show a trend towards a more theologically formalized threefold order, including a focal role for the bishop. Writing to the Christians in Smyrna, Ignatius enjoins them to

> follow the bishop, as Jesus Christ followed the Father, follow the presbytery, as the apostles ... reverence the deacons as the commandments of God. Wheresoever the bishop appears, there let the people be, even as wheresoever Christ Jesus is, there is the Catholic Church.

This text, and others similar to it, in Ignatius are often signalled as the first clear reference to the existence of the threefold order and the emerging monarchical episcopate. The threefold analogy for bishops, presbyters and deacons appears in different forms: in his letter to the Trallians, he claims the deacons represent Jesus Christ, the bishop God the Father, and the presbyters God's council. If we try not to read these through the lens of later development, they may not actually be as formal as they first appear, and certainly neither version represents an unambiguously hierarchical ordering (Pinnock, 1991).

There is a scholarly consensus around the view that as the Church grew, at some point the practice began of appointing a 'presiding elder' among the body of the presbyters of the local church community. In due course, this was extended to encompass responsibility for oversight of a group of churches across a locality, as a result of which the offices of 'elder' or 'presbyter', and 'overseer' or 'bishop', became distinct. By the late second century, Irenaeus of Lyons is developing ideas about a succession of bishops, traceable back to the apostles and safeguarding the continuity and consistency of orthodox teaching across both time and space. It is notable that the title of the work in which Irenaeus expounds this doctrine is *Adversus Haereses*: MacCulloch observes wryly that 'he was popularizing a concept with a prosperous future in Christian consciousness: heresy' (2010, p. 143); and so, it became possible to be a 'heretic' on grounds of erroneous belief about ecclesial order as much as about doctrine, a notion conspicuous in the New Testament by its absence. The politically desirable quality of *unity* came at a high cost for a Church under threat of persecution from without and heresy from within, something seen most vividly in the ministry of Cyprian of Carthage.

Heresy, unity and ministerial order

Cyprian became Bishop of Carthage (in present-day Tunisia) in 249, and shortly afterwards a major persecution of Christians took place, during which a large number capitulated under pressure and renounced their faith. A major controversy ensued about how those who had lapsed should be treated if they desired readmission to the Church once the persecution was over. The Bishop of Rome, Cornelius, ruled that those who had fallen into apostasy could be restored to the Church after a due process of penance, catechesis and evidence of perseverance in faith and good works, a position supported by Cyprian. However, Cornelius was challenged by a rigorist group that deemed the lapsed incapable of returning to the faith, as in denying it they had forfeited the gift of the Spirit bestowed in their baptism. They consecrated one of their number, Novatian, as a rival bishop in Rome, and the schism spread to North Africa, where bishops were consecrated in opposition to Cyprian in 252. Until his martyrdom in 258, Cyprian was embroiled in a further dispute about whether Christians who had been baptized by Novatianists should be re-baptized if they rejoined the regular Church: he took the view that they should, as baptism by schismatics (heretics) was invalid. But Stephen, who succeeded as Bishop of Rome in 254, argued against re-baptism on the grounds that the grace of God is bestowed objectively in baptism and is not dependent on the standing of the minister.

These are more than arcane and antiquated disputes because they highlight the changing interpretation of the nature of ministerial order, especially episcopacy, the efficacy of the sacraments and the impact of both of these issues on the understanding of Church unity. Initially, Cyprian's principal concern as a bishop for unity was wholly pastoral: the tone of his early *Proposals to the Church of Carthage about the Lapsed* (250), for example, is considered and cautious. He gently chides those presbyters who have rushed rather too quickly to the readmission of the lapsed to communion, and goes on to advise them about careful pastoral measures to bring them to rehabilitation. Unity in the Church, while focused in the bishop, is to be achieved and maintained through the operation of a true Christian character: pursuing reconciliation, practising mercy, fostering communion and peace.

Over time, Cyprian's tone became markedly more authoritarian, resulting in his historical reputation as the arch-institutionalizer of Church and ministry in his elevation of the office of bishop (Melinsky, 1992, pp. 42–3). But the critical factor for the legislative institutionalization of ministerial order was not so much due to Cyprian as to the triumph of the Roman view on the matter of baptism by schismatics, in the doctrine of *ex opere operato*: 'that the sacrament ... was valid whoever performed it if it was done in the right form and with the right intentions' (MacCulloch, 2010, p. 175). In this doctrine of a Church able to dispense the grace of God by means of an impersonal mechanism of sacramental leverage, the inherited language of orders of ministry maintained its continuity with the primitive Church, but its meaning underwent a transformation in response to the theo-political controversies of the day.

Ministerial order from the Middle Ages to the Reformation

The collapse of the Roman Empire was a profound shock to the Church that massively influenced new directions in theological and ecclesiological thinking. Notably, Augustine developed a totalizing narrative of the relationship between Church and world within the providence of God, while monasticism flourished as a movement of renewal pursuing a more disciplined, spiritual and communal way of being Christian. But the eventual establishment of the Holy Roman Empire set the definitive direction of travel, in which the ministry of the Church adhered ever more closely to the imperial patterns put in place under Constantine (his impact is treated further below in the section on 'Hierarchy and people movement'). The clergy became an 'order' (*ordo*) or class within society, admitted by a rite of ordination, originally the Roman ceremony of admission to one of the higher orders in distinction from the common people (*plebs*). They were integrated into the civic structures, from which other ecclesiastical terms were also derived, such as 'diocese', 'parish', 'vicar' and 'cathedral'. By the high Middle Ages, bishops, priests and deacons could be said 'only in a limited sense' to be 'the same' offices as they were within the Church of the first two centuries (Davis, 1967, p. 139).

Movements of reform, when they came, were quick to issue a challenge on this front. Already in the late fourteenth century the Lollards, followers of John Wycliffe, declared that the 'priesthood which began in Rome ... is not the priesthood which Christ ordained for his apostles' (*Lollard Conclusions*, 1394). When the Reformation eventually became unstoppable in the sixteenth century, Luther declared that there was no difference of 'estate' between persons in so-called 'spiritual' (clerical) and 'temporal' (lay) occupations. He asserted that 'a priest should be nothing in Christendom but a functionary', and thus it is perfectly possible for a priest to step down from his office and become 'a peasant or a citizen like the rest' (*Appeal to the German Nobility*, 1520). Likewise he argued that as episcopal functions are only exercised in the name of the congregation(s), rather than being invested in the person of the bishop, it follows for example that a group of Christians stranded in a desert place, in the absence of a bishop, could appoint and order their own ministries.

In Geneva, Calvin was prepared to vary the orders and structures of ministry towards what he considered a more biblical pattern, believing the only essential marks of the Church to be the preaching of the word and observance of the sacraments. Melinsky, however, notes how even Calvin's ostensibly 'biblical' church order 'owed as much to the republican style of government in Swiss cantons as to the New Testament' (1992, p. 81). With Martin Bucer, Calvin 'asserted that the New Testament described four functions of ministry, pastors, doctors [teachers], elders and deacons' (MacCulloch, 2010, p. 633). Here the term 'elder' (presbyter) subsumes within its meaning the concepts of 'oversight' or *episcope*, reflecting the primitive pattern in which these two orders appeared to be interchangeable, and leading to the Presbyterian form of church governance (Lindberg, 2010, p. 314). Others who wanted to eliminate hierarchical authority altogether formed the loosely related family of Congregationalist churches. At the most radical end of the spectrum, the Society of Friends (the Quakers) insisted that all forms of differentiation of status among Christians should be abolished (Robert Barclay, *Chief Principles of the Christian Religion as professed by the people called the Quakers*, 1678).

The threefold order in modernity

Approaches to ecumenical *rapprochement* over ministerial orders within the Anglican context varied in their generosity over the course of the twentieth century. In its *Letter To All Christian People*, the Lambeth Conference of 1920 proposed that any future united Church must embrace 'a ministry acknowledged by every part of the Church as possessing not only the inward call of the Spirit but also the commission of Christ and the authority of the whole body'. Rather than insisting that this must mean the inherited Anglican pattern, the bishops went on only to suggest rather meekly, 'may we not reasonably claim that the Episcopate is one means of providing such a ministry?' In 1938 the Church of England's Doctrinal Commission Report *Doctrine in the Church of England* went further, conceding that 'the myth of a single New Testament form of ministry' should not be used 'to justify one present-day church order to the exclusion of another' (cit. Greenwood, 1994, p. 14).

In this spirit, the Church of South India, inaugurated in 1947, was able to bring together Anglicans, Congregationalists and Presbyterians with an affirmation that 'all the ministers of the uniting Churches will ... be recognized as equally ministers of the united Church without distinction or difference'. Measures were put in place for an episcopate, with the proviso that 'this does not involve any judgment upon the validity ... of any other form of ministry'. The Dogmatic Constitution on the Church issued by the Second Vatican Council in 1964, *Lumen Gentium*, shows ecumenical influence in affirming the common priesthood of the faithful *alongside* the ministerial or hierarchical priesthood, and in the idea of the 'collegiality' of bishops (MacCulloch, 2010, pp. 969–70). The 'Lima text' of the World Council of Churches 1982, *Baptism, Eucharist and Ministry*, stated that churches should 'recognize their respective ordained ministries if they are mutually assured of their intention to transmit the ministry of the Word and sacrament in continuity with apostolic times'.

However, a follow-up report on issues arising from Lima a decade later noted that mutual recognition was often being impeded by 'a tendency to identify this with the personal ministry of bishops and ... with the historic episcopate'. This is evidenced in the Report of the Archbishops' Group on the Episcopate (1990), which refers in a somewhat coy fashion to 'those Churches which, in the emergency situation of the sixteenth century, departed temporarily or until the present day from the threefold pattern of ministry' (p. 3), treating the dissenting communions of the Reformation as prodigal churches that will hopefully one day see the error of their ways and return to the fold.

A recurrent debate runs through these ecumenical engagements between advocates of ministerial order as 'divinely given for all time' and those who see it as a pragmatic response to circumstances. In an era where the Church occupies a dominant social position, the 'divinely given' model carries plausibility; but the more the Church loses that position, the less plausible the model seems. Once the Church becomes marginal, a model that responds to social change by both successive and concurrent adaptations looks far more convincing. The advantage of this adaptive view is that it does not necessarily require the jettisoning of outdated models to make way for new ones, but rather recognizes that *none* enjoy protected status, and *all* may have their uses in certain times and places. The Church should neither cleave to 'catholic order' nor constantly hanker after rediscovering the 'authentic early Church', but rather consider the particular adaptations that constitute a creative response to the challenges of the present.

The remainder of this chapter will retrace the journey through Church history in relation to the other three major contested issues identified earlier. All three of these cut across the foundational principles of the 'threefold order' and modify or call into question the way it is understood. Burkhard refers to the conclusion of Hans Küng that 'the threefold order ... is *a* [emphasis mine] legitimate expression of apostolic leadership', but 'other, possibly more charismatic or "Pauline" ways cannot be excluded', and 'this is not a limitation but a benefit for the church' (Burkhard, 2004, p. 77). This reference to 'other, more charismatic ways' introduces the issue discussed in the next section.

Charismatic endowment and juridical office

The New Testament and the Patristic era

As early witnesses to the primitive Church, both Luke and Paul in their different ways place an emphasis on the Spirit as the creator, energizer and shaper of the Christian community. For Luke, the story flows from the outpouring on the day of Pentecost with its miraculous gift of languages and harvest of conversions, together with signs and wonders performed by the apostles in continuity with the ministry of Jesus. For Paul, it is the nature of his dramatic conversion experience as a direct visitation of God wholly outside the structures and authorities of his own religious background. This leads him to an independent-minded mission understood to be under the immediate guidance of the Spirit, and the resulting creation of a new kind of community described as the 'body of Christ', animated by the diverse gifts and ministries of the Spirit. Luke's later account is somewhat rose-tinted in its desire to present the phenomenon of the Church as a success story; Paul's view is more honest, arising as it does from immediate personal and often painful experience and expressed in the form of 'occasional' writings that were not designed to create a narrative for posterity, but often to address a crisis.

The Archbishops' Group on the Episcopate make the familiar point that in the post-New Testament period, there was 'a movement from the sacramentally bestowed charismatic endowment of an "order" to the juridically bestowed power of an "office"' (1990, p. 30). Despite the hints of a more settled institutional pattern in the later documents of the New Testament, especially the Pastoral Epistles, this was far from yet being a definitive shift. William Countryman insists that the Holy Spirit 'has not composed the existing patterns of church life and theology as a tidy and unalterable package for all time' (2012, p. 10). Writing of the extraordinary ministry of Philip in Acts, who begins as one of the 'seven deacons' and goes on to become a travelling evangelist, he concludes that the Spirit's distribution of ministries may often be improvisational: 'we are not in charge' (p. 93). Likewise, Burkhard argues (citing Yves Congar) that 'in emergency situations the Holy Spirit might very well intervene to preserve apostolic office by ... an extra-institutional principle' (2004, p. 36).

The judgement of history has tended to be clouded by the fact that often the advocates of the Spirit found themselves on the losing side: and, typically, this was registered by branding them as heretics. The first testing ground for this came late in the second century with the Montanists, who brought a radical ministry of prophecy, often accompanied by ecstatic phenomena and an attack on the growing 'worldliness' of the Church (Melinsky, 1992, p. 38). One noteworthy recruit was the North African lay theologian Tertullian, who had argued forcefully for the authenticity of the faith deriving in the first place from its continuity and consistency with the witness of the apostles. For Tertullian, Montanism passed the test, as it was clear that from apostolic times spiritual gifts such as prophecy should be expected in the Church. There needed to be internal mechanisms for discernment in respect of such ministries: prophetic utterances should be 'examined with the most scrupulous care, in order that their truth may be probed' (Tertullian, *On the Soul*, 9). It is likely that the Montanists could have been judged sufficiently orthodox in their basic theology (MacCulloch, 2010, p. 139; Melinsky, 1992, p. 38), were it not for their unauthorized leadership and ecstatic practices making them unacceptable to the evolving institutional Church.

By the end of the second century, Montanism was condemned: 'raptures and visions are forced out of the Church ... and the words "prophecy" and "charisma" disappear from circulation' (Melinsky, 1992, p. 39). Despite this, 'pneumato-charismatic' and 'official-sacramental' approaches clearly continued to coexist at the time (c. 215) of the *Apostolic Tradition* of Hippolytus (p. 37). A little later, Origen, in his writing *Against Celsus*, defended a charismatic conception of 'church' and expressed some scorn for the spiritual quality of the bishops and other clergy of Alexandria who were products of the increasingly institutionalized system (Melinsky, 1992, p. 40). MacCulloch notes that the clash between a model of authority rooted in 'monarchical episcopacy and the threefold ministry' and 'the random gift of prophecy' has recurred time and again throughout Church history. He quotes the priceless comment in a Victorian textbook, 'if Montanism had triumphed, Christian doctrine would have been developed, not under the superintendence of the church teachers most esteemed for wisdom, but usually of wild and excitable women' (MacCulloch, 2010, p. 140).

From the Middle Ages to the Wesleyan revivals

Commenting on the origins of dissent from the eleventh century on, MacCulloch notes how groups such as the Friars could offer a form of dissent from within, an alternative expression of Christian life, ministry and mission to the highly centralized, law-governed institution (2010, pp. 401–3). By the year 1300, the western Church was experiencing more frequent episodes of dissent – for example, from the 'Spirituals', a radical wing of the Franciscans (pp. 410–11, 558). The Reformation unleashed among its various streams those more radical groups who provoked debates on issues between formal education/authorization for ministry and free charismatic vocation: 'not a unified movement but rather a loose network of local or regional groups', 'a mobile fellowship of conventicles' (Melinsky, 1992, pp. 82–3, referring to the Anabaptists). As we have seen, the most radical rejection of official authorization comes with the Quakers, who represent a tradition for which ministers are only authentic on the basis of a communally recognized charismatic endowment.

The Evangelical revivals of the eighteenth and nineteenth centuries including the 'Great Awakening' under Jonathan Edwards and others in America, and the Wesleyan movement in Britain, saw further incidence of charismatic phenomena including prophecy, healings and people falling into a state of ecstasy in the context of preaching or worship. As a lifelong Anglican of an originally High Church persuasion, John Wesley wrestled with the conflicting demands of his tradition, the new patterns of ministry and mission he was convinced were necessary for the spread of the gospel, and the building up of the congregations being developed from his tours of preaching. The innovative structure of class meetings, local preachers and society stewards set up among the Methodist congregations signalled a sharp challenge to inherited Anglican models of ministry, ultimately making it impossible for the Methodist movement to remain part of the Church of England.

The revivalist movements are forerunners of the emergence of Pentecostalism in the early twentieth century; the threads of this story will be taken up again in Chapter 6.

People movement and institutional hierarchy

From the New Testament to the Christendom era

It can hardly be denied that the Church began as a 'people movement', initially made up of Jews who had come to confess Jesus as their Messiah, and soon also embracing Gentiles with the message of Jesus as Lord and Saviour. They were inspired by Jesus' teaching and example, energized by the conviction that he was raised to life after his crucifixion, that his Spirit was now with them, and possessed of a strong sense of a mission to proclaim the news of the Kingdom of God. Gathering converts, they began to form communities of disciples, meeting in homes, praying together, circulating and listening to remembered accounts of what Jesus did and taught, and sharing in bread and wine in memory of him as he had instructed the apostles on the night before he died. Spreading across the lands of the eastern Mediterranean, they attracted attention as something new, dynamic and potentially subversive on the religious scene, and both opposition from the Jewish establishment, and scepticism and suspicion on the part of the Roman authorities, soon made life harder for them. Paul's letters testify to the ethical challenges, power struggles and mixed fortunes of these early Christian communities. If they were to survive beyond the first flush of missionary zeal and charismatic effervescence, they would need to develop an institutional infrastructure to sustain them.

Institutionalization is a fact of life and a necessity for the extension of an original movement over time and space. This section interrogates the particular form of institutionalization as *hierarchy*, and enquires into alternative historical developments that were able to conserve more of the distinctive character of the people movement. Geoffrey Barraclough observes that 'beginning as a series of cells within the Jewish communities of the Diaspora, the church developed into an organization that eventually paralleled that of the state itself' (Barraclough (ed.), 2003, p. 32). This journey begins within the first 40 years after the death of Jesus, as Paul draws on his elite status as a Roman citizen and a distinguished Jewish teacher to begin to introduce a measure of organization into the Christian communities he founded. Frend calls this 'Paul's establishment of Christian synagogues, with their ministries staffed by permanent officers (presbyters and deacons)' (2003, p. 46). MacCulloch agrees that 'Antioch [where Paul was first based] and Jerusalem seem to have found their models for ministry in the organization of the Jewish Temple and its hierarchy' (2010, p. 131).

As yet, however, these early structures were not fully hierarchical:

MacCulloch compares Paul's arrangements to Wesley's setting up of a 'mobile "itinerant" ministry alongside a settled and locally based one', in what he aptly calls an 'effort at improvising oversight in mission conditions' (2010, p. 131). A crucial step towards further institutionalization comes as the itinerant ministry dies out, and increasingly (as in the Didache) there is a suspicion of travelling self-styled 'apostles' and 'prophets' who might 'turn up' in a Christian community claiming some kind of immediate authentication by God of their ministry and message (p. 132). The denunciation of the Montanists as heretics in the second century removed a potential impediment to the development of more formalized hierarchical models.

Over the next two centuries, the roles and functions of Christian ministry were altered by two significant developments in the contextual understanding of ministerial terminologies. The first occurred within the Church's theological tradition, in part as one element of a broader move to claim the Hebrew Scriptures as sacred Christian texts (Cunningham, 1990). This facilitated the gradual infiltration of Old Testament terms and concepts such as *hiereus* and *sacerdos* (Greek and Latin respectively for the cultic priest) into the treatment of Christian ministry. The second originated not from within the Church but from the surrounding society. Following the conversion of the emperor Constantine, Christianity acquired the status of official religion of the Empire, leading to the assimilation of the offices and functions of the Church to Roman culture and organization (Melinsky, 1992, p. 57).

It is a matter of dispute whether 'conversion' is the appropriate term for the nature of Constantine's attachment to the Christian faith from 312 onwards. MacCulloch suggests 'he came to a deeply personal if rather capricious involvement in the Christian faith' (2010, p. 191); Alistair Kee argues his experience was 'not conversion, but an exchange of divine patronage' (1982, p. 14), in essence an act of political expediency. Both agree however that Constantine's embrace of Christianity was in pursuit of an imperial strategy, which had drastic repercussions for the nature of the still developing offices and orders of Christian ministry. The alignment of the Christian minister with both the sacrificing priesthood of the temple, controlling access to the divine, and the ruling class of the empire, enforcing civil order, was powerful indeed.

The Middle Ages to the Reformation and beyond

The rise of monasticism led to many of the aristocracy granting lands for the foundation of religious communities and the building of churches, resulting in a 'proprietary Church', the legacy of which passed to the Church of England with its system of patronage, and incumbency as institution to a 'living'. By the height of the medieval period in England, 'the iron of feudalism had entered deeply into the Church's soul' (Melinsky, 1992, p. 70). Priests multiplied in appointments sustained by private patronage, where offering the Mass became the key priestly function with or without a congregation: the 'true Body of Christ' was no longer the Church either assembled or dispersed, but the Eucharistic host. Some clergy were minors, others illiterate, absentees or holders of multiple offices (pp. 68–9).

In all this we see the perpetuation only formally of the 'historic threefold order' of ministry. Margaret Aston writes of 'enormous numbers of people … admitted to lower clerical orders, many of whom never reached or aspired to the priesthood' (2003, p. 161). The seeds of reformation are sown initially through lay movements, such as the Hussites and Lollards, reacting against the tightly authoritarian line of papal and priestly control and the 'tension between the church defined as ecclesiastical hierarchy and … as a community of faithful believers' (p. 156). Beneath the surface of the all-powerful medieval ecclesial system, it was possible to discern a counter-movement for which, as Aston puts it, 'the structured hierarchy is dispensable, and it sometimes seems as if the church is most alive when that hierarchy, subject to Gospel appraisal, is most in question' (p. 170).

Theologically, the conception of ministry changes with Luther's 'priesthood of all believers'; but structurally, this does not settle the question of hierarchy over against 'people movement'. Luther's concern was more for the restoration of universal access to the Scriptures, in order that lay people might exercise their own judgement on their meaning and thus be empowered to challenge papal teaching, than for reform of the orders of ministry as such. In his *To the Christian Nobility of the German Nation* (1520) Luther had urged the laity to 'take back control' of the Church from the clerical hierarchy (Evans, 2008, p. 121), but his anxiety about social disorder, and his belief in the need for the 'godly prince' to maintain the societal arm of God's governance of the world, made him unable to support the side of the peasantry in the uprisings led, among others, by the Anabaptist radical Thomas Müntzer in 1525.

The greatest challenge to ecclesial order came therefore from the more radical wing of the Reformation: Müntzer conceived of church as 'a democratic – synodal communal polity' in which 'through the inner witness of the Spirit, power is given to the people' (Lindberg, 2010, p. 133). In England, the Puritans demanded 'a Presbyterian form of government, placing control of the church in local congregations and ministerial associations rather than in episcopal hierarchy' (Youngs, 2003, p. 201). In Europe, some Anabaptist 'brethren' such as the Mennonites looked for an even more far-reaching deconstruction of ecclesiology, often worshipping 'in what would now be called "house churches" with no officially recognized system of overarching ministerial oversight' (Evans, 2008, p. 153).

The Elizabethan Settlement for the Church of England (the *Via Media*) preserved the essential features of the pre-Reformation ministerial order, including the succession of bishops. Only after Elizabeth's death, and the accession of James I in 1603, did Puritan groups repeat their demands for more radical reform in the so-named *Millenary Petition,* reputedly signed by a thousand English clergy. Their chief concerns were for clergy to be competent preachers and for the reform of malpractices such as the holding of appointments in plurality, rather than with the organizational hierarchy. During the Civil War, the Puritan 'Solemn League and Covenant' of 1643 looked to the abolition of 'prelacy', defined as 'Church government by archbishops, bishops, their chancellors and commissaries ... deans and chapters, archdeacons, and all other ecclesiastical officers depending on that hierarchy'. The 'Savoy Declaration' of 1658, made under the Protectorate of Cromwell, spells out a strongly 'independent' ecclesiology. There are only 'particular churches', no worldwide or 'catholic' Church; churches comprise 'members' and 'officers', the latter being pastors, teachers, elders and deacons, chosen by the congregation and appointed by prayer and the laying on of hands.

Those Puritans who had earlier sailed to the New World, in the face of Charles I's refusal to countenance their demands, were already putting these principles into practice by establishing their churches 'far away from the influence of bishops' as 'virtually autonomous bodies governed by the members of each parish rather than by an episcopal hierarchy' (Youngs, 2003, p. 210). MacCulloch finds this 'paradox of an established Reformed Church with an all-embracing system of parishes like England, but run by local assemblies of the self-selected godly' (2010, p. 721) a significant factor in encouraging the remarkable diversity of church life that became the norm in America (p. 731). John Wesley recorded his experience of a meeting of Moravian brethren during his missionary venture to America in 1736: he felt himself transported back to the days of Paul and the early house churches, and vowed to bring something of this back to the Church of England (Evans, 2008, p. 189).

The lay-led class meeting structures Wesley devised, with their practices of mutual confession of sin, and encouragement to persevere in holiness, undoubtedly succeeded in introducing a new charism of lay leadership and devotional intensity into the established Church; hierarchy, however, was not so readily disturbed, and indeed Wesley had no particular desire to dismantle it. The resistance of hierarchy to being dislodged was still being noted in the heyday of the Movement for the Ordination of Women in the 1980s (Clark, 1984): not surprisingly, given that hierarchy very literally means 'sacred' (and therefore untouchable) order. Finding alternative formulations therefore takes centre stage in the more radical contemporary reimaginings of ministry, as we shall see in later chapters.

Christianized society and distinctive community

The early centuries

Underlying much of what has been discussed in this chapter is a major issue of missional objectives and the purpose of ministry: is the ultimate goal to fashion a Christian society, or a distinctive Christian community *within* society? And, depending on how this question is answered, is authorized ministry a public representative role with rights of access to all sectors of society in the interests of a broad understanding of Christianization, or is it more specifically directed at congregational formation and the cultivation of a kind of alternative society?

The essentials of these questions are already present in the Donatist schism, which plagued the Church through much of the fourth century. Caecilian, Bishop of Carthage during the early years of the reign of Constantine, was recognized by Rome only on condition that he adhered to the line set by Stephen, Bishop of Rome in Cyprian's time, that sacraments performed by heretics are valid if carried out according to proper procedure and with a right intent. The North African churches, committed to the opposing view, consecrated Donatus as a rival bishop to Caecilian, and the split continued for several decades. The Roman position was eventually defended definitively by Augustine, who as Bishop of Hippo, in present-day Algeria, was well-placed to take on the Donatists. Whereas they, 'proud of their unblemished record in time of persecution', had 'proclaimed that the Church was a gathered pure community' (MacCulloch, 2010, p. 304), Augustine argued that the sacraments must provide a reliable guarantee to the recipient that God's grace is conveyed through them, regardless of the worthiness of the minister. This assurance was needed on account of the mixed nature of the Church in which some 'live wickedly' and may be 'sunk in heresies or in pagan superstitions' (Augustine, *De Baptismo*).

The early Church rejected Donatism as heresy, just as it had done earlier with Montanism. The Donatists insisted that the sacraments are not *ex opere operato* but require worthiness in the minister; the Montanists had privileged the gifts of the Spirit to all believers. Rome's rejection of both these positions can be seen within the context of the growing tightening of institutional constraints by a centralized hierarchy, beginning in the third century and advancing rapidly post-Constantine. If the objective of Christian missionary expansion is the Christianization of societies, unfettered access of all to the Spirit's blessings can be viewed as a dangerous thing, a potential threat to the social order. Accordingly, an authoritative ecclesiastical structure with its episcopally led and ordained hierarchy of ministers is needed to guard and administer such access.

In the same way, in a Christianized society it has to be recognized that levels of religious commitment will vary: a duly authorized hierarchy of ordained clergy will be able to ensure that God's grace is appropriately administered without prejudice from any moral considerations about who is *fit* to do it. Conversely, the Montanist ideal of the free availability of spiritual charismata, and the Donatist requirement of personal qualification to minister in God's name, make sense if the missional objective is to create a distinctive colony of Christian believers living amid, yet in a sense apart from, the wider society with its religiously mixed nature. Here was a debate that would run and run.

From the Middle Ages to the Reformation and beyond

By the Middle Ages 'the Church was a compulsory society, entered by baptism', with 'the full apparatus of a state, with laws, taxes, a great administrative machine, and power of life and death' (Melinsky, 1992, p. 60). A compulsorily Christianized society cannot be other than a 'mixed body' (*corpus permixtum*), as Augustine recognized, and accordingly a 'two-tier' system of religious devotion evolved in which 'the truly Christian way ... was followed only by a minority, by monks and hermits, regular canons and clergy' (Morris, 2003, p. 145). The Church sought to enforce moral rigour for ordinary people by legal and theological means, for example in the doctrine of Christian marriage. For the clergy, celibacy was a way of ensuring that the moral demand was set at an even higher standard. Thus 'in many different ways ... the clergy asserted their power to regulate the lives of the laity, as well as establish their distinction from lay people' (MacCulloch, 2010, p. 373). The 'double standard' persists to this day in the Church of England's official position on same-sex relationships, in which lay people are permitted to enter civil partnerships or marriages, but clergy are required to adhere to a supposedly 'higher' or more rigorous moral commitment to sexual abstinence.

These developments fundamentally reshaped the roles and functions of Christian ministry, together with the nature of the relationship between clergy and laity, as ordained ministry became more about regulating and enforcing the practice of the laity than about the communal living out of the gospel. At the Reformation, Luther seemed to reject the double moral standard for clergy and laity, writing to the 'Christian nobility' that the distinction between a 'spiritual estate' of popes, bishops, priests and religious and a 'secular estate' such as nobles, artisans and farmers was invalid: 'all Christians are truly of the spiritual estate, with no difference among them but that of office' (Luther, cit. Melinsky, 1992, pp. 73–4). Faced however with the dilemma of a 'mixed Church', Luther simply shifted the focus of the two-tier system from a clergy/laity divide to one between leaders and led: his reform in the end turns out to rely heavily on the exemplary piety of the 'godly prince', the secular authority, and therefore exposes the Church to the risk of a different kind of captivity.

In England, the famous *Via Media* of Anglicanism forged in the reign of Elizabeth I offered another solution to the problem of a distinctive Christian Church within a nominally Christian society. Richard Hooker insisted that '*no* form of polity is exclusively prescribed in scripture' (Melinsky, 1992, p. 93), and put the emphasis on the *visible* Church as a 'society' – that is, not just an 'assembly' that has no existence when its members are not 'assembled'; but not an invisible 'communion' either. As a visible Church it is necessarily also a mixed body; but its apostolic nature and continuity with the primitive Christian communities are guaranteed in its doctrine, liturgy and sacraments (Hooker, *Laws of Ecclesiastical Polity* III.i, pp. 7–8).

The English Puritans were not satisfied with this apparent 'halfway house' model of Reformation. A leading Puritan divine, Thomas Cartwright, published in 1572 a set of 'admonitions' to Parliament, demanding the abandonment of both episcopacy and the Book of Common Prayer, which Puritans regarded as still much too close to the Roman Mass (Melinsky, 1992, p. 95). The failure of these demands led to a hardening of attitudes on episcopacy in the Church of England; nevertheless, most Anglican divines at this stage still maintained that although episcopacy was of apostolic origin, it was not of the 'essence' of church, and therefore non-episcopal churches were still churches. During the Civil War and the Protectorate under Cromwell, with the short-lived ascendancy of the Puritans, the differences between Puritan and Anglican ecclesiology became much more sharply defined: the Restoration brought about the exclusive insistence on episcopal ordination and ministry that has persisted to the present time, and more than once proved the decisive stumbling block in the way of ecumenical advances.

The Westminster Confession of 1643 makes a clear distinction between the 'visible' and 'invisible' Church: only the latter is wholly true and pure as it consists of God's elect, whereas the visible Church is 'subject both to mixture and error'. The Confession retains a relatively moderate position on the distinctiveness of the earthly Christian community, by contrast with a classic Puritan text such as John Owen's *The True Nature of a Gospel Church*. Owen insists that bodies claiming to be churches must *'visibly answer* the description given of gospel churches in the Scripture'. Owen dismisses the view of Anglicans like Hooker that the Church cannot be pure, as to settle for the mixed Church of the 'Christianized' society is to accept a position that falls far short of God's ambitions for the redemption of souls and the transformation of lives. Similarly, the continental Anabaptists 'turned to local congregations of voluntary members who regarded themselves as altogether set apart from the state' and 'aspired to communal solidarity as a holy people' (Lindberg, 2010, pp. 190, 210).

The debate about the distinctiveness of the Church is an intractable one, but its very intractability might well be a source of strength in the postmodern climate. The view that the true Church can only be identified by the right belief and conduct of its members, ruling out the idea of a 'national Church' with its mixed character, relies on lofty ideals that prove extraordinarily difficult to achieve in practice. But there is now an opportunity for a fresh approach to the Christianization of society, on a model that differs from that of the Christendom era, in no longer being predicated upon a dominant institutional Church in close alliance with the State. Where Christendom modes of church are losing traction and many of their features are dwindling into vestigial remains, the question can be raised anew of what a distinctively Christian presence in the public arena that is *not* world-denying, separatist and sectarian might look like; we shall return to this in Chapter 9.

Conclusion

This chapter has taken soundings from the history of the Christian churches to develop a portrait of the contested field of ministry, its orders and structures, roles and functions. While Catholic order has sought to integrate these elements around the threefold order of bishops, priests and deacons, historically this has not always been the hallmark of ministerial orthodoxy, and even where it has been, this sense of continuity has been maintained only at the cost of accepting a wide range of interpretations of the theological meaning and practical responsibilities of the three orders. The chapter has explored three particular areas in which the contestation of ministry has led to recurring debate and dissent: the axis between ministry as charismatic endowment and institutional authorization; the ordering of ministry through hierarchical structures alongside its emergence from a grass-roots movement of the people; and the contrast between the fundamental theological visions of a broad-based and 'mixed' Church within an officially Christianized society, and the Church as a distinctive and committed Christian community set within a broadly secular or (sometimes) hostile environment.

These tensions and polarities underline much that is debated at the present time, as the churches in the post-Christendom West attempt to develop strategies for engagement in the alien world of the emerging social and cultural environment. In the next two chapters, we shall return to the foundational questions of the threefold order and the meaning and practice of ordination itself in the changing context.

3

Threefold Disorder: Diaconal, Presbyteral and Episcopal Ministry Today

In the previous chapter, I offered a reading of important developments in the theology and practice of ministerial ordering during key periods in the history of the Christian Church. The theme holding the narrative in the chapter together was the perpetually contested nature of ministry. In the case of the 'threefold order of bishops, priests and deacons', this contested quality holds true not only with respect to debates between those churches that do, and those that do not, explicitly embrace this framework for authorized ministry, but also between and *within* churches that do. Although the terminology may exhibit continuity and consistency among these churches, both the meaning of the terms and the practical ways in which the ministries come to expression are frequently variable and always contextual.

In this chapter, the diaconal, presbyteral and episcopal expressions of ministry will be examined in relation to a number of contemporary debates, engaging chiefly with sources designed to bring ideas informed by good scholarship to a wider church constituency, with a view to influencing ongoing strategic thinking about ministry in the contemporary context.

Ministry in three dimensions

A familiar strategy over the last 20 years or so has been to recast the threefold orders in terms of essential characteristics and functions of ministry, rather than referring them in the first instance to individual roles. One of the best-known examples has been the work of Steven Croft (1999, new edition 2008), which provides a useful starting point for the discussion in this chapter. Croft's agenda supports to some extent the position argued in this book, in that he acknowledges that expressions of ministry are culturally contextual:

All through history, the Church has reacted with the culture in which it has found itself ... Each generation of Christian people has needed to understand the times and the culture in which it is set and respond accordingly ... Different times and seasons in the Church call for different patterns of ministry and mission, even though the Gospel message itself may be unchanging. (2008, p. 3)

Three aspects of this opening statement raise issues to be addressed in this and subsequent chapters. First, there is the question of the extent to which the reaction of the Church to the surrounding culture cannot only be about *understanding* it, but must also allow for the Church being *changed* by the process. Second, the assertion that although patterns of ministry and mission may change but 'the Gospel message itself' does not, may be an oversimplification, since medium and message cannot be so easily distinguished. Third, to admit the need for different patterns of mission and ministry in response to cultural context implies at least the possibility that no one pattern is definitive as a theological 'given', but all are provisional.

Croft (chapters 4, 7 and 11) comprehensively examines all the New Testament texts that refer to *diakonoi, presbuteroi* and *episkopoi* (deacons, presbyters and bishops), concluding that they can be read as referring not only to individual ministries, but also to three dimensions present in all ministry. This 'not only, but also' reflects Croft's assurance that the roots of the Church of England's developed pattern of the 'threefold order' can indeed be found in the soil of the New Testament. However, his analysis could also support the view that if the texts were approached without assuming the 'threefold order', they could be seen as reflecting a pragmatic and adaptive response to changing circumstances. This would bring Croft closer to the findings of James Dunn, whose analysis of the texts leads him to conclude that in the New Testament there is 'no greater diversity than that apparent in the various concepts of ministry', and that the only 'focus of unity' that can hold together the 'divergent patterns of ministry ... with any consistency' is 'Jesus and faith in him' (2006, pp. 131–2).

Threefold ministry and trinitarian ecclesiology

In recent work on ministerial theology, a popular way of retaining the view that the ordering of ministry reflects much more than pragmatic necessity in response to socio-cultural context is to argue from trinitarian principles. This position, worked out in detail in the influential ecclesiology of the Orthodox theologian John Zizioulas (1985), is associated in the British context particularly with Robin Greenwood, who puts the issue this way:

> Some churches ... allocate no permanent roles to their ministers and so the relationships ... are purely provisional and functional. In a trinitarian ecclesiology ... the ordering of ministries is more than a haphazard pragmatism ... The Church's ordering images the *perichoretic* reciprocal movement between Father, Son and Spirit. (2009, pp. 98–9)

Greenwood works through this position with an impressive consistency, both here and in his earlier work on priesthood (Greenwood, 1994). Nevertheless, while it can be granted that ministerial order is not merely a matter of pragmatism, it is a massive leap from here to claiming that its theological basis rests on privileged insight into the inner relations of the deity.

Helen Morris casts doubt on the model of 'social trinitarianism' as a basis for ecclesiology, on the grounds that it tends to lead away from the 'real' church into abstraction (2019, pp. 59–64). She points out that Zizioulas deploys the trinitarian model in support of a *hierarchical* structure of church, contrary to those (for example, Greenwood) who see it as favouring a more 'egalitarian' model (p. 60). The problem here is the risk that the inherited 'threefold order' is assumed, in whatever form, and the trinitarian theology is appropriated to defend it. Another example of this is found in the Report of the Archbishops' Group on the Episcopate, who assert that the Church's institutional framework is 'an incarnational expression' of participation in the trinitarian community (1990, p. 9). The problem with all such claims is that it is not clear whether they are to be read as statements of fact, exhortations to the Church to conform more closely to an ideal, or speculative proposals about a mystical, 'true' Church. Trevor Beeson commented tartly on the Group's report that although their 'doctrine of church order could not have been higher', relating it to the practical challenges facing episcopacy today 'proved to be beyond the group's capacity' (2007, p. 237).

Another advocate of a trinitarian ecclesiology, Christopher Cocksworth (2008), engages with the question of whether the ordering of the Church is implied in the gospel. He begins with Michael Ramsey's argument in *The Gospel and the Catholic Church* that catholic order in and of itself is already 'a development which grew in the Gospel ... which expresses the Gospel ... is an utterance of the Gospel' (Ramsey, 1990, p. 57, cit. Cocksworth, 2008, pp. 100–1). Cocksworth's conclusion is that he cannot go quite all the way with Ramsey:

The Gospel does mediate principles for the life and order of the church which belong to its essence. But do the principles of, for example, oversight, local leadership and costly service require embodiment in appointed persons to oversee (*episcopoi*), to teach and lead (*presbyteroi*) and to serve (*diakonoi*) in such a way that without them, we must say with Ignatius, that 'no group can be called a church'? (2008, p. 103)

His answer follows Miroslav Volf (1998), whose trinitarian theology of ministry focuses on the Spirit, whose procession from the Father and the Son validates the distribution of a multiplicity of *charismata* among all members of the church. Volf is content that 'all important functions' can be gathered under the three broad categories of episcopal, presbyteral and diaconal ministry (1998, pp. 247–8, cit. Cocksworth, 2008, p. 104). Hence Cocksworth concludes that 'the leading, teaching and serving functions of those ministries need to be fulfilled in some way through the church's various office holders', not necessarily by bishops, presbyters and deacons as historically understood. He therefore tilts the balance away from Ramsey's prioritization of the catholic over the local, which leads to the view that the ordering of ministry by local churches must be dependent on a formally recognized universal order. Instead, he prefers Volf's evangelical location of responsibility for ministerial functions 'in the Christ-confessing and Spirit-filled life of the local gathering of Christians' (p. 105).

Even so, it is still not quite clear just how far Cocksworth is prepared to let the notion of 'dimensions' or 'functions' of ministry challenge inherited positions. In a section headed 'the minister as a sign of the priestly people' (pp. 245–6), he chooses to use the term 'presbyters' in preference to 'priests', allowing himself to appear to be making a proposal that could require the Church to change quite radically. But he does not state plainly whether the 'presbyters' he wants are identical with what 'priests' already are within the Church of England. He writes about 'ministries of apostolic overseers, congregational leaders and servants of the kingdom' (Cocksworth and Brown, 2006, p. 216, cit. Cocksworth, 2008, p. 257): are these to be identified with 'bishops, priests and deacons' as the Church of England understands them, or is he allowing the possibility of valid alternatives? The words are capable of either a radical or a conservative interpretation, and this is a problem that besets all attempts to reconfigure the 'threefold order' in other terms, such as 'dimensions'.

In the present situation, the churches cannot afford to limit their innovative initiatives to a tight conformity with inherited ministerial theology: at the very least, wider ecumenical conversations are required which can take account of the insights of independent and emerging churches. For example, writing from a Brethren (Independent) perspective, John Baigent argues that God did not necessarily intend 'to control practice for all time and all circumstances' (2006, p. 15). Rather than a blueprint, the New Testament implies a minimum requirement of 'every-member ministry', plus some form of recognized local leadership. The guiding principles include equality of status (no hierarchy); recognized leadership, with a suitable terminology determined by the context (i.e. they do not have to be called 'elders', 'ministers', 'bishops', or whatever); and the avoidance of any definitive clergy/lay distinction (pp. 16–17). The following discussion of the threefold orders will allow for a broader dialogue with this kind of position alongside the inherited model.

Diaconal ministry

Origins and evolution

Diaconal ministry took its cue from the Lucan narrative of the appointment of the 'Seven' in Acts 6 to look after the fair distribution of food to the widows of the community and to serve at the table. This led to a more or less universal understanding of *diakonia*, as 'the specific kind of selfless, caring, and loving service that characterized Jesus in his dealings with the lame and rejected men and women who people the gospel narratives' (Collins, 2002, p. 8). How to embody this expression of caring and loving service within a formalized order of ministry soon became problematic, and despite notable exceptions such as the third-century St Lawrence the Deacon and the medieval St Francis of Assisi, the Catholic tradition soon saw the diaconate dwindle into a year of apprenticeship prior to ordination to the priesthood.

The churches of the Protestant Reformation made some attempts at reviving the order, by setting up orders of deacons within the church specifically to undertake a ministry of social welfare (running orphanages, hospitals, almshouses and so on). In particular, this sometimes provided a recognized ministerial role for women, as with both Lutheran and Anglican deaconesses: the portrayal of the diaconate as a suitable ministerial role for women has a long pedigree. As recently as 2017, a survey found continuing controversy over the issue of whether the permanent diaconate should be seen as a pathway to ordained ministry for conservative evangelical women whose churches barred women from positions of leadership giving them authority over men ('Poll uncovers obstacles to the diaconate', *Church Times*, 20 January 2017).

On the whole, the Reformation failed to re-appropriate the diaconate, which remained a transitory ministry, seen as secondary or minor (Hall, 1991, pp. 1–8). The changes in training for ministry in the nineteenth century (see Chapter 11) omitted to pay any serious attention to the diaconate. At Vatican II (1962–65) the Roman Catholic Church proposed a 'permanent diaconate' (exclusively male, but candidates could be married), to exercise a 'ministry of the word, of the liturgy, and of charity' (cit. Collins, 2002, p. 10). Subsequently most major denominations have revisited the question of diaconal ministry with a view to distinguishing more clearly between diaconal and presbyteral forms of ordained ministry; in some churches, deacons remain on the 'lay' side of the lay/ordained line.

In the Church of England, the report *Deacons in the Church* (1974) broached the possibility of abolishing the diaconate altogether. The ordination of women as deacons in 1987 renewed interest in trying to define the nature and functions of the diaconate, particularly in view of the coexistence in the church of (lay) deaconesses and (ordained) women deacons, but in 1988 the report *Deacons in the Ministry of the Church* struggled to capture the distinctiveness of the deacon's ministry. The report *Deacons Now* (1990) focused primarily on the experience of women deacons, in the period between their introduction in 1987 and the vote to allow women priests in 1992. Following the ordination of women to the priesthood in 1994, the diaconate once more took a back seat until the House of Bishops issued their report *For Such a Time as This* (2001), which reignited interest at least in thinking about a distinctive diaconate, if not to any great extent in practice. In the Church of England, the great majority of deacons are still 'transitional', serving a one-year term prior to ordination to the priesthood.

Fresh approaches and unresolved issues

In common with all recent thinking about the diaconate, the 2001 report was influenced by the extensive research carried out by the Australian scholar John Collins, originally in the 1980s but reprised and updated at various points since (Collins, 2002). Collins undertook a massive lexical examination of the usage of terms with the root *diakon-* throughout the New Testament and other documents of the earliest period of the Christian Church. He concluded that 'caring and loving service' did not accurately represent the principal semantic field of these terms when interpreted in context. On the words of Jesus in Mark 10.45, 'the Son of Man came not to be served but to serve, and to give his life as a ransom for many', Collins argued that as Jesus was speaking here about the mission committed to him by his Father, the one who sent him and whom he came to serve, the emphasis is on Jesus' sending and obedience to his mission rather than on the caring nature of his deeds. The Acts 6 passage was essentially a red herring: Luke nowhere refers to the men appointed by the term 'deacons', and the emphasis is on their being appointed to this specific task on behalf of the apostles, and being authorized to carry it out, rather than on the particular nature of the task.

On the other hand, Collins observed that where the designation of individuals as 'deacons' (*diakonoi*) does occur, such as in the Pastoral Epistles and the first verse of the letter to the Philippians, it is paired with the term *episkopoi*, or overseers. This suggests a twofold pattern, in which the pairing reflects the partnership between those who are authorized for particular ecclesial tasks (*diakonoi*) and those who, in the name of the whole Church, authorize and oversee them (*episkopoi*). *Diakonia* may be defined as 'conscious mission with divine authority and with the mandate to be a go-between in contexts of conflict and suffering' (Collins, 2002, p. 19). Deacons are authorized representatives of the apostolic community who are sent into the world to *get things done* on behalf of the gospel. Those who are ordained as what used to be called 'permanent', now (better) 'distinctive' deacons, seem to straddle aspects of both Collins and the traditional models. Some have a very church-based ministry with a strong emphasis on liturgical functions and pastoral care, while others have a more 'out in the world' role, such as town centre or local retail chaplaincy.

Collins's work continues to stimulate debate about the prospects for the regeneration of the diaconate, and it raises a number of largely unresolved critical questions. First, if Collins is right, what might it mean to claim that this form of diaconate is one part of a threefold ordering of ordained ministry? In some contexts, it is chaplains who would appear to be carrying out the kind of missional ministry Collins has in mind, but relatively few chaplains are actually deacons, and growing numbers are not ordained at all (chaplaincy is discussed further in Chapter 7). Second, in the Church of England at least, what would be the relationship between Collins's deacons and the ministry of Readers? A few dioceses have sought to rebrand (lay) Reader ministry as either a distinctive (ordained) diaconate, or as 'Licensed Lay Ministers': the first move raises questions about why those who are licensed to preach and lead worship should have to be ordained, and the second about what the difference between licensed lay ministers and deacons would be. Third, rebranding deacons as the authorized apostolic emissaries of the Church into the world carries a risk of a new clericalization of ministry similar to that which occurs when the priest is seen as the 'public representative minister' par excellence: where does this leave lay people as witnesses in the world of work and daily life?

The failure to clarify the diaconate has repercussions for the remaining ministries within the threefold order. The view that the orders are cumulative, not successive (i.e. once a deacon, always a deacon, even when becoming a priest or a bishop), makes good theological sense, but it does little to settle the question of what the diaconate ought to be. Diaconal ministry cannot be seriously engaged with in the process of reimagining ministry without allowing it to interrogate the distinction between ordained and lay (the subject of the next chapter).

Presbyteral ministry

Priest or presbyter

'In the earliest Christian congregations, the elders were the supervisors, which is another way of saying that the presbyters (or priests) were the bishops' (Rorem, 1990, p. 17). Presbyteral ministry derives from the recognition of those in the congregation with spiritual maturity as suitable persons to exercise oversight of the community. The concept of the 'elders' has ancient anthropological roots. The etymology is the same for *elder*, *presbyter* and *senior*: all are comparatives meaning simply 'older'. This does not mean that presbyters need to be 'old' in years: that is why Paul writing to Timothy urged him not to let anyone despise him on account of his youth (1 Tim. 4.12) – he may have been young in years, but his faith was mature. Originally, then, presbyters are 'senior Christians' who command the respect and trust of the congregation, and they are also always and everywhere plural. Even when a presiding elder was elected from among their number, this presidency was not exercised in a monarchical way, but collegially as *primus inter pares*, first among equals.

The English word 'priest' has a complicated semantic history. Etymologically it is a contraction (most probably via Old French) of the original Greek *presbuteros*, or 'elder' (Latin *senior*). However, as we have seen, in the early centuries of the Church the theology of Christian ministry came to absorb many elements of the sacrificing priesthood of the Old Testament. The Hebrew word for the temple priest, *cohen*, is rendered *hiereus* in Greek and *sacerdos* in Latin, terms familiar via such English words as 'hierarchy' and 'sacred'. This word is never used to designate a Christian minister in the New Testament, but only Jesus (for example, as our 'great high priest' in the Letter to the Hebrews), or the whole Church as a body (a 'royal priesthood', 1 Peter 2.9).

However, the early English versions of the Bible (notably Wycliffe, 1395) used the same word, 'priest', to translate both the Old Testament *hiereus* and the New Testament *presbuteros*, reflecting the medieval theology of priesthood. The Reformation scholar and translator of the Bible into English (1525), William Tyndale, was well aware of this anomaly:

> There is a word in Latin *sacerdos*, in Greek *hiereus*, in Hebrew *cohan*, that is minister, an officer, a sacrificer, or priest; as Aaron was a priest, and sacrificed for the people, and was a mediator between God and them. And in the English should it have had some other name than priest [because] ... another word is there in Greek, called presbyter, in Latin senior, in English an Elder, and is nothing but an officer to teach, and not to be a mediator between God and us. (*Doctrinal Treatises*, p. 255)

It is interesting that Tyndale, recognizing the derivation of 'priest' from presbyter, suggests that it is *hiereus* that ought to be translated by some other word than 'priest', rather than 'priest' being reserved for the cultic priesthood of the Old Testament and a different term found for the Christian minister. Linguistically speaking he is right, but it is probably too late to retrieve the more etymological sense of 'priest' and divest it of the hieratic sense, so that as a result the same word has to do duty for both.

This is noticeable in the literature on rethinking ministry, where contributors tend to adopt the usage that reflects their church tradition. Thus, for example from the evangelical side, Croft (2008, chapters 7 and 8) unambiguously takes his cue from the equation of 'priest' with 'presbyter', and only briefly (pp. 100 ff.) discusses the influence of the derivation from *hiereus*. Lewis-Anthony, on the other hand, as an Anglican moderate or 'Affirming Catholic', turns naturally for his model of priesthood to Michael Ramsey's classic *The Christian Priest Today* (Lewis-Anthony, 2009, pp. 77 ff.), with no mention of 'presbyter' at all. Whether a person more instinctively thinks 'presbyter' or 'priest' when considering this order of ministry will significantly affect the approach they take to its renewal, especially in respect of the idea of 'ministerial priesthood', to which we now turn.

Ministerial priesthood

A universal priesthood?

One way of approaching the idea of 'priesthood' that owes more to *hiereus* than to *presbuteros* is to claim for it a broader and more universal status than purely what is found in the Hebrew Scriptures, as this will result in a validity that can persist even alongside the 'presbyter' of the New Covenant. An example of a monumental effort to defend and expound such a view can be found in Kenneth Mason's *Priesthood and Society* (1992, revised edition 2002). Mason relies on a theory of 'natural' or 'universal' priesthood that underpins all expressions of ministerial priesthood: 'The necessity of priesthood operates in all societies ... priesthood is primarily an articulation of social relationships in such a way that the sacred becomes manifest through them' (p. 55). Just as the Church is both a divine creation and a human institution, in Christian priesthood 'certain social and institutional necessities for community identity and relationship are ... made to serve as symbols pointing beyond themselves' (p. 110).

The most interesting aspect of Mason's work is his view of how priesthood serves the subversive and precarious processes of 'anti-structure' that reveal the demand 'that all human life, as pursued in all social contexts, shall be opened up to God' (p. 68). It is the role of priesthood to handle these processes, through symbol, ritual and religious performance (liturgy). In principle, every Eucharist is a contribution to this process; we have to live in the world of structure, but with an experience of anti-structure that relativizes our perspective on this world. Mason draws on Victor Turner's *The Ritual Process*, with its ideas of passage through temporary 'liminal' (threshold) experiences in which an anti-structural condition of *communitas* is achieved, that 'allows those who pass through it to change, and ... the society from which they have been parted to receive them back changed' (p. 63).

In order to be able to handle responsibly the symbolism and ritual that will accompany people through the anti-structural moment (pp. 112–13), priesthood requires universal recognition and must reside in the person as well as in the role and function. I would argue that Mason's view of priesthood will be intensely resistant to being systematized into a single 'correct' form; the qualities of priestliness it envisages do not sit naturally with the structures, roles and expectations for which the Church customarily selects, trains and deploys its ministers. This is the challenge for all approaches that place priestly quality of life at the centre of their definition: they may well end up identifying all kinds of people who excel in this role without being ordained as priests, and conversely many who *are* in ordained ministry for whom this is not at all their own perception of their role, nor where their natural aptitudes lie. The dilemmas of this can well be illustrated from the sub-division of ministerial priesthood known as 'public representative ministry'.

Public representative ministry

A principal example of this approach can be found in the collection of essays edited by Sam Wells and Sarah Coakley (2008), and the theological reflections on this model of priesthood in a second volume from the same source, the 'Littlemore Group' founded by Coakley and Wells (Martin and Coakley (eds), 2016). Coakley puts it like this:

> In an established church in particular, the dog-collared figure bears more weight of expectation and longing (or alternatively, of revulsion and loathing) than he or she may consciously know. The priestly office, even in secularized Britain, still comes with such burdens and possibilities ... When priests efficaciously enact their priesthood, then, there is this quiet quality of vicariousness or 'representation' in what they do. It is a demanding, and often discomforting place in which to stand. (Wells and Coakley (eds), 2008, pp. 3–4)

In the same volume, Rowan Williams makes explicit the links with the priesthood of the old covenant: 'Priesthood works, classically, through the supervision of *sacrifice*, the processes by which peace-making gifts are offered to the divine reality so that sacred order may be restored' (p. 173). True, he does go on to affirm that Jesus has fulfilled this work of restoration once and for all, so that 'priesthood is over and sacrifice is now unnecessary', as the Reformers taught. However, he does not believe that this means the Church can dispense with the public priestly task: 'this priestliness in respect of the society we inhabit is focused in the person of the Church of England's priests' (p. 179). The priest is the 'trustee' of the time and space cleared by God, the space for restoration and grace, reconciliation and hope. It is not first and foremost about 'leadership', nor even about teaching; these happen 'only as and when the priest has learned what it is to inhabit a place and to speak from that place into the community's life' (p. 181).

Magdalen Smith vividly portrays this role in its joys and burdens:

> Our presence has the potential simultaneously to jar and comfort, depending on who we encounter and what the occasion is. We are still 'odd' and unusual ...; many people simply don't know what to make of us or how to relate to us ... we sometimes become representative of something unpleasant in a person's history ... we jar and clash with people's already worked-out understanding of society in our post-modern and reductionist Western world-view. Yet for others there is a recognition; we are a soothing and comforting presence in the community. (2014, p. 11)

There are stark contradictions here: 'to jar *and* to comfort'; or, in Coakley's account, 'expectation and longing' or 'revulsion and loathing'. Hoyle too describes an 'extraordinary task' that invites failure, that Jesus promised 'the world will hate you', that priests 'can cause us worse distress by doing their work well', because of the uncomfortable message with which they are charged (2016, pp. 60–1). Priesthood in this model requires enormous reserves of resilience to manage the discordant reactions priests may provoke and the conflicting expectations they elicit (Allain-Chapman, 2012). These issues will be explored further in the next chapter in the context of a wider discussion about ordination, and in the final chapter in relation to the handling of role and person in ministry.

The priesthood of the parson

In light of the demands of ministerial priesthood understood as public representative ministry, it is hardly surprising that books designed to help clergy cope are on the rise (Edmondson, 2002; Clitherow, 2004; Ison (ed.), 2005; Lewis-Anthony, 2009; Oliver, 2012). Lewis-Anthony describes as 'Herbertism' the model of parish ministry that came to be regarded as normative in the Church of England, summarized in the following terms:

> His story is a triumph of the *mythos* of the Church of England, the story we tell ourselves, to root ourselves in the soil and society of England, to show that, despite all the vicissitudes of the centuries, reformations, dissolutions, indolence, decay, revivals, disputes and decline, we are both *the* Church of England and the Church *of* England. This land is our land, and George Herbert is the guarantor of our title to it. (2009, p. 22)

Resonances of this model can be detected in the titles of such works as Wells and Coakley's *Praying for England* and Stephen Platten's *Rebuilding Jerusalem: The Church's Hold on Hearts and Minds* (Platten, 2007). Lewis-Anthony develops a sketch of Herbertism in action by drawing on the well-known handbook by Forder, *The Parish Priest at Work* (1959), the classic manual for the benevolent paternalism, or authoritarianism with a cheery smile, that was the dominant model for Anglican parish ministry for much of the last century. It is a model in which the parson is the centre of everything in both church and community; the parson runs everything, advises everyone about everything, shows up everywhere and is available 24/7 to respond to all manner of need with tea and sympathy.

To illustrate the crisis in this model, Lewis-Anthony cites Nicholas Stacey's eventual disillusionment with parish ministry, following the relative failure of his innovative community ministry at Woolwich in the 1960s significantly to increase the size of the regular congregation (Stacey, 1971). Stacey made three proposals for radical reform which Lewis-Anthony quotes with interest: 'that 90 per cent of clergy should seek secular employment ... the Church must divest itself of the burden of so many unnecessary buildings ... [and] there needs to be a parallel "stripping down", of what is taught and what is believed in' (Lewis-Anthony, 2009, pp. 38–9, cit. Stacey, 'How the Church could survive', published in *The Observer*, May 1965). Stacey was right, half a century ago, about the need for a much more radical overhaul of all the Church's structures and systems than its hierarchy were prepared to contemplate. But Lewis-Anthony focuses largely on the sheer fact of the parson being expected to do far too much; hence the later chapters advocate better management of time and resources and a more disciplined rule of life. The book turns out to be more about helping the clergy cope with ministry in the existing system than about envisaging far-reaching change to it.

Most accounts of representational priesthood ultimately insist very strongly on a role that only the priest can occupy, that is much more than functional. While God distributes gifts through the Holy Spirit, for the whole body of Christ as 'laity', there is a separate, distinct and unique gifting for a 'special priesthood not possessed by other Christians ... different in essence and higher in dignity than the ordinary faithful' (Davis, 1967, p. 139): this is the Catholic position classically expounded by Moberly in his *Ministerial Priesthood* (2012, originally published 1897; see Greenwood, 1994, pp. 7–11). By contrast, those for whom 'priest' unambiguously denotes 'elder/presbyter' are operating a single-track approach: Christ bestows all gifts for ministry in the same way, so that 'priesthood' comes not as a special, individual calling but only from and through the community.

Greenwood (1994 and 2009) has offered an analysis that aims to unite the perspectives of 'presbyter/elder' and 'priest', by anchoring the theology of priesthood in a relational, trinitarian pattern. Some understandings of priesthood are principally Christological, based on the priest as in some way representing and imitating Christ, and others are pneumatological or 'charismatic', prioritizing the diverse gifts of the Spirit for the whole body of Christ over any kind of ministerial priesthood (Pickard, 2009); Greenwood urges that a trinitarian foundation permits the best of both worlds. At its best, Ordained Local Ministry (OLM; see further in Chapter 5) was able to model for the Church at large a synthesis of these two approaches to priesthood. OLMs were expected to exercise their ministry within the context of a collaborative team; but precisely because they were local through and through, deeply embedded in the communities that had nurtured their faith and their vocation, as well as very often providing the context for their daily employment and their social life, they also had the potential to fulfil the kind of role the contributors to Wells and Coakley are writing about.

It is noteworthy, however, that when Greenwood invited a sample of parish clergy to reflect on what 'energized' them in their ministry, the data suggested strongly that the key factors were overwhelmingly personal and individual (2009, chapter 2). The moments that made the respondents feel 'here I am truly expressing my priesthood' appeared less in line with his collaborative model for priestly ministry, and more in keeping with the model in *Praying for England*. This shows that there is something within the role of 'priesthood' that is not adequately captured by the more prosaic 'presbyter', but this is much more significant for their ministerial identity for some clergy than for others. The question is how this might be reflected in a reimagined ministry, beyond the 'one size fits all' practice of ordination to the priesthood that smooths over the very real differences.

Presbyterate and episcope

Writing about how clergy manage the different demands on their time, Croft observes that for some, 'the whole of ordained ministry becomes more and more focused around presiding at the Eucharist' (2008, p. 20). Croft sees this as negative, but this is not necessarily the case, since Eucharistic presidency is precisely the role that lies at the heart of presbyteral ministry, gathering the people and creating with them the central act of worship that gives expression to their ecclesial identity. Those who have the distinctive charism and calling to preside should not necessarily be expected to be 'leaders' or 'managers' in a secular sense; they may not always be the chief preachers; nor necessarily responsible for being the 'public face' of the Church, or suited to being pioneer missioners. For some, being 'focused around presiding at the Eucharist' may be their exact vocation, the embodiment of local *episcope*.

Greenwood argues that this role of presidency within the local church community, as distinct from 'leadership', harks back to the earliest times when *episkopos* and *presbuteros* were one and the same. The people are 'asking [their priest] for the time being ... to be *episkopos*, the one who persuasively draws together and holds the values of the community' (2009, p. 101). He maintains that this 'understanding of God as a communion of personal and diverse relations ... offers a vision for a priest to be "in charge" without becoming merely separate or superior'. He proposes the image of the 'navigator', who 'will stimulate and resource the community in recognizing its own overall responsibility for the shape and quality of its ministry and mission' (p. 116). The 'navigator' metaphor is a helpful alternative view of how local *episcope* ought to be exercised in a Christian context, but as an individual role, in the present cultural climate in the Church, great care will need to be taken to avoid it being co-opted into a subtle form of enhancement of the power of bishops, to which we now turn.

Episcopal ministry

As we have seen, Collins claims to have unearthed the primitive 'binary' model in which ministry is ordered into *episcope* and *diakonia*. The first is the exercise by the council of presbyters of the calling to preside over the household of the Church, animating and orchestrating its life in the pluriform harmony of the Spirit. The second comprises the sending out of commissioned envoys into the world with the authority of the *episcope* to serve the apostolic mission. Certainly, at least as late as the fourth century, the early Church does not seem to have conclusively distinguished bishops from presbyters. Two questions immediately arise. The first concerns what justification there is for regarding episcopacy as a fully fledged 'third order' of ministry rather than a senior level of the presbyterate. The other arises once the attempt is made to link the earlier concept and practice of *episcope* with the reality of the structures within episcopally ordered churches today, and also to interpret the model with respect to other churches that do not have 'bishops' as such.

Order and office

The Archbishops' Group on the Episcopate (1990) defend episcopacy as a genuine 'third order'. In consideration of ecumenical difficulties with this, they note that in rejecting the episcopate, Presbyterians and Congregationalists had good reason in the sixteenth and seventeenth centuries to 'resist claims to personal power held by bishops in their own right' (p. 65). They explain that Lutherans retain a vision of episcopacy as among those 'rites and ceremonies' that can be varied by local (regional) churches, because 'the distinction of the "orders" of priest and bishop' is seen as 'post-apostolic, and of human not divine origin' (p. 70). They accept that even for Anglican theologians such as Hooker, episcopacy was always seen as of the *bene esse* of church rather than the *esse*: an episcopal structure is to be preferred, but non-episcopal communions are nonetheless genuine churches (p. 86).

The Group therefore try to quell the fears of Protestant churches about insistence upon episcopal ordination as a prerequisite for recognition of their ministries, claiming that the monarchical, prelatical character of bishops has given way to a model of collegiality and servanthood. Despite this, a somewhat less reassuring picture also characterizes the report. The Group strongly defend episcopacy as a third *order* of ministry rather than just an *office* (pp. 152–3). The distinctions here become rather technical, but in essence whereas an 'office' may be shared and temporary (for example, it lapses on retirement), 'orders' are a permanent state that can only be conferred and held individually. The Group affirm the teaching of Vatican II on the distinctive 'ordination' gifts conferred to bishops (pp. 53–4), giving expression to the idea that bishops are *sui generis*, not just presbyters writ large. Episcopacy is 'mystical' as well as structural, on account of the embodiment of catholicity and apostolicity in the person of the bishop by virtue of episcopal ordination (p. 142). In a striking phrase drawing on Lossky, the bishop embodies the unity-in-diversity of the Church: 'the bishop is the *poluplethia* ['multi-plenitude'] in his person, the many in the one' (p. 9).

The lofty calling of the order of *episcope* interpreted in this manner brings us to the second area of critical debate, which is whether the model is deliverable under contemporary conditions. Because of all that bishops symbolize in their person, delegation of roles and responsibilities is difficult: it 'leaves the ultimate pastoral responsibility in the hands of the bishop' (p. 177). Appointing more suffragans to assist the diocesan bishop does not really help, because the suffragan is merely 'the bishop who acts in the place of his diocesan when delegation or occasion requires', as an 'episcopal vicar'. 'It is a sharing of identity ... he might be described as taking his diocesan's "episcopal presence" with him ...' (pp. 198–9). This is an extraordinary concept that surely seems to saddle both diocesan and suffragan alike with a relationship between role and person that is almost impossible to sustain while retaining personal integrity, not to say sanity.

The diocese as the local church

The question of the sheer practicality of episcopacy understood as set out in the previous section is brought into sharp focus in the case frequently made for regarding 'the diocese' as the basic unit of 'the local church'. This position is articulated in the first ARCIC Report on Authority (1976), para. III.8: 'The unity of local communities under one bishop constitutes what is commonly meant in our two communions by "a local church", though the expression is sometimes used in other ways.' This appeals to the early Patristic understanding that 'where the bishop is found, there is the Church': the presence and practice of *episcope* effectively identifies the Church locally.

In this respect the diocese precedes the parish, which is seen as a more functional entity that developed in close alliance with socio-economic units (typically villages); to put it another way, the parish is sociologically but not theologically significant, whereas the diocese is both. However, as initially the presbyter and the bishop were one and the same, it follows that so too were the parish and diocese, and we should not read back into the primitive context an interpretation that makes it seem more similar to the present structures than it is. The doctrine of the diocese as the 'local Church', in England at least, sounds like an ecclesiological assertion lacking empirical evidence for its truthfulness. By contrast, 'the parish has, without question, been the primary embodiment of Anglican social space' (Andrew Rumsey, 'A Kind of Belonging', *Church Times*, 2 June 2017; see, further, Rumsey, 2017).

The ecclesiology of the diocese as the local Church is commended by the Church historian Colin Podmore, although there is a hint of a quali-fication in his reference to 'a' rather than 'the' local church: 'The diocese is not an aggregation of parishes; rather, it is (in the technical sense) a "local church", of which the diocesan bishop is the "principal minister". It is ... a portion of the people of God gathered around the diocesan see and its bishop' (2008, p. 2). For Podmore, episcopal authority remains theologically and structurally separate from that of the Synod, so that while he concedes that the Church of England since 1970 has required its bishops to govern in consultation and collaboration with synodical processes, he is lukewarm about the idea that the Church is 'episcopally led but synodically governed' (p. 4):

> While it is true that the Church of England's bishops are charged with governing their dioceses synodically ... the phrase can be heard as im-plying that the Church of England is governed by synods ... The Synod cannot usurp the responsibilities which the members of the House of Bishops have, individually and collegially, by virtue of their episcopal ordination and office. (2008, p. 10)

This position has been criticized by Malcolm Grundy, arguing that the move towards a re-enhancement of episcopal authority over against more democratic patterns of governance, and the prioritizing of the diocese over other units of church organization (including the ecumenical dimension), militates against effective *episcope*. It tends to privilege leadership in the 'authoritative' domain over what he calls the 'organic' (2011, pp. 112 ff.), and plays down the communal and collaborative dimensions of the exercise of the ministry of oversight. Bishops need to focus less on working with each other as a kind of closed fraternity (*sic*, being until recently an all-male enclave, in England), and more on engaging in a ministry of presence at all levels of the Church and with its people and communities.

To assert, therefore, on purely theological grounds that the diocese is the local Church is to fall foul of the social reality of the present circumstances of the Church of England. First, 'the parish' has been firmly established in society for centuries as the basic unit, not only of the Church's social presence but also for a long period as the basic civil territorial division as well, which gives it a much sharper profile in the popular perception than the diocese. Second, since the Church is established, and therefore its bishops have a multiplicity of roles (not to mention their means of appointment), the function of 'local oversight' is virtually unrecognizable in reality. Third, the diocese as a unit has become far larger (with the possible exception of Sodor and Man) than the picture painted above presupposes. We cannot buck social reality by means of theoretical ecclesiology alone, however fine and pure it may be.

As an illustration of how the doctrine *might* be seen as empirically true, suppose that the Christian faith is spreading and taking root in Barnsley. Little Christian congregations or cells, groups of followers of the Way, are springing up in various places. Several meet in people's homes ('the church in Eileen's house'). One gathers teachers, parents and children in a primary school. Some meet in hospitals or pubs. There is one at the Metrodome Leisure Centre. Each one is under the leadership of local elders raised up from among their number. As time goes by, members of these scattered and diverse groups make contact with one another and the idea begins to take shape that it would be good for them to work together in various ways, to facilitate and broaden their mission to the town as a whole. Gradually a kind of federation comes into being until the day comes when the churches decide to set up a unifying structure with a 'presiding elder' or superintendent as their figurehead: a respected, mature, pastoral and mission-minded leader to be their public focus, elected from among their local elders. And so, by such means, the office of 'Bishop of Barnsley' comes into being, whose diocese is 'the Church in Barnsley', which on that definition becomes 'the local Church'.

In the context imagined above, the model of the 'diocese as the local Church' could actually become workable, and serve to facilitate the apostolic, or missional, function of bishops. Within the existing structures, however, the model creates centripetal forces that impact on episcopal ministry in problematic ways. First, the impossible demands already recognizable in the expectations of churches about the roles and responsibilities of their parish priests are transferred to the episcopate in equal measure. This can be seen in Cocksworth's account of the legislation for Bishops' Mission Orders, permitting bishops in the Church of England to authorize pioneering initiatives that may entail setting aside some rules such as the inviolate nature of parish boundaries (for example, to allow a 'church plant' from one church into another parish). Such initiatives seem entirely episcopally dependent:

> With their oversight of multiple congregations, their authority to ordain, their capacity to inspire and encourage, their ability to adapt the rules and conventions of the church and their responsibility as guardians and interpreters of the faith and their powers to establish new congregations, bishops have a unique gospel-driven opportunity to release the apostolicity of the church for the sake of the kingdom of God. (2008, pp. 259–60)

This all-embracing agenda sounds very much like a major enhancement of the role of bishops.

A further problematic outcome of this approach is that when every diocese is viewed as the basic 'local Church' unit, presided over by a bishop as leader in mission, it becomes more important for the Church nationally that the bishops are 'all singing from the same song sheet' (M. Bunting, cit. Furlong, 2000, p. 157); as Martyn Percy puts it:

> The bishops seem to be obsessed with agreeing with each other on issues of contention, so as to present a united front to Church and society ... Instead of being offered two or three tracks of truth, in which people can live, move and journey, the laity are all too frequently offered one episcopally-backed line to walk on ... Monological unity feels imposed and restraining, and is alienating. (1998, p. 139, footnote 34)

The result is the disappearance of the maverick, independent-minded, stirrer-up of controversy type of bishop. Brown and Woodhead characterize those now being appointed as the 'safe rather than sorry' variety; they need to be 'managerially competent, and forever on message'. They lament that 'the long line of colourful Anglican bishops like David Jenkins ... came to an abrupt end'; and this was no accident, for 'ensuring that there would never be another David Jenkins had been one of the aims of the Carey years' (Brown and Woodhead, 2016, p. 187).

Episcopal ministry, therefore, struggles to escape from the effects of long-standing historical circumstances that led to the diocesan patterns currently in place, and a conservative theology that seeks to maintain that situation and indeed to encourage a fresh enhancement of the bishops' role independently of more democratic structures of church governance. Meanwhile, the drive from those like Greenwood, schooled in the 'local ministry' movement, is for the relocation of *episcope* to parish and benefice level. In collaborative ministry the congregation corporately become more 'priestly' and the ordained priests need to become more 'episcopal'; this is all the more so when the ordained minister has pastoral charge of multiple local churches (Grundy, 2015). The dogma of the priority of the diocese as the 'local Church' looks increasingly irrelevant set against this backdrop: for the practical purposes of ministry, the 'supra-local' level is that of the benefice or group of churches, within a deanery or circuit, for which an individual minister has responsibility, and it is here that the challenge to work out what *episcope* means comes home most forcefully.

Conclusion

In a controversial article, 'The Episcopacy of All Believers' (2010), the American Episcopalian theologian Marilyn McCord Adams offered a forthright critique of ecclesiological models that enhance the role and office of the bishop, above and beyond all reasonable expectation of being able to fulfil it, based on 'the over-identification of the Church as Body of Christ with the Church as visible historical society acting through humanly devised institutions' (p. 15). She castigates what amounts to an idolatry of the institutional Church that purports to be able to claim that particular arrangements for the ordering of ministry can be seen as mirroring and expressing God's intentions for the Church. On the contrary, all such arrangements are provisional and fallible; 'take away the historical contingencies of human institutional arrangements, and what we have are the diaconate, the priesthood, and, yes, the episcopacy of all believers!' (p. 22). McCord Adams considers that orders contain nothing that resides uniquely in particular ways of structuring them: there is 'no ontological deficit that would prevent any and all Christians from functioning in any or all liturgical functions now assumed by ordained clergy'. God is always several steps ahead of us, offering the vision of fresh patterns for changing times, for *episcope* just as for diaconal and presbyteral ministries.

This chapter has taken a critical overview of developments within the interpretation of the so-called 'threefold ordering' of the ministry of bishops, priests and deacons. What is revealed is that the foundational sources are insufficient to justify a single, consistent theological and practical understanding of these ministries; and even in a church that, like the Church of England, practises ordination as though it were a clear, agreed concept, it remains essentially contested. In each case, there are divergent views about what the ministry is and how best it might be structured, and where necessary reimagined, to meet contemporary needs. Underlying all these debates and diversities, the proverbial 'elephant in the room' (as we saw initially when discussing diaconal ministry) is the meaning of ordination itself and the difference between clerical and lay ministries. The next chapter therefore turns its attention to the theology and praxis of ordination.

4

Interrogating Ordination: Ontology, Function and Gender

The previous two chapters have pursued trajectories through the history of the Christian churches and into the contemporary context to construct a picture of the contested nature of ministerial order, seen in alternative accounts of diaconal, presbyteral and episcopal ministry. The chapters that follow this one will focus on a number of influences and developments in ministry that have fed into strategies for renewal over the last 50 years or so. But first, this chapter is devoted to the issue that frames and constrains all innovations in ministry, namely the question of ordination itself, and how it too is susceptible to conflicting interpretations.

The chapter is in four parts, beginning with a critical theological reflection on ordained ministry as 'set apart', arising from a moment in my own experience (an earlier version of this section was originally published as Williams, 2000). The second part considers the persistence of 'clericalism' in the church, and makes a provisional assessment of how the ministry of women priests and bishops might be affecting it. Picking up the themes of contestation and adaptivity in ministry, the third part offers some reflections on the vexed question of mutual recognition of ministries between the churches. Finally, I present a tentative reframing of the domains of the language of 'ordination' and 'priesthood' respectively, to suggest a more flexible practice, adaptable to contemporary needs.

Set apart?

Some years ago, I came away from the diocesan Ordination of Priests with two words going round in my head: 'set apart'. Nine times they were spoken by the bishop, at the anointing of each of the candidates: 'I anoint you with this holy oil *as a sign that you are set apart this day as a priest* ...' The simple syllables, *set*, *apart*, *this*, *day*, resounded like drumbeats announcing a portentous and irreversible turn of events. Here, it seemed, was a key exegesis of the entire liturgical text: an act of *setting apart* was the defining moment. It is especially striking that these words are not part of the authorized ordination liturgy in the Church of England, but additional words the bishop had chosen to use. I set myself to ponder on the particular connotations of the term.

Clearly there are theological traditions for which it is absolutely crucial. For example, in an article headed 'Holy priests are set apart, as the Church is from the culture', the Roman Catholic Archbishop of Glasgow, Philip Tartaglia, offers a vivid account of set-apartness as an essential consequence of the priest's iconic representational role:

> Our secular culture can't help but see us as odd and out-of-date, even scary – but nevertheless strangely attractive … it's a misguided theology of ministry that encourages priests to think of themselves as 'just like everybody else'. We're certainly not better … But we're different … That's why our most spiritually mature lay friends love us, but treat us *as priests* … As priests, we can't go back and become 'merely human' again, because we're not. (2017)

I find there is something quite unnerving about such a view, expressed with such monumental confidence. The Australian theologian and bishop Stephen Pickard echoes my own experience in finding 'troublesome' the use of the term at ordinations (the phrase 'set apart' does appear in the Ordinal of the Anglican Church in Australia). He asks, 'have we not here an unintentional example of clericalism, that most pervasive of all problems that has beset the Church … Clerical inflation is a well-attested strategy in times of pressure and doubt concerning identity and function' (2009, p. 155). As a metaphor for the priestliness of priesthood, then, 'setting apart' invites further investigation.

There is a whole cluster of terms that signify distance or separation as the defining quality of a relationship between persons or things: *apart from, above, below, in front of, behind.* By contrast, a different set of words specifies proximity or connectedness: *among, between, amid, within, alongside.* This suggests that the choice of a term of distance or separation to locate priest in relation to people is not purely fortuitous: there must be some element of conscious preference here over, say, among or amid (for example, 'as a sign that you are set among the people this day as a priest …). There is a resonance here with Emile Durkheim's (1915) definition of the sacred, or holy, as 'things set apart and forbidden', like the untouchable objects of pre-modern societies, surrounded by the power of *tabu*: set apart to channel, convey and somehow *make present* the ineffable divine. This is certainly the idea behind Mason's 'universal priesthood', discussed in the previous chapter.

Does this therefore capture something of the essence of ordained Christian ministry? Certain apprehensions, even 'great tides of doubt and fear' (Hoyle, 2016, p. 1), are a frequent and perhaps proper response to the prospect of ordination. Mason goes so far as to suggest that this act inducts a person into a life that 'has a dangerous, disturbed quality ... family relations are strained, his wife wonders what she has married, the children are famous for their oddity ... people react strangely to him' (2002, p. 1). As a curate, Lincoln Harvey admits that the experience of ordination 'changed me in a way I did not like: it had taken me away from the people, as well as moving me nearer to them' (Ross-McNairn and Barron (eds), 2014, p. 28). In this understanding, since they are no longer lay persons, priests are *ipso facto* 'set apart', sacramentally stamped by God as different, with a new priestly character.

Is this then what a priest is, 'a walking sacrament'? So that, when someone sees a priest passing by, they are reminded of the existence of God (a disquieting experience)? If this is so, can this kind of ontological set-apartness possibly avoid attracting to itself other rather more problematic kinds? The theological 'otherness' of priesthood readily turns into a whole set of projections of apartness on to priests by society at large: morally, in that priests must be holier than the rest of us, so woe betide them if they fail; spiritually, in that priests will have perfect prayer lives and always be untroubled by doubts; culturally, in that priests mustn't drink (too much) or smoke or know anything about sex; or socially, in that priests live in some other world and aren't part of 'ordinary life'. The BBC sitcom *Rev*, about a London inner-city parish priest, addressed these projections in an acutely observed, entertaining but often very poignant way. Churches without a tradition of 'priesthood' experience it too: as Neil Summerton writes from the Brethren tradition, 'in the minds of the "laity", at least sub-consciously, the minister is often still in a class set apart' (2006, p. 37).

If then you are a priest and the world knows it, there's no escaping the feeling of being different. You bear a load of religious symbolism; you incur a weight of cultural expectations; you receive, and are expected to accept, a plethora of personal projections. You are immensely privileged to share in the profound moments in people's lives, and entrusted with amazing confidences. You have a surprising degree of access to institutions. What kind of a phenomenon is this? Few could doubt that here, in this thing called 'priesthood', there is something significant, and maybe even socially necessary, as Mason believes. The conclusion I have reached is that priesthood thus conceived is capturing something genuine: but it is not specifically Christian and is misrepresented by being bundled together with ordination for Christian ministry, and with the role of presbyter in the local church.

In the Hebrew Scriptures, the term 'priest' refers to the Levitical (Aaronic) priesthood, 'set apart' to handle holy things that ordinary mortals are forbidden to touch. We have already seen in the previous chapter how this meaning of priesthood infiltrated the interpretation of the New Testament *presbyter* in the early centuries of the Church. Today, such a concept of priesthood would seem to be an inescapable feature of a once partially Christianized, now post-Christendom and partially pre-Christian (or pagan) culture. Its notion of set-apartness resonates with (usually patriarchal) models of society in which roles and status are defined by locating persons within a structured system in which relative value attaches to the position occupied vis-a-vis others, that is *above*, *below* or *on a par with but at a distance from* them. But no individual can achieve status or value solely by virtue of occupying a position 'above', 'below' or otherwise 'distinct from' someone else.

That is why contemporary theology reimagines the Trinity in favour of a model that shows how the intrinsic value of persons is only realized insofar as they are able to flourish in an environment of mutuality (e.g. Soskice, 2007, chapter 6). Steve Taylor (2019) draws on Soskice's work to provide the foundations of an ecclesiology for new expressions of church: in such an understanding it would make little sense to single out 'apartness' as the central or definitive characteristic of ordained ministers. In separating clergy so sharply from everyone else, it puts asunder what should be kept together, and risks endorsing heroic individualism instead of relationality and *koinonia* in the Spirit.

The interpretation of Christian priesthood in terms of 'set apartness', then, has problematic consequences for clergy roles and the social expectations of them. Not least, it is a model that bolsters a form of clericalism, 'a form of power structure which attributes all power of sacramental celebration, theological knowledge and decision-making to ... members of the clergy on [sic] whom this kind of power is imparted by ordination' (Watson, 2002, p. 68). This raises an important question about how we do our theology, and especially ecclesiology and ministerial theology, since churches and ministers exist empirically in the world and are therefore influenced by it. Does our theology merely serve to justify inherited patterns of ministry, or can it be proactive in changing them? To paraphrase Karl Marx, the theologians have interpreted ministry in various ways; the point, however, is to change it. In the next section, the question to be considered is whether the ordination of women as priests and bishops might be such a catalyst for change.

Ordination, gender and clericalism

Shortly before the first, abortive 2012 vote in the General Synod on the admission of women to the episcopate, the *Church Times* published a letter from a bishop who had decided not to support the measure. One of the reasons given for this decision was his anxiety that the consecration of women might change the theology of episcopacy. This seemed to me a revealing admission, given that it is the bishops who define the official theology of the Church, and therefore the theology of episcopacy (and indeed of everything else) has hitherto been defined exclusively by men. Once this patriarchal privilege has been overthrown, it is only to be hoped and expected that the theology will indeed change, as women too have a share in defining it; but why did this bishop seem to see this as a threat?

It is outside the scope of this book to rehearse in detail the arguments of those opposed to the ordination of women, but a valuable set of documents assembled by Podmore (2015) demonstrates how the debate about women's ordination, including admission to the episcopate, raises acute questions about the way we do our theology. An illustration of this would be the seriousness and detail with which several contributors are *still* arguing for the relevance to the case against women's ordination of the Fatherhood of God, the maleness of Christ, and the inclusion by Jesus of only men among the apostles. In this light it is essential to be aware that the admission of women to priestly and episcopal ministry will not be sufficient to dislodge the hold of clericalism on the Church without a radical rereading of the theological traditions that have underpinned a patriarchal and hierarchical model (Watson, 2002, pp. 66–77).

This, however, will not come about without a struggle. A peaceful settlement of women's entry into ordained ministry, including episcopal ministry, must not be achieved at the cost of simply conforming women to a pattern already set in the all-male environment (Hoad, 1984). A provocative expression of the folly of extending ordained ministry to women without any consideration of the need for radical change in the culture of priesthood came from Maggie Ross, in a collection of essays marking the first ordinations of women to the priesthood of the Church of England (Walrond-Skinner (ed.), 1994). Ross argued that the pathology of clericalism would be perpetuated if all that happened was that the existing system 'sucked in' the women duly ordained and otherwise remained unchanged:

> Clericalism ... is a kind of contagious sickness. It is inherent in a hierarchical system. It infects clergy without distinction and without their

knowing. It sets them apart as a class, which is a very different matter from the setting-apart of holiness that indwells the interior solitude of each human being. Clericalism is inherently destructive, both to the person who is already infected and to those affected, and therefore often infected, by that person's life; it perpetuates the classic co-dependent cycle and its denial. (1994, p. 106)

Rosemary Ruether sees clericalism as 'a development which essentially transforms the community into hierarchically ordered castes of clergy and laity' (Watson, 2002, p. 68). This was part of the reason for the Catholic theologian Charles Davis's decision to leave the priesthood, which caused huge shockwaves in the Church after the end of the Second Vatican Council: 'the making of the Christian minister into a priestly class, set apart, and possessing a priesthood different in kind from the rest of Christians, disrupted the Christian community. It led to the degradation of the laity' (Davis, 1967, p. 141). In the words of Richard Roberts, 'the ordained hierarchy came to conceive itself by means of an identity which, in asserting itself, correspondingly denied theological identity to the other, that is the laity' (1989, p. 161). Ruether argues that a situation disadvantageous to women is thereby built into the system, because the clergy-laity binary arrangements are 'essentially modelled on … the male-female binary in which the male is seen as the dominant, the strong and the normative, while the female represents that which at best complements the male' (Watson, 2002, p. 68).

This unhappy legacy of clericalism means that careful and reflective listening to the fresh voices being brought to ministerial theology from the perspectives of ordained women is needed, not least because these women have inhabited the Church for many years from the standpoint of lay people experiencing the ministry of ordained men. It is important not to be naive about this: Bishop Penny Jamieson warns that it will be no small task to overcome the ways in which 'the structures and institutions in which women are beginning to take leadership have been formed and shaped by conceptions of leadership that derive from a long history of authoritarian, monarchical and patriarchal practice' (1997, p. 14). Further, Jane Shaw cautions against the assumption that women in leadership in the Church will automatically bring about transformation because they are 'more "naturally" pastoral, less competitive and more empathetic and collaborative' (2010, p. 89).

Despite this, Shaw affirms that 'those who come into the centre of power from the margins and a history of exclusion can often see it differently, with fresh eyes' (p. 90). Accordingly, with this caveat against simplistic assumptions about gendered behavioural characteristics, a few soundings are taken here from the work of women clergy writing about their ministry, on becoming 'insiders' after many years of exclusion from the guild of the ordained. Shaw herself is convinced that this 'seeing differently' can lead to 'influencing' and in due course 'practising differently':

> The entry of women into leadership roles has prompted us to reflect on what leadership ... might be in the churches ... the Gospel teaches that all are made in the image and likeness of God, that all are radically equal, all ... have gifts to offer, but ... too few have the opportunity to exercise these gifts, and our leadership models do not necessarily encourage it. It is therefore incumbent upon us ... to enable and encourage all to exercise their gifts, to flourish as women and men made in the image of God. (p. 93)

From the perspective of former exclusion, Shaw is able to discern how leadership styles in the Church have failed to facilitate many in discovering and exercising their gifts, and to see such releasing as a central function of ministry.

Penny Jamieson insists on the priority of the *relational* in Christian leadership, oriented to the cultivation of community; such leaders

> are inclusive and open in their relations, and find it a privilege to welcome into their number people who are misfits elsewhere in society. These leaders are skilled at recognizing and affirming the gifts that God has given and they encourage their use ... They co-ordinate the community, ensuring that all are working together and that the efforts of each person contribute effectively to the whole. (1997, p. 144)

This is a description of a style of ministerial leadership that maintains openness about difference as people tell their stories and the community develops its sense of identity and purpose. In the light of the trustful relationships that result, there follows the effective release and distribution of spiritual potential, gifts and graces. In Jamieson's case, it is relevant that the leadership style she is describing refers to episcopal ministry. It is notable that this is in no way an abdication of leadership, an accusation sometimes levelled at those who are committed to a collaborative style by others in a more traditional mould, as well as by those who favour a more charismatic type of 'up-frontness'.

The vexed question of the representative function of Christian ministry in relation to the divine, and the cultural role and *persona* of the priest, is explored by Ali Green in a vision for women's priesthood derived from a contextualized, gendered and adaptive theology that 'breaks the male monopoly' and 'opens up possibilities for a female symbolic':

She represents the ability of women everywhere to mediate the divine, not by escaping from but by celebrating their embodied, gendered nature. From this flows the promise of flourishing to all women – and to men also, through the destabilization of the traditional symbolic of godlikeness, power and domination associated with the masculine. (2009, p. 16)

Here again there is an emphasis on the celebration of difference and an undermining of inherited assumptions about the possession and deployment of power; the notion of 'destabilizing' is highly significant in the context of adaptive ministry. Green expects that women's ministry will reflect back on fundamental theology because the introduction of the feminine into a centuries-long exclusively masculine domain cannot help but make an impact, and she is ready to use the language of disruption and perspectival shift, not only in relation to ministerial practice, but also to 'the Christian story':

The woman priest has caused a collision between the community's tradition and the continuing revelation that informs Christian identity. This collision has given rise to new interpretations, embedded in women's experience and spirituality, which have begun to enrich and deepen our narrative of faith ... The shift she causes in the identity of priesthood necessarily means a shift also in the Christian story which the priest represents. (p. 163)

Women in ordained ministry are emphasizing difference, relationality and mutual flourishing, with the expectation of a reframing of fundamental models and assumptions about ministry. These considerations are of vital relevance to the wider ecumenical conversations about the mutual recognition of ministries. The reception by the churches of the priestly and episcopal ministry of women might be able to point the way ahead for the churches to live generously in celebration of a diversity of ministry that requires neither denominational exclusivity nor ecumenical uniformity.

Mutual recognition of ministries

We have noted earlier that disputes about ministry have been a major factor in provoking conflict and schism throughout Church history since at least the time of Cyprian. Highly ontological, top-down understandings of ordination are a critical obstruction to ecumenical progress. In 2011, the issue was brought into vivid relief by the media attention given to three Anglican bishops who converted to Roman Catholicism, in part on account of the moves in the Church of England towards the consecration of women bishops. A memorable image of the event was that of the moment when the three now ex-Anglican bishops, duly ordained as Catholic priests, were vested with their new stoles by their wives, who stepped forward at this significant moment to help their husbands into their new role (Stanford, 2011).

There is a profound irony in the refuge that some clergy unable to accept the ordained ministry of women have sought by defection to the women-free zone of the ministry of the Roman Catholic Church. These Anglican bishops, like all other defecting clergy, had to be re-ordained as priests in the Catholic Church, because the Roman Church does not believe that they were validly ordained in the first place. Ever since the Reformation and the re-writing of the ordination rites by Cranmer, the Catholic Church has doubted the sufficiency of Anglican ordinations. Notoriously, in 1896 Pope Leo XIII, in his papal bull *Apostolicae Curae,* declared them to be 'entirely null and void'. Although the *Final Report* of ARCIC I made some progress towards a possible resolution of this issue, and proposals were prepared for consideration by ARCIC II, the process was halted by Pope John Paul II, at least in part owing to the move towards women priests and bishops in some parts of the Anglican Communion (see Greenacre, 2014, pp. 121–4). In 1998, Cardinal Joseph Ratzinger, as he then was, reaffirmed Pope Leo's teaching as binding, and it has never been revoked, even if the present tendency is to treat it as a matter of 'doubt' about Anglican orders rather than outright rejection.

For traditionalist Anglicans like these bishops, the admission of women to the episcopate muddied the waters considerably with regard to the recognition of ministries. As long as the Church had women priests, but not bishops, it was possible simply to avoid the ministry of a woman if you did not believe her genuinely to be a priest. Once there are women bishops, however, you can no longer judge the authenticity of a male priest unless you also know the gender of the bishop who ordained him. In sum, clergy converting to Catholicism out of an anxiety about living in a Church where there may be other clergy whose orders are not valid because they were conferred by a woman bishop, are submitting themselves to a communion that believes precisely this about their own orders, that they are not, or may not be, valid because they were conferred by an Anglican bishop. Even Greenacre, from his Anglo-Catholic perspective, acknowledges how absurd this will appear to some who ask, 'as a serious question and sometimes as a taunt, "Why worry about Rome's refusal to recognize women priests when it refuses even to recognize our *male* priests?"' (2014, p. 124).

This is one reason why the Church of England has continued to make special provision for clergy and parishes unable to accept the ministry of a woman priest or bishop, or of a male priest ordained by a woman bishop (and, for some, even a male priest ordained by a male bishop who also ordains women). When the Church attempted a few years ago to appoint a traditionalist Catholic, who did not ordain women, as a diocesan bishop, the volume of protest from within the diocese led to the candidate's withdrawal. Emma Percy, a priest in the diocese concerned, commented that the Church hierarchy, while expressing 'deep pastoral concerns for those who cannot accept the ministry of women', did not seem so exercised on behalf of 'women who find their ministry fundamentally undermined by the theological views of one with whom they are to share a cure of souls' (*Church Times*, 3 March 2017). This then is an ecclesiological minefield where the attempt to safeguard the tender theological consciences of some only serves to offend the sense of justice of others on gender equality. 'Mutual recognition of ministries' is therefore always a hot potato, and we need to enquire a little further into the sorts of criteria that might make the process easier in the future.

The tone in which the Church of England conducts discussion about this tends to be rather condescending where the Free Churches are concerned. In June 2019, for example, the General Synod debated whether 'eucharistic presidency by Methodist presbyters not ordained as priests by bishops in the historic episcopate can be "gladly borne" as a "temporary anomaly"' (Davies, 2019). But bountiful toleration until the errant church returns to the parental bosom is not enough. In pursuit of a fresh approach, the Catholic scholar Burkhard notes that the ARCIC document on 'Ministry and Ordination' (1979) states that 'mutual recognition presupposes acceptance of the apostolicity of each other's ministry' (Burkhard, 2004, p. 168, footnote 5). Across the range of ARCIC reports, the adjective 'apostolic' is applied to many aspects of the Church, any or all of which might contribute to defining 'apostolicity': apostolic 'tradition', 'community', 'faith', 'teaching', 'witness', 'mission', 'authority', 'order' and 'leadership' (pp. 168–9). He therefore argues that the Catholic statements themselves furnish a basis for a much less juridical, institutional approach to mutual recognition of ministries.

Burkhard proposes that the idea of 'validity' of ministries needs to be revisited, since mutual recognition has become 'the obstacle that defies resolution' in ecumenical engagements (2004, p. 225). Going beyond the mere test of 'liceity', that is, the property of being 'licit', in conformity with canon law (pp. 220 ff.), he suggests that the churches might consider 'ritual, charismatic and ecclesiological' models of validation (pp. 226 ff.). The 'ritual' test entails a judgement whether 'what the other church does' can be seen as sufficiently consonant with historic traditions, as for example when 'ordination' is practised as the means of 'installation' into a ministry, as in Lutheranism. In the charismatic perspective, the criterion is whether the other church can be seen as bringing to expression a genuine movement of the Spirit, for example by looking at its 'fruit'. The ecclesiological test turns on whether the non-conforming expression of ministry can be validated on the basis that the community practising it can properly be seen as 'ecclesial' (pp. 226 ff.). All of these criteria depend on a theology that argues inductively from contemporary ecclesial experience, rather than deductively from dogma ostensibly founded in divine revelation. The approach acknowledges the possibility of granting legitimacy to alternative understandings of what contested concepts such as 'ordination', 'priesthood' and 'episcopacy' might mean, within a broader recognition of ecclesial character.

So far in this chapter I have advanced a critique of a model of ordained ministry that 'sets apart' the recipient of the order from the 'laity', and have begun at least a preliminary enquiry into whether and how the inclusion of women in ordained ministry will challenge or change this theology. I have then discussed the possibility that mutual recognition of ministries might be granted, both within and between churches, in less juridical and dogmatic ways in order to encourage and enhance communion and inclusion. I now want to gather up the issues with a proposal, in the form of a 'what if?' kind of experiment in free thinking. My proposal is that the terms 'ordination' and 'priesthood' come into clearer focus if understood as belonging to different spheres of discourse, and that a recognition of this would considerably reduce the obstacles to both ecumenical collaboration and ministerial experimentation.

Rethinking the terminology of 'ordination' and 'priesthood'

Although it is usual to discourage students from citing Wikipedia as an academic source, I will transgress the rule here, because the definition of ordination it gives illustrates all the problems:

> Ordination is the process by which individuals are consecrated, that is, set apart and elevated from the laity class to the clergy, who are thus then authorized (usually by the denominational hierarchy composed of other clergy) to perform various religious rites and ceremonies. (https://en.wikipedia.org/wiki/Ordination, accessed 12.09.2019)

'Set apart', 'elevated from the laity class to the clergy', 'denominational hierarchy': all the elements are present that have already been subjected to critical scrutiny in this chapter, and elsewhere in the book. But the key issue I want to highlight is the shift of register that occurs between the language of 'set apart and elevated', and that of 'to perform various religious rites and ceremonies'. There are many procedures that have the effect of authorizing people to undertake practical responsibilities, but these are not normally described in terms of 'setting apart', still less of 'elevation' to a different class of person (other than ennoblement, perhaps). The language that pertains to 'making someone into a priest' is transformative and focused on the person; the language of authorization is much more functional and task-oriented.

The root of the term 'ordination' in the Latin *ordo*, *ordinari* signifies the orderly appointment of a person to a position in Roman society, with the recognition or bestowal of the authority to perform the particular functions proper to it. In the earliest days of the Christian Church, the need for such recognition soon arose, but there was no higher status or class into which to 'elevate' those whose ministries were to be recognized. Melinsky, for example, refers to the New Testament Church as 'this remarkable organization without constitution or rank' (1992, p. 23). Writing around 200, Tertullian, who was probably the first to use *ordinatio* to refer to appointment to Christian ministry, declared that 'the difference between the Order [the priesthood] and the people is due to the authority of the Church'; where there is 'no bench of clergy', as he puts it, 'when necessity arises, you have the rights of a priest in your person' (*De Exhortatione Castitatis*, 7). Thus, he denies a special 'class' of clergy, arguing only for necessary church *order* as a publicly owned and accountable way of managing power to act.

Ordination, then, can be seen as originating in the management of power within the ongoing institutional life of the Church, beyond the early, free charismatic phase (Percy, 1998). To be ordained is to receive, traditionally by the episcopal laying on of hands, recognized public authority to exercise a ministerial function in which potentially hazardous spiritual power is involved. Hence ordination is intrinsically bound up with function, since decisions about who may do what are at the heart of what makes it necessary: who may preside at the Eucharist, or preach, baptize, marry, anoint the sick, or ordain? In most Protestant and non-conformist traditions, such questions about practical responsibilities underpin the development of 'offices' (rather than 'orders') in the Church, which imply 'responsibility rather than status' (Summerton, 2006, p. 44). However, within the Catholic tradition, ordination has come to denote a sacramental rite of passage from the lay to the clerical state. The ordained person by definition belongs to the 'estate' of the clergy; by the same token a lay person is simply, negatively, one who has not been ordained.

Nevertheless, Pickard has argued that 'Catholic ontology versus Protestant functionalism' doesn't quite capture the real issue, because in both models 'ministries have strong relations to the centre and weaker relations to each other' (2009, p. 159). He maintains that it is necessary to speak of both ontological and functional dimensions to ordained ministry, and that ordination 'has unmistakeable ontological weight' (p. 161). The way to overcome the dichotomy is to be clear that both function and ontology must be understood relationally: ministerial functions and tasks are to be undertaken with the laity, and the 'formative' aspects of ministerial 'being' are intrinsically related to the 'becoming' of the ecclesial community. 'Neither ordained nor other ecclesial ministries can be what they are without the other' (p. 154). We will return to this in the next chapter, but at this point while agreeing broadly with Pickard's analysis I would want to offer a slightly different take from his on the relationship between the ontological and the functional.

I would argue that the language domain of 'ordination' is about appointing and authorizing the 'official' in the interests of order, whereas that of 'priesthood' is about identifying and nurturing the 'personal' in the interests of communion (*koinonia*), and problems arise when these are reversed or confused. For example, Ian Aveyard points out the tensions created for some clergy by the mismatch between being 'ordained' to 'priesthood', but then 'appointed' to 'incumbency', which will entail leadership whether the priest likes it or not (Aveyard, 2013, pp. 36 ff.). Ordination is more properly about appointment (function), and priesthood is about person (ontology), and cannot be secured by authorization or appointment. Both a wholly ontological reading of ministry and a wholly functional one create a binary system (ordained/lay), which leads to clericalism. Pickard identifies this in both the Catholic 'Father knows best' form and the Protestant 'CEO' or management/leadership model (p. 159).

Croft (2008) expresses regret that in struggling to handle the competing demands of ordained ministry, some clergy 'are drawn down the route of abandoning the distinctiveness of ordination altogether'. In the perspective of this book, however, the 'distinctiveness of ordination' is precisely one of the contested issues to be addressed. A functional view of ordination allows for the public authorization of a maximal diversity of ministries, whether 'lay' or 'ordained' in traditional terms, spreading the load much more widely in terms of roles and responsibilities. At the same time, this leaves the way clear for the particular qualities of priestly character to be identified, validated and nurtured in appropriate persons across the full range of ministries. Distinctiveness is retained, but without the damaging concentration of all the roles and functions in the one person who wears the badge of the 'ordained'.

My proposal, then, is that ordination is a concept which needs to be seen not as creating an ontological category, but as a process of public authorization for a range of ministries intrinsically bound up with function. Priesthood, on the other hand, is a concept that should not be defined in terms of certain ministerial functions that are reserved to it, but rather as a potential quality of many different ministries. For example, the 'Ephesians 4 list' of apostles, prophets, pastors, teachers and evangelists expresses ministry by means of a range of functions into which a person might properly be 'ordained', in the sense of being publicly appointed and authorized by prayer and the laying on of hands. Significantly, however, 'priesthood' is not on the list, because any or all of these ministry functions might be performed by persons who are either lay or ordained, and all of them might display the personal qualities of 'priesthood' when this is being construed in terms of person and character rather than function.

Conversely, distinguishing the concepts of ordination and priesthood in this way would generate a richer ecology of ministry. More people would be 'ordained', because there would be a full range of ministries to which they could be appointed; and more people would be recognized as 'priests', because their special qualities as public representative Christians ('the holy person in the midst', as a colleague of mine used to say) could be acknowledged without being tied to particular ecclesial functions. As Countryman puts it:

> A priest is one who lives in the presence of God and can assist others to enter that presence ... this kind of priesthood ... is going on all around us, all through our lives. We all perform priestly acts, and we are all ministered to in priestly ways – not only by ordained priests, but by old friends, by wise mentors, even by complete strangers. (2012, p. 26)

In this chapter I have critiqued ideas of priesthood and ordained ministry that foreground 'set-apartness' as the key distinguishing quality, suggesting alternatives that give more emphasis to the dimensions of relationality, mutuality and community. I have offered some reflections on the contribution that the inclusion of women in the priesthood and episcopate might be making towards shifting perceptions of the character of ordained ministry. I have explored an alternative approach to how ministries might be mutually recognized both within and between churches, making more use of 'bottom-up' criteria drawn from theological reflection on experience rather than 'top-down' application of dogmatic positions. Finally, I have explored the possibility of thinking about ordination and priesthood as concerned respectively with appointment to particular ministerial roles and functions, and formation in a distinctive character that might be manifested within any of those roles. We now move on to examining some of the principal streams of renewal and rethinking of ministry developed within the mainstream churches in response to social and cultural change.

5

Shared, Lay, Local and Collaborative: The Road Less Travelled

We saw in Chapter 2 how the principle of diversity in ministry can be supported from an examination of the earliest history of the Church. It has never proved possible to derive once and for all a single pattern of ministry from the New Testament. At the very least, a variation of models is discernible between the early, indigenous Jerusalem church and the churches planted around the Roman Empire in Gentile territory by St Paul and his associates. In Britain the earliest history of Christianity shows distinct differences between the ancient 'Celtic' patterns of organization of ministry and mission and the Roman models which eventually superseded them (Bradley, 2003; but see also Bradley, 2018, for a more critical reappraisal of 'Celtic Christianity'). Today we are becoming aware that the 'threefold order of Bishops, Priests and Deacons' enshrined in the Ordinal does not of itself dictate with any precision how ministry is actually to be provided and deployed locally. In this chapter, we move on from questions of ordering to matters of practice: how models embracing a plurality of ministries working together have been proposed as better serving the needs of the contemporary Church.

The first part of the chapter looks back at a representative selection of reports and other documents published mainly by the Church of England in the late twentieth century (see, further, Kuhrt, 2001, chapter 5). These reveal a recurring concern to recommend greater diversity and flexibility in the practical provision of Christian ministry, but also a lack of any consensus around a way forward. Close attention is given to 'Local Ministry', developed especially in an Anglican context from the 1980s into the new century, including the introduction of 'Ordained Local Ministry'. This is followed by consideration of critical issues for collaborative ministry, including the persistent challenge of clericalism, the need for an appropriate leadership style, and the place of 'vision'. The final section examines how collaborative ministry might impact upon three key areas of ecclesial practice: the planning and leading of worship, the expression of inclusive fellowship, and the pursuit of adult Christian learning. Earlier versions of some of the material in this chapter can be found in Williams, 1998 and 2004.

Shared, lay, local and collaborative ministry: reforms, reports and recommendations

In the 1960s, the appetite for church reform was keen in some quarters, while a complacent traditionalism held sway in others (for an entertaining overview from someone who lived through it all, see Beeson, 2007, chapter 2). A strong reforming tradition flourished among a number of younger clergy, several of whom became curates or incumbents under the episcopacy of Mervyn Stockwood at Southwark in the early sixties, including most notably Nicholas Stacey at Woolwich (see Stacey, 1971). Their interests were represented by the Parish and People movement, led by such figures as Trevor Beeson and Eric James, and together with Bishop John Robinson they came to exemplify what became known as 'South Bank Religion' (for a journalistic account, see Mehta, 1965, pp. 67–97).

These reforming clergy shared a frustration with the ecclesiastical machinery which they had inherited, and a desire to see more flexible structures designed to enable the Church to engage with a changing world. For example, writing in the magazine *Prism* in February 1965, Eric James argued that for the Church to 'serve and penetrate the world as it is ... will necessitate a breakdown of the old structures of Church life and the development of far more unstructured patterns'. John Robinson had already envisioned a new structure in a volume of essays written before he became a bishop (Robinson, 1960), which included a strong advocacy of the priesthood of the *whole* Church (pp. 72–82), and a proposal for the 'house church' as a structure to facilitate the expression of this (pp. 83–95), something very close to what has in more recent times been termed 'cell church'. He chose to return to this theme in his follow up to *Honest to God*, aptly entitled *The New Reformation?* (1965, pp. 25–31, 88–100).

But many of the reformers experienced disillusionment with what they saw as the failure of the Church establishment to recognize the urgency of the need for change. This was expressed forcefully by Nicholas Stacey when he resigned, not only from his ministry at Woolwich, but from parochial ministry altogether, for a career with the Social Services:

> The structures as we have them of full-time clergymen and lots of buildings and a large number of organizations, and the Church's role as a sort of Third Estate of the land, with the bishops in the House of Lords

and the status of the hierarchy, all that has massively declined and will continue to decline. (cit. Bentley, 1978, p. 40)

An important institutional response to the perceived need for change, that was much welcomed by Stacey and like-minded colleagues at the time, came in the 'Paul Report' of 1964, *The Deployment and Payment of the Clergy*, which addressed most of the issues that were the cause of Stacey's exasperation (Stacey, 1971, pp. 230–1).

Leslie Paul was known as a layman with strongly held views about the reform of ministry, possessing sociological expertise as well as a keen theological mind (see Paul, 1968). His report went much further than expected in laying bare the structural problems brought about by the Church of England's organizational life being geared to institutional patterns that had long since passed away, such as feudalism and a predominantly rural society. He recommended reshaping the entire parish system, abolishing the clergy freehold, developing group and team ministries, and encouraging lay ministry by means of adult theological education, delivered through a system of house churches similar to that proposed earlier by Robinson. As his report was the work of an individual, a commission was set up to discuss it, emerging with most of its proposals intact, in the 'Morley Report' of 1967 (chaired by Canon Fenton Morley of Leeds Parish Church). It was, however, roundly rejected by the Church Assembly as it came under attack from several senior bishops.

Nevertheless, efforts to innovate persisted. In 1968, the report *A Supporting Ministry*, from the Ministry Committee of the Advisory Council for the Church's Ministry (ACCM, as it then was) recognized that 'many would see the man-power situation as a sign that God is leading his Church to discuss new forms of ministry for the new age in which we live' (p. 14). In response, the committee recommended the development of an 'auxiliary' non-stipendiary (unpaid) ministry. Although their proposals were exclusively clerical, the different types of non-stipendiary ministry (NSM) they envisaged were interesting in the light of later developments (the language at that time is of course gender exclusive):

A man, already exercising Christian leadership in a local church, might be ordained to work in that local church, while retaining his secular occupation. Alternatively, a man might ... identify himself with an area of particular need and ... work there. Thirdly, a man, already exercising Christian leadership in a secular situation, might be ordained to exercise his ministry in that secular situation ... but also help in a local church as well. (p. 18)

In these three cases we see, broadly, the options that evolved over time into Ordained Local Ministers, Sector and Pioneer Ministers, and Ministers in Secular Employment.

The proposals were not new ideas but helped to generate wider attention for the innovative forms of ministry and training that had been pioneered since 1960 by the Southwark Ordination Course, launched originally by John Robinson when Bishop of Woolwich. Ministers in Secular Employment (earlier termed 'worker priests', based on a model being trialled in the Catholic Church in France, and developed in a different form by Nick Stacey in Woolwich) were perhaps the most far-reaching of the innovations in terms of shifting the focus of ministry from the congregation to the wider society, but over time they became increasingly vulnerable to the centripetal drag of the parish as 'available' clergy, especially on Sundays, for making up the shortfall in stipendiary numbers (see Lees, 2018). In the 1970s, the focus of the Church's energies for ministerial reform shifted away from the more ambitious proposals and towards the challenge of declining clergy numbers, rather than declining congregations.

The radical cause was not helped by subsequent reports such as *The Future of the Ministry* (General Synod of the Church of England, GS 374, 1978), in which the House of Bishops asked General Synod to affirm 'its recognition of the continued need for a full-time paid ministry of at least the present size' and 'the Church's willingness to provide the resources required to train that ministry' (Resolution 4). It is noteworthy that the title of this report reflects the continuing assumption at that time that the term '*the* ministry' would be understood as referring only to full-time stipendiary ordained ministry. The report now appears backward-looking and barely in touch with the massive social and cultural changes placing inherited forms of ordained ministry under pressure; its aspirations were thrown into disarray by the failure to achieve anywhere near the target level of recommendations for training of 400–450 per year.

Two years later, the Church of England's Ministry Co-ordinating Group attempted to take stock of the situation in the light of the preceding discussions and reports. In *The Church's Ministry – A Survey* (Ministry Co-ordinating Group of the Church of England, GS 459, 1980), a seemingly promising change of direction occurred: the group suggested that it might be better to begin 'with a description of the ministry of the whole people of God before proceeding to identify the particular ministries which exist, within which the role of the ordained ministry finds its place' (para. 6). However, almost immediately, the group rejected its own suggestion (para. 7):

The understanding of ministry as a shared responsibility is of great potential significance *for the future* [emphasis mine]. But the extent to which it has yet actually affected the basic assumptions and expectations of the majority of church people must not be over-estimated.

As a result of this view, that a greater variety of ministries, especially lay, would be highly desirable, but the Church at large isn't ready for it yet, a curious ambiguity runs through the report. Different categories of ministry are carefully identified: non-stipendiary ministers, deaconesses, licensed lay workers, Church Army officers, Readers, members of religious orders, paid employees of churches and diocesan offices, as well as 'normal' parochial clergy. Key questions are asked: 'how far is it right to include any or all of these in a national ... strategy? ... how far should accreditation or licensing be extended? ... how far is it necessary for the various but sometimes overlapping categories to be more clearly defined?' (para. 34). But little progress is made, because whereas 'what is required, clearly, is ... that there should be a wider acceptance in the Church of the ministry of lay people' (para. 102), it remains the case that 'some lay people in the Church of England still regard a full-time ordained priest as the only properly authorized minister of the Church' (para. 95).

There is always something disingenuous about a Church report that says, in effect, that of course *we* (the committee producing the report) are far-sighted enough to grasp what needs to be done, but 'the laity won't wear it'. Arriving at this impasse, the group resorted to the hope that Synod would nonetheless see its way to enabling some more long-term, visionary thinking about the future to take place, and it was out of this that the famous Tiller Report, *A Strategy for the Church's Ministry* (1983), eventually emerged. Like the Paul Report, it was intended as a stimulus to discussion which would have the unity and forcefulness of a single person's vision. John Tiller, then the ACCM chief secretary, certainly fulfilled that brief. Hoyle (2016, p. 10) comments that with Tiller, familiar assumptions about ministry 'began to look less and less sure ... our theology started to sound provisional'.

Tiller's strategy was rooted in four changes in ministry he identified as already taking place, one negative and three positive. First, the parochial system was coming under increasing strain, owing to falling clergy numbers and insufficient ordinations. Second, there was a growth in the vitality of lay ministries. Third, specialist ministries were developing steadily among the clergy. Fourth, dioceses were taking greater strategic responsibility for ministry deployment (para. 54). Tiller therefore sought to build a strategy that would seize the opportunities created by the positive developments he had identified rather than trying to remedy the negative one. He argued that the case for a collaborative understanding of ministry was now proven, certainly at a theological level (chapter 8). Conversely, there were clearly ways in which the existing parochial system, and the leadership of full-time paid clergy, militated against this (chapters 9 and 15). What is at stake is how to mould the institutional arrangements of the Church to embody more effectively a variety of ministry functions, ordained and lay.

Tiller saw a remodelled eldership (presbyterate/priesthood) as the key to this (chapter 13): the leadership of the local church should always be plural, with eldership being both ordained and lay, both local (indigenous) and diocesan (catholic). The eldership would be organically related both to the wider *episkope* (oversight) represented by the diocese and the corporate *diakonia* (service) expressed through the local church body. This is the ecclesiological rationale underlying Tiller's much-criticized proposal for a dual system consisting of local, unpaid clergy working alongside lay people as part of a ministry team, and a diocesan 'pool', on the paid payroll, available to be deployed where needed according to their distinctive ministry gifts. Tiller observed that many clergy who have transitioned from parochial ministry into chaplaincy valued the job satisfaction that accrues from this sense of devoting the lion's share of their time to the exercise of their specific gifts. He advised that 'every servant of God is called to a specialist ministry – the one which effectively employs that person's particular gifts' (paras 164–65). But, as with much else in his report, there was more than enough ecclesiastical long grass into which such ideas could be kicked at the time.

As though Tiller had never been, five years later a further Discussion Paper from the Ministry Co-ordinating Group (1988), *The Ordained Ministry: Numbers, Cost and Deployment,* was extremely cautious about offering any encouragement to alternatives to traditional parochial ministry. Tiller is dismissed in a brief paragraph, and the group suggest it is still too early to assess what impact the Strategy has had (para. 24); elsewhere a single paragraph (59) is given to 'Other Ministries'. This 'ACCM Green Paper', as it was known, was nevertheless remarkably optimistic in its assessment of the possibility of maintaining and affording a continuing overall coverage of stipendiary ministry into the twenty-first century. In the deanery where I was serving at the time it resulted in a resolution by the Synod to maintain the existing structure of parochial ministry, including increases in clergy numbers where desirable, together with a commitment to raising the finances to pay for this and to fostering the vocations to make it possible. Handed the opportunity by its ministry thinkers to reaffirm the status quo, the representatives of the Church at local level were more than happy to do so.

In 1993, a report of the Advisory Board of Ministry (as it had by then become), *Order in Diversity*, raised for the first time the possibility of the need for a significant decline in paid numbers. The report broached the possibility that a fresh theology of ministry, and an overhaul of ministry structures to enable it, might be needed. Unfortunately, however, it stopped short of offering an actual strategy for developing experimentation in diversity, and it met with a reception at best lukewarm, at worst hostile, in the General Synod. In an article in the *Church Times*, John Tiller quoted from *Order in Diversity*, that 'rather than being the one who was thought of as the main agent of the Church's mission, the clergy are now seen as "enablers", "trainers", "resource people", "managers", and "discerners of people's gifts", *as well as being* [emphasis Tiller's] pastors, preachers, and leaders of the worship and life of the congregation'. He commented that it is this 'as well as' that both condemns the parochial clergy to an impossible task and reduces lay ministry yet again to 'helping the clergy'.

It is worth interjecting here that even at the present time, a clergy recruitment drive still forms part of the Church of England's strategy for renewal (for a thorough account of the Church's approach to vocations, recruitment and selection, see Reiss, 2013). Reporting that the latest vocations target would almost certainly not be met, a spokesperson said, with characteristic equivocation, 'whilst the news remains encouraging, we will be looking more carefully at what longer-term projections might be telling us' ('Growth in clergy vocations slows', *Church Times*, 2 September 2019). It would seem to me that the demographics of church attendance suggest that the longer-term prospects for clergy recruitment, under the present system for discerning of vocations, selection, training, deployment and the 'mechanics' of ordination itself, would not be promising.

The preceding series of reports paints a picture of a Church dragged only reluctantly towards a recognition of the theological validity, and ecclesiological and missiological necessity, of shared, collaborative and diverse patterns of ministry. Group and Team ministries did come into being, but they only brought together clergy to share ministry, and formal Team Ministries had an awkward hierarchical structure of Team Rector, Team Vicar(s) and Curate(s). Reforms of the legal structures of tenure of office for the clergy have taken place, but not in a way that significantly altered ministerial practice. Lay ministry has massively increased over the last 40 years, and this is to be applauded, but with the reservation that in many cases it has multiplied individual ministries more than it has nurtured genuinely collaborative teamwork. Given that lay ministry does not necessarily mean shared ministry, and shared ministry does not always include the laity, the advocates of collaborative ministry are looking for something more: a local church as a non-hierarchical, organic communion that releases the creative contributions of all, with maximum encouragement of diversity and interdependence.

Not long after the Tiller Report was quietly consigned to the pending file, a number of dioceses were launching schemes for the development of Local Collaborative Ministry, forming parish Ministry Teams within which vocations to a range of ministries would emerge, including Readers, Pastoral Ministers, Evangelists and other lay ministries, together with, controversially, Ordained Local Ministers. The vocation, selection and training of these deacons and priests would be cultivated and contextualized within the local church and community, and their ministry exercised wholly in that context (Advisory Board of Ministry, 1998; Greenwood and Pascoe (eds), 2006; Torry and Heskins (eds), 2006; Bowden et al. (eds), 2011). The influential *Stranger in the Wings* report (ABM Policy Paper No. 8, 1998) offered an overview of this emerging experimental field and suggested guidelines and principles for good practice, especially in collaborative ministry. The report offers the following definition:

> Collaboration is at the heart of the development of shared ministry, a sharing between laity and clergy of their fundamental vocation arising from their baptism. LNSM [Local Non-Stipendiary Ministry, later known as Ordained Local Ministry] grows from and is an expression of the shared ministry of Christians in a particular locality, setting apart within the whole church certain men and women for the particular role of priest in that community, serving within a coherent team of clergy and laity. (para. 3.3, p. 27)

Stranger in the Wings had a noticeably different character from the other reports documented above, because it was neither a top-down episcopal statement nor produced principally as an answer to the question 'how can we compensate for the declining numbers of full-time clergy?' Instead, it drew on the developing experience of a growing movement in Britain, the USA, Canada, Australia and New Zealand, encouraging 'approaches to Church envisioned as the people of God working together and sharing responsibility for the mission that God has entrusted to them' (Greenwood and Pascoe (eds), 2006, p. viii). This work was resourced and researched by the Edward King Institute for Ministry Development from the 1980s to early in the new century; the EKI journal *Ministry* published theological and practical commentary and critique on the emerging patterns of collaborative ministry throughout this period. In 1999 an international symposium was held in San Francisco drawing together practitioners reflecting on practice from across the world (for a collection of writings documenting the development of the American experience of 'total ministry', see Borgeson and Wilson (eds), 1990).

The *Stranger in the Wings* report rounds off the list of documents on ministry strategy under consideration in this chapter. It is important now to pause and explore in more detail the theology and practice of the collaborative models of ministry it commended. One significant feature of these developments is that they arose in a number of pioneering dioceses and spread through networks, conferences and key personnel writing and speaking about their ideas and advising like-minded colleagues in other dioceses. Local Ministry Schemes initially evolved in a very ad hoc way, with little centralized guidance, and imaginative diocesan personnel essentially making it up as they went along. This quality of improvisation extended to the devising of programmes for training Ordained Local Ministers on diocesan schemes, outwith the established provision of theological colleges and courses. Although this kind of spontaneous expansion and improvisational character was vital for encouraging entrepreneurial flair and a culture of permission-giving, it also laid the movement open to certain challenges from more conventional Church sources less favourably disposed to innovation.

Three challenges to collaborative ministry: local, clerical and missional

The first contentious issue for critics of Local Collaborative Ministry related to the priority of the 'local' for ecclesiology, often raised by churches of a Catholic tradition. Volf puts it well:

> The church nowhere exists 'above the locally assembled congregation, but rather in, with, and beneath it'. A congregation is the body of Christ in the particular locale in which it gathers together ... A particular denomination, the local churches in a cultural or political region, or the totality of local churches can be called 'church' only in a secondary rather than a strictly theological sense. (1998, p. 138, quoting Otto Weber)

Dan Hardy notes the tensions this theological perspective can produce. The Church 'as traditionally predefined' defines norms and standards centrally, deriving from the 'greater church', and thus standardizes ideas and practices of ministry and enshrines requirements in policies and legislation. By contrast, Local Ministry affirms the openness of ministry to all according to their gifts, as a consequence of their baptism, and that the diverse ministries are 'radically oriented to the varying task of meeting the needs of others' (Hardy, 2006, p. 145). Whether and how far local variations can deviate from centrally established norms therefore raises tensions that have never been resolved, and are likely to emerge with equal force as Fresh Expressions and Pioneer Ministries continue to evolve, as we shall see in Chapters 8 and 10.

The second bone of contention turned upon the impact of collaborative ministry on traditional clergy roles. Diocesan Local Ministry Schemes typically offered churches a developmental process for the establishment of shared and collaborative ministry within the everyday life of the church, in which clergy and laity were expected to participate together, with additional training in collaborative ministry provided specifically for the clergy as part of their Continuing Ministerial Education. It was not unusual to encounter resistance to this training from clergy who suspected that their authority would be undermined, or that they would be left without a clear role. For example, Clitherow worries that some priests may feel 'disempowered' by collaborative ministry (2004, p. 52), and Hoyle fears that shared ministry may turn into a competitive striving and a source of conflict (2016, pp. 132–3). Sadly, there is no short-cut to collaborative ministry that lets the vicar continue business as usual.

Some clergy have been keen to enrol on diocesan programmes, but (knowingly or otherwise) have retained a model of lay ministry as merely helping the clergy, or limited to a process of delegation of tasks without a sharing of responsibility, authority or leadership. Where collaborative ministry has begun to sow in the minds of local Christians the revolutionary thought that they 'really are the church', clergy are not always as delighted as one might hope when they encounter the creative energies flowing. Many find it very hard to accept that a Local Ministry Team may comprise imaginative, highly motivated and deeply committed Christian people who have a strong vision for their church and its development. This problem often occurs with the arrival of new clergy who are determined to start again from scratch with their own ideas, and instances of clergy unilaterally taking decisions, and summarily dismissing lay ministers or disbanding ministry teams, are not uncommon. The problems are illustrated in the unhappy story recounted to the theologian Ruth Page by a long-serving diocesan Adult Education Adviser:

Meeting a lay reader at a Diocesan Synod I asked how things were going. In tears, she described how a new incumbent had decided that preaching and teaching were *his* gift. After years of valued and full ministry of leading groups and preaching she had been 'stood down'... A few days later a vicar rang up incensed because a lay member of his congregation had been invited to help with some diocesan training and the request had not been channelled through him to determine what his lay people should or should not be invited to consider. Shortly afterwards a clergyman who has seen himself as being facilitative and encouraging of lay ministry was brought up short as he became aware of how constantly he talked about 'my parish', 'my people', 'my patch', as though somehow he owned them. (Chris Peck, cit. Page, 2000, p. 83)

A third criticism was made by those who suspected that Local Collaborative Ministry is essentially a *conservative* initiative, designed only to compensate for the decline in stipendiary clergy. In my own diocese, the bishop was rather non-committal until he encountered one or two 'good news stories' about certain participating parishes, whereupon, without consulting the Ministry Scheme staff, he announced that it would now be a target for every church in the diocese (239 in all) to produce an OLM. Croft fears that some of this enthusiasm may suggest that collaborative ministry 'can be understood to assume' that ways of being church do not need to change (2002, pp. 27–8), whereas 'if the problem is the way we are church then no amount of renewal of ministry will solve it' (pp. 48–9). He is right in maintaining that the Church's problems go much deeper than can be solved by finding scores of new clergy in the form of OLMs, but mistaken to assume that this is what Local Collaborative Ministry is fundamentally all about.

This misconception has been recognized by writers in the field. Greenwood has criticized 'a tendency for Local Ministry to be seized upon and repackaged to shore up inherited but exhausted patterns of Church', rather than a resource to help churches discover 'how to be a community that finds and serves God's mission' (Greenwood and Pascoe (eds), 2006, p. 3). Similarly, Daniel Hardy comments that it was often regarded 'much less as a new kind of way of "being church" than a way of providing priests locally where none were otherwise available' (2006, p. 131). There is a telling comment from Jessica Martin: 'When there are not enough priests to go round, lay incarnational presence is absolutely vital' (Martin and Coakley (eds), 2016, p. 28), as if this were only needed where there is a priest-shaped gap to be filled. It is clear then that too often, Local Collaborative Ministry has indeed been viewed by senior church leaders and others as a way of keeping the show on the road.

But what if it should turn out to be precisely a way of steering the show *off* the road, swerving the Church into the rough tracks and undergrowth of off-road driving? What if it should turn out to be a pioneering outback route into uncharted territory where we unexpectedly come upon God, beckoning the company of Jesus' disciples into a strange land where the familiar churchy landmarks have vanished? Unleashing experimental and adaptive models and patterns of ministry risks setting in motion a train of events that cannot easily be contained by the usual mechanisms of institutional control in the Church. The genie is out of the bottle, even though it would better serve the inherited ways of doing things to put it well and truly back in.

Responding to the critical issues about the priority of the local, the role of the clergy, and the allegation of a 'maintenance' rather than a mission ethos in Local Collaborative Ministry, the next section will examine more closely the requirements of appropriate leadership for collaborative ministry and the place of missionary vision.

Leadership and vision in a collaborative ministry context

At a diocesan meeting of Rural Deans called to explore the potential for collaborative ministry in their deaneries, one (charismatic) remarked that, 'I always feel that collaborative ministry is a way of making it much harder for me to be able to deliver my vision', and another (Anglo-Catholic), memorably, that, 'I could never try this in my patch because if I let go of control they'd all be at each other's throats.' But whose 'vision'? And what 'control'? The clerical model of leadership has been distinctly that of the priest 'in charge', the source of all vision, going it alone, striving both to care for and to inspire the dependent flock. John Leach, formerly Director of Anglican Renewal Ministries, expresses reservations about collaborative ministry and leadership teams because 'in many cases the leader is the visionary. He or she senses from God what the direction is to be, and then leads the people in that way' (1997, p. 11).

This concept of 'visionary leadership' suggests energetic, charismatic clergy who can come into a struggling parish and turn the church around. The Church of England is actively promoting the recruitment of leaders with missionary gifts, among which the ability to build and sustain vision is paramount. The *Mission-shaped Church* report (Archbishops' Council of the Church of England, 2004) recommended that particular resources be put into the identification, selection and training of ordained ministers with missionary and pioneering gifts: 'those involved in selection need to be adequately equipped to identify and affirm pioneers and mission entrepreneurs' (p. 147). Such people have clear and necessary gifts. Nevertheless, they are often not team players, and frequently less skilled in putting in place the foundations to ensure the good work carries on when they leave.

In a section headed 'appropriate local leadership', the report acknowledged this, warning that 'if pioneers are to establish work that endures, they quickly need to become team leaders ... *There can be a tension between the visionary and the relational, team-building elements of leadership* [emphasis mine]. Both elements are essential if the work is to last beyond an initial burst of enthusiasm' (p. 133). Accordingly, the draft guidelines for the identification, training and deployment of these Ordained Pioneer Ministers, published in late 2005 in consultation with Fresh Expressions, noted that 'pioneer ministers may well need to develop new patterns of ministerial leadership. Bishops' Advisers will need to be sure that candidates are self-motivated within a team context and are able to enable and motivate others.' 'The ability and desire to work in a team and collaboratively' is listed as one of eleven 'core elements' to be looked for in such candidates.

Included with the guidelines, a letter from Steven Croft, of Fresh Expressions, and Paul Bayes, of the Church of England's Mission and Public Affairs Division (and both now senior bishops), to principals of the various institutions of ministerial training, makes explicit that pioneering ministries should also be encouraged within Local Ministry Schemes. In keeping with this, one of the illustrative scenarios for Pioneer Ministers given in the draft guidelines is for an OLM deployed into a 'fresh expression of church' being pioneered within her own parish: to support her training, 'a ministry development team is formed from those already exercising leadership in the church'. In addition, the Church of England's generic Learning Outcomes for ministerial training now require that in order to be licensed to a post of incumbent status, clergy should 'demonstrate effective collaborative leadership and the ability to exercise this in a position of responsibility' (Archbishops' Council of the Church of England, 2006, p. 70).

All of this material is indicative of a growing recognition in the Church's thinking of the links between leadership, collaboration and mission. Collaboration is not an abdication of individual leadership responsibility, and nor is visionary quality a licensing of maverick individualism. Secular leadership theory has coined the phrase 'post-heroic leadership' to denote the alternative (see Crevani, Lindgren and Packendorff, 2007). One of the best Christian expositions of this is provided by Penny Jamieson:

> Rather than beginning at the centre or the top, as a hierarchical structure would indicate, one should look within the community and ... start with the 'infinitesimal mechanisms' which each have their own story, the exchanges and relations between individuals. (1997, p. 10)

However, the picture is by no means fully formed. If, therefore, the Church is to put into practice its good intentions with regard to identifying and training clergy who will exercise leadership in a way that is both missionary (and visionary) *and* collaborative, it will need to seek out resources that help to hold those elements together in a creative synthesis.

In her Christian Research Lecture 2004, *Strategic Thinking and its Impact on Leadership*, the management consultant Gillian Stamp writes helpfully about strategic leadership qualities. The leader is endowed with curiosity, interested in people with an insatiable desire to find out more about them, how they tick, what is going on between them. S/he displays humility, in the sense of recognition of the limits of their own knowledge and the consequential openness always to fresh learning. There will be the exercise of discernment, being open to what may be happening, reading the signs of the times, helping others to gain insight and so make their own decisions. Then leaders will facilitate the process of conceptualizing, 'seeing the wood for the trees', going beyond the mass of detail to see the big picture and the connecting threads and patterns within situations. They will require the imagination to help people see things from a variety of standpoints, and the foresight to ask questions about ultimate aims and the direction of travel required in order to attain them.

As another helpful resource, *Stranger in the Wings* lists the characteristics of good practice for clergy and laity working collaboratively in ministry (1998, pp. 29, 32–3, 43–4). Leaders need to be 'willing to act as guide, adviser and consultant rather than benevolent dictator or efficient delegator' (p. 32), and should aim to promote 'a shared vision', and affirm 'a wide variety of gifts and skills'. They will cultivate an attitude of 'flexibility and openness to change' across key areas of church life, including 'sharing in the leading and planning of worship', 'good communication between groups and individuals' and 'continuing learning, corporate and individual' (p. 29). Notably, the report acknowledges that this consultative style brings with it costs for the kind of leaders who are in a hurry to get things done. Sometimes, they must be prepared to accept that their ideas will 'be postponed or rejected' (p. 32). In devoting time to consultation and planning with the ministry team, and making provision for training and support, they will need to understand that 'collaboration is better, but is not usually easier or quicker' (p. 33).

These are all vital qualities for the kind of approach needed to endorse with full seriousness the roles and responsibilities for leadership in the emerging missionary Church. In the remainder of this chapter, I want to put some flesh on the bones by drawing attention to how the 'people's church', as the company of disciples, rich in ministries, all working together as the body of Christ, might look in three important areas of the Church's life.

Marks of a collaborative church

The Church at worship: the laicization of liturgy

Public worship is an area of the life of the Church that has moved from being something of a 'one-man band' leading a passive congregation, to a situation where there is likely to be a 'sharing out' of particular tasks, such as reading lessons, leading intercessions and administering the cup at Holy Communion. These are significant first steps along the way to an expression of collaborative ministry, but there is scope for much more. Within the Church of England, the challenge comes from the way in which the ordering and leading of worship are matters of legislation. Anglican identity and doctrine are liturgically maintained and expressed, and this gives rise not only to much synodical discussion of detail, but also to an immense reliance upon liturgical professionals. Authorized liturgies need to be 'correct': in line with mainstream catholic tradition, doctrinally orthodox, and biblically sound. There is a price to be paid for all these good and desirable things: the removal of the direct involvement of the people in articulating the voice of authentic worship, as what is permitted is given back to them only after it has passed through the hands of the experts.

Michael Perham, then a major player in the Church of England's Liturgical Commission, acknowledged that 'if in this post-modern world where choice is inevitable ... you treat people as adults, you spell out to them the freedom they are being given' (2002, p. 39). However, although 'treating people as adults' might seem to be a good thing, he feared that 'if you extend freedom, and create a culture of freedom, *people will then claim it* [emphasis mine], rather unthinkingly, even in the areas in which it has not been given'. This anxiety about people claiming (too much) freedom results in extreme caution in matters of worship and liturgy. There is an important issue here about whether 'quality control', so to speak, is better achieved by tighter legislation, or by taking lay education more seriously.

A more positive view of lay freedoms is possible: to take the risk of cultivating projects in which laity and clergy might work together locally, as the people's church creating the people's liturgy, supported by effective education and good resources, rather than constrained by legislative controls. Janet Morley offers an insightful account of the process of creating liturgy as a collaborative grass-roots project:

It is my observation that the effort to put together a form of liturgy that can be assented to and 'authorized' by the whole group involves a significant loss of innocence. The question about how we can worship together, what *exactly* we are communally prepared to confess as our faith, arises in a poignant way ... It questions the kind of clericalism whereby the form of worship is simply 'produced' by an expert; and it raises in a very practical way the issue about how particular words for worship are authorized by the groups that recite them. Where people are taking on this task at grassroots level, working on new liturgies both nourishes and helps to develop a new kind of Christian community. (1988, p. 35)

Morley's vision of lay participation in the design and delivery of worship captures a number of points of huge significance for collaborative ministry across the board: the 'loss of innocence' that makes the old paternalistic ways of doing things impossible; the poignancy and power of really needing to engage seriously with what is believed; the intrinsic relationship between the words used in worship and the faith stories of the community.

The approach taken by Tim Lomax also emphasizes the variety of ways in which churches can move away from the reliance on worship as a 'performance' delivered from the front, to an audience, and work creatively and collaboratively on worship that reflects their context and common life (2015, pp. 23 ff.). Even a cautious, 'quintessentially Anglican' approach can seek to bring the old and the new into creative liturgical interaction by 'starting where people are' and allowing the worship to develop within that cultural field (p. 36). This can often be combined with the 'praxis' model where worship is created in tandem with church action on social and community issues, which Lomax associates with the work of Ann Morisy (2004), and her concept of 'apt liturgy' (2015, pp. 32 ff.). At the more radical end of the spectrum, there are maximally diverse multi-media or 'liquid' approaches that can be challenging and even confrontational in crafting acts of worship that present how Christianity profoundly questions aspects of contemporary culture.

We shall return to these more radical expressions of collaboratively produced worship in Chapter 10. Closer to the mainstream, Mark Earey has contributed a constructive study of how churches might be tempted to greater creativity in worship, rather than simply treating *Common Worship* (in the design and implementation of which he was a significant player) as a collection of 'off the peg' set texts. He concedes that it is a problem that 'the inherited "mood" in the Church of England is still that liturgy is about control' (2013, p. 42), seeking instead to create a situation in which 'trust, creativity, experiment (with accountability) is the norm, and central control is the exception' (p. 141). His proposal is that in place of a large body of legally authorized liturgical texts combined with fairly minimal permissions for use of alternatives on specified occasions, the Church should legislate for a small core of principles and frameworks for designing worship, with certain basic texts centrally 'commended' for use, and provision to enable local commendation of other materials at diocesan level (pp. 119 ff.).

These considerations about worship will be developed in Chapters 6 and 10, in relation to the influence of Pentecostalism, and then in the context of a culture of postmodernity.

The Church as community: transcending tribalism

As in the case of the vicar who feared what might be unleashed if he dared to encourage collaborative ministry in his church, community in the Church (Greek *koinonia*, or fellowship) is often a greatly devalued concept. Commonly, a sense of 'togetherness' may spring from shared concerns, as in a working party, a pressure group, or a sports club; or from a shared lifestyle or indeed simply from close proximity, or from likemindedness. But the challenge is to ask what happens if the fellowship the Holy Spirit creates brings people together who do not share any of these bases, people who are simply unlike each other in every way (Moltmann, 1997, p. 89). Within the context of the Church, there can indeed be no other kind:

> It is only the complex diversity of gifts and energies which makes a living and viable unity possible. If it is simply a case of 'birds of a feather flock together', the people who are no different from each other will become a matter of indifference to one another ... For the community of Christ, on the other hand, acceptance of other people in their difference is constitutive. (pp. 59–60)

In this case, 'the Christian congregation is a matter of trust' (p. 99). It is costly to achieve unity in fellowship at this level, and involves enduring pain and resolving conflict.

Peter Selby uses the terms 'ethnic' and 'ecclesial' to describe the contrasting understandings of unity. Ethnic, or tribal, unity is achieved and maintained by means of the *esprit de corps* of those who belong. This can manifest in different types of church. There is the small congregation which insists, 'we are a very friendly and close little fellowship here', but in practice 'close' means 'closed'. By contrast, there is the large and thriving evangelical church to which people are attracted from miles around who carry the same card, in doctrine and churchmanship. In the first case, newcomers cannot break in at all; in the second, they are welcome as long as they hold the right views. Selby warns his fellow bishops against falling into the trap of licensing likemindedness: 'Among the most dangerously half-true understandings of the role of bishops is that they are to be the focus of unity in the Church', a concept all too 'capable of exploitation under the impulse of tribal self-defence' (1991, pp. 59–60).

The future will require a radical deconstruction of inherited institutional models in order to free the people of each worshipping community to 'be church' in a manner appropriate to who and where they are, rather than simply drawing their character from the tradition of their clergy. With this liberation, they will be much better placed to handle diversity in unity than the traditional institution is likely to be. An example of this is the prolonged agony of the official attitude of the Church of England towards gay people, both lay and ordained. As long as there exist conflicting opinions strongly held, within the House of Bishops as elsewhere, no 'firm lead' can be taken, since an *appearance* of unity must be maintained. However, what is being preserved by the bishops is always a form of 'tribal' rather than truly 'ecclesial' unity: just enough emphasis on the theology of inclusivity for them to *seem* affirming of the LGBT minority, but just enough moral disapprobation to keep on board the powerfully anti-gay lobbies that often have strong representation among some of the most flourishing and affluent churches of their dioceses. Meanwhile, in practice, many congregations take a far more relaxed attitude towards their gay members, and indeed to gay clergy, including some who are living in committed relationships with partners.

In its practice of fellowship, the vision is for the worshipping Christian community to take authority with full authenticity, on the basis of its own experience and recognition of the common life of *agape* in the Spirit: 'this is who we are'. Such communal authority will take precedence over both the timidity of institutional hierarchies and the bullying tactics of vested interests. Writing from within the Pietist tradition, David Williams argues that the 'conventicle' (a non-hierarchical, non-systematized small-scale gathering) offers a suitable environment for addressing 'the problem of multiplicity and unity', and pursuing the aims of 'restoring true humanity' (2015, pp. 43–4). The Church of England at its best managed to do this in resolving the debate about women bishops, but has so far failed to do so over homosexuality. This issue of how the Church handles questions of unity and diversity therefore leads directly into the third area, of the Church as a learning environment.

The Church as a learning movement: 'listening not debating'

The nurturing of collaborative ministry will move the Church away from lay education based on the 'confirmation class' model, where the pupils sit at the feet of the minister, who shares with them the riches of the Christian tradition by means of devotional talks, in accordance with his or her personal preferences. In the educational dimension of the Church's life, the expectation of deference to experts on the part of the untutored has been as strong as anywhere: 'church leaders traditionally gave attention to teaching Christians the proper doctrines and beliefs' (Hawkins, 1997, p. 11). This reflects the hierarchical model in which truth is seen as a stream flowing from its ultimate source with God, down through such mediations as Scripture and tradition, to be handled and dispersed by those duly trained and steeped in these resources, down to the waiting faithful. By contrast, Hawkins argues that the task of the contemporary church leader as educator is to create and nurture an environment in which 'the whole people of God can shape and reshape meaning within a community of shared practice, continually clarifying those meanings in the light of a deeper understanding of the revelation made known in Jesus Christ' (p. 11).

This complements the approach of Schillebeeckx, who argues that leaders who hold a teaching office must not overlook the various 'mediations' of the work of the Spirit, including 'above all the mediation of the structured people of believers themselves, here and now in the stream of time' (2000, p. 221). Thus 'the democratic participation of everyone ... in a theologically responsible way ... must play a role at precisely this level'. Debating, in the manner of a Church synod, which is geared towards establishing the supremacy of one argument over a contrary one, has no place in this collaborative and communal learning process, which is rooted in careful listening and oriented to the advancement of understanding.

In her treatment of learning as a mutual and collaborative process, Katherine Nevins finds resources in the work of Philip Spener, one of the founders of German Pietism (Nevins, 2015, p. 56). The non-hierarchical common priesthood of all believers ensures that love of God and neighbour governs the relationships that should pertain between students and teachers, who are also to be role-models and mentors. Humility and openness to correction are vital to the creation of an authentic learning community (pp. 57–8). All of this envisages a 'learning ecclesiology' that 'views the church as a schoolhouse of faith' (Hawkins, 1997, p. 67), rather than the 'pastoral ecclesiology' that regards leadership principally in terms of teaching and caring for the people. In the collaborative church, this learning and teaching ministry subjects all those taking part to exposure, risk and vulnerability, but equally to the joy of discovery. As the Quaker writer and teacher Parker Palmer puts it:

> Forced to listen, respond and improvise, I am more likely to hear something unexpected and insightful from myself as well as others ... As we learn more about who we are, we can learn techniques that reveal rather than conceal the personhood from which good teaching comes. (1998, p. 24)

The classic error is that 'driven by fear that my backstage ineptitude will be exposed, I strive to make my on-stage performance slicker and smoother' (p. 29): a drastic misstep into inauthenticity that can easily afflict ordained ministers just as much as teachers.

Conclusion

This chapter has traced something of the long story of the churches' quest for new ministry strategies to meet the demands of the present day. The favoured trajectory has been towards ministry that is more lay, shared and collaborative, and more local and contextual. Sometimes, these aspirations have been used as a thin disguise for keeping the traditional show on the road, but there have also been valid and praiseworthy efforts to promote a genuinely collaborative energy within an inherited church structure that is not always hospitable to such a move. Local collaborative ministry initiatives in particular have tried to reimagine church leadership and coax into being a fresh 'take' on ordained ministry as the 'priestly person' who is recognized and validated by the community. The final main part of the chapter offered some snapshots of the collaborative church, in its approach to worship as a corporate and contextual creation, its fellowship as a joyful celebration of difference and its Christian formation as a deep collective reflection on the traditions of faith in the light of experience.

But there is a long way to go. Ordination services continue to declare loud and clear that whatever other varieties of ministry there may be, *this* is the one that really counts. Churches in a so-called 'interregnum' continue to repeat the mournful mantra, 'when the new vicar comes ...' and services still take place at which the new arrival is feted with flowers and fanfares and proclaimed as the dawn of a new era. But the energy for gospel life, ministry and mission belongs at the heart of the gathering of the people of God as the body of Christ wherever they are to be found.

Whenever and wherever the Church is being given back to the people, the people who constitute the Church are coming to a fresh apprehension of just how exciting, if daunting, a prospect that is. In the next chapter, attention turns to one of the most significant engines for rebooting the Church along these lines in the twentieth century, the Pentecostal tradition and its offspring in the mainstream churches, the charismatic movement.

6

Distribution and Difference:
The Pentecostal and
Charismatic Inheritance

Encountering a movement

In the first part of this chapter, I want to adopt a somewhat different style by writing in autobiographical mode. At the age of 20, I was a student in Cambridge, finding my way rather unexpectedly into a practising Christian faith. During the academic year 1973–74, the buzz word in Christian Union circles was the 'charismatic movement'. Members of my college CU were reporting exciting developments at a parish church in a workaday part of town well away from the historic university area. A new vicar had arrived at this church having formerly been a Pentecostal pastor, and was leading the congregation's worship into the heady zone of 'spiritual gifts': it was becoming the place to be. I went along on a Sunday evening, to experience a two and a half hour long Communion service incorporating extended periods of worship songs led by a guitar group, a 40-minute Bible sermon, people who wanted to be prayed for coming forward for the laying on of hands, people praising God with hands raised, people swaying, weeping, embracing, and 'singing in the Spirit' that sent shivers down the spine. I was hooked.

With the guidance of Christians of longer standing than myself I soon learned that this was a new movement that seemed to be sweeping through the Church. An American Episcopalian priest called Graham Pulkingham had come over from the States to tell his own story of renewal (Pulkingham, 1972; Harper, 1973), bringing with him a worship group called the Fisherfolk, who introduced many of the early charismatic choruses that began the process of gently revolutionizing the musical dimensions of worship in many an ordinary church. There was news of a young evangelical minister, David Watson, who had revived a struggling church in York, St Cuthbert's, before eventually decamping into the nearby St Michael le Belfrey, adjacent to York Minster, when the congregation got too large. This and other centres of charismatic renewal dotted around the country became like places of pilgrimage. At the same time, back in the Christian Union, prayer groups were springing up spontaneously where students sought spiritual blessing and gifting in ways the conservative evangelical elders of the CU tended to disdain. They thought it was all very emotional: you were supposed to trust in facts not feelings and, in any case, they taught that those rather outlandish gifts like speaking in tongues were only ever intended for the apostolic era and had died out since.

I learned many years later that Graham Pulkingham died in 1993 as a disgraced figure, having confessed to sexual misconduct during his ministry as an influential charismatic leader and founder of an experiment in Christian communal living (Duin, 2009), one of several high-profile instances of charismatic leaders going seriously astray. This led me to think that those evangelical elders may well have been on to something in their reservations: the charismatic milieu could too easily come under the spell of a dangerous cult of personality, and it saddens me that today's inheritors of the charismatic mantle so often seem to value a leadership style very much focused on the individual leader's drive and vision, as though lessons have not been learned. But this is now, and that was then: the more the conservative evangelicals disapproved, the more the charismatic element grew.

Back at home for the 1974 summer vacation, I decided to hunt for the charismatic movement locally. There was just one vicar in the town at the time who turned out to be committed to it, even though many of his congregation weren't enthusiastic. He pointed me in the direction of the Renewal Fellowship, a monthly gathering where teaching was regularly delivered by a retired Pentecostal Holiness preacher, Cecil Cousen, who now lived locally (for more on Cousen, see Hocken, 1986, pp. 25–37). He spoke of his delight that the movement of the Holy Spirit to which he had devoted his life's ministry was at last being manifested in the mainstream churches. I travelled with friends into the heart of the Yorkshire Wolds to an isolated farmhouse, to discover a dozen or so people assembled, hosted by the farmer and his wife, for charismatic prayer and worship. In a nearby village, the vicar had a vision to convert the vicarage into a centre for renewal with conferences and days where Christians hungry for change in their churches could come to receive teaching and ministry, and share together in worship with the spontaneity and spiritual dynamism of the renewal movement (Hoyle, 2003).

Back in town, I was told about a prayer meeting for young people held every Friday evening in the home of a woman who belonged to the local Elim Pentecostal church. The group ranged from quite young pre-teens into early twenties, and they joined in extempore prayer, laid hands on each other and sang choruses with eyes closed and hands outstretched with palms uppermost in front of them. An invitation was always offered to any who wanted to receive the Holy Spirit – to be 'baptized with the Spirit' – to be prayed for, which after a few weeks I did. At the time, the experience did not seem overwhelming, to be honest; but I do recall after leaving the house that I ran all the way home with a song in my heart.

I am trying to convey something of the heady atmosphere of these early days of charismatic renewal. There was a real sense of Christianity reinvented as an underground movement, an alternative society, a spiritual force at work to change the face of the Church and ultimately of the world. It seemed a kind of radical deconstruction of church, a back-to-basics, bottom-up re-creation of a people's church, a secret discipline, a holy subversion of conventional religion, and I thought it was the future. But, of course, it wasn't; at least, not in the way I had thought, in my youthful enthusiasm and inexperience. And yet, in another way, it *was* and *still is* the future: which is what I want to go on to say more about. Soon after leaving university, I found myself in a Pentecostal chapel on the south coast of England. The building was crumbling, the congregation a motley crew, the worship in some ways shambolic; but the spiritual 'hit' was tangible and the folk cared for one another in a way that put most other churches I'd experienced so far to shame. And so: why Pentecostalism matters.

Historical streams

The beginnings of Pentecostalism are generally traced to William Seymour's church at Azusa Street in Los Angeles, where a notable revival occurred in 1906. Seymour was a black pastor ministering in a tough and dangerous urban environment blighted with poverty and racism. The Pentecostal revival brought together the characteristic evangelical themes of conversion and holiness with the additional expectation of a profound religious experience of 'baptism in the Spirit'. This entailed the phenomenon of speaking in tongues, often accompanied by other occurrences such as healings and exorcisms, and dramatic physical manifestations interpreted as the direct working of the Holy Spirit. At the time, the movement was largely dismissed by the evangelical 'establishment' because of its origins in a poorly educated black environment, and its theology was rejected as 'unscriptural'. Pentecostals were driven to form their own denominations, principally the Elim and Assemblies of God churches.

In its origins, Pentecostalism reinvents church from below, from the margins, from the poor and the discriminated against. It initially set its face against elites and hierarchies and regarded the inherited churches as irredeemably tainted by worldliness, class and racial prejudice and the formalities of 'respectable religion'. There is a journalistic account of the Azusa Street meetings, published in the *Los Angeles Times* in April 1906, written by Frank Bartleman, a sympathetic observer:

> ... coloured people and a sprinkling of whites compose the congregation, and night is made hideous in the neighbourhood by the howlings of the worshippers who spend hours swaying forth and back in a[n] ... attitude of prayer and supplication ... Divine love was wonderfully manifest in the meetings ... It was a sort of 'first love' of the early church returned ... The 'baptism' [of the Spirit] as we received it in the beginning did not allow us to think, speak, or hear evil of any man. (Frank Bartleman, *Azusa Street*, p. 54, cit. Mitchell, 2011, pp. 153–4)

It was a spirituality that drew on elements of both the 'Pietist' and 'Puritan' roots of evangelicalism, placing a strong emphasis on the experiential dimension of faith and the expectation of dramatic manifestations of spiritual experience, while often rejecting 'worldly pleasures' such as dancing, cinema or alcohol (for a useful overview, see Kay and Dyer (eds), 2004, pp. xix–xxxiii).

Roger Haydon Mitchell judges that the early accounts place it beyond doubt 'that a countercultural, non-hierarchical unity of male and female, black and white, rich and poor characterized the embryonic movement' (2011, p. 154). Seymour was recognized as the de facto leader, but no hierarchical structures or symbols were put in place (for example, according to Bartleman, no pulpit). Early Pentecostalism was particularly hospitable to the ministry of women, and there are some notable examples of women preachers attaining celebrity status, such as Aimee Semple Macpherson (1890–1944), founder of the International Church of the Foursquare Gospel, who filled stadiums, built megachurches and pioneered radio evangelism.

The flavour of this subversive ministry from the margins is well captured in the British context in the person of Smith Wigglesworth (1859–1947), the working-class Bradford evangelist who was baptized in the Spirit under the remarkable pioneering ministry of the Anglican Alexander Boddy in Sunderland in 1907 (Wakefield, 2007). As an Assemblies of God pastor, Wigglesworth developed an international reputation as an evangelist and healer. His depiction of the core Christian experience is vividly conveyed in the following passage:

It is not a touch; it is not a breath; it is the Almighty God; it is a Person; it is the Holy One dwelling in the temple not made with hands. Oh, beloved, He touches and it is done ... Pentecost is the last thing that God has to touch the earth with ... If you do not get this you are living in a weak and impoverished condition which is no good to you or to anybody else. May God move us on to a place where there is no measure to this fulness that He wants to give us. (Smith Wigglesworth, 1922, 'Filled with God', cit. Kay and Dyer (eds), 2004, pp. 57–8)

Wigglesworth's no-nonsense and sometimes confrontational style belied an impassioned desire to see the power and presence of God at work to alleviate human sickness and suffering. In December 1936, he attended the conference of the Apostolic Faith Mission in Johannesburg and stayed at the home of its general secretary, the Pentecostal minister David du Plessis. While there, Wigglesworth burst into du Plessis' office and delivered what has become a famous word of prophecy; du Plessis records the event like this:

'Come out here!' [Wigglesworth ordered]. Without hesitation, I moved around the desk and walked toward him. 'Yes, Brother Wigglesworth.' He put his hands on my shoulders and pushed me against the wall, not roughly, but certainly firmly. He began to speak, and I knew he was prophesying. What followed was a remarkable and, to a Pentecostal in 1936, heretical message. The Lord would pour His Spirit upon the established Church, he said, and the ensuing revival would eclipse anything the Pentecostals had experienced. And David du Plessis would be mightily used by God to bring acceptance of the Pentecostal message to the established churches. (Jonas Clark, undated; see also Hocken, 1986, pp. 18–21)

Soon afterwards, an opportunity opened up for du Plessis to begin to explore the possibility of bringing together world Pentecostalism through a series of international conferences, which in due course expanded into an ecumenical initiative. In 1954, du Plessis attended the second assembly of the World Council of Churches, and for the rest of his life (he died in 1987) he was at the forefront of the advocacy of charismatic renewal across denominational boundaries, including cooperation with the Roman Catholic Church, something unthinkable for earlier generations of Pentecostals. Thus came about, from an originally illiterate Bradford plumber, via an initially conservative South African Pentecostal pastor, one significant thread of development of Pentecostal influence upon world Christianity.

David Martin argues that Pentecostalism was successful because it was 'voluntary, global and hybrid from the beginning' (2011, p. 68). This matches Chris Baker's observation that early Christian expansion tended to be to 'hybrid' communities, meeting-places and melting-pots of culture, such as seaports: from the start, the message was proclaimed differently in different places, in a multiplicity of tongues (2009, pp. 151, 153). Pentecostalism crossed social and cultural barriers and made a nuisance of itself in the face of the contempt of establishment religion; Martin describes Pentecostals as 'religious entrepreneurs setting up shop for themselves, and running their own show' (2011, p. 70). An instance of this was the restoration by some Pentecostal churches of the 'fivefold ministry' of apostles, prophets, evangelists, pastors and teachers derived from Ephesians 4.11 (Kay, in Kay and Dyer (eds), 2004, p. 167). Within this framework, Kay argues that apostles and prophets in particular 'would be able to challenge ecclesiastical hierarchies based upon established structures'.

Not surprisingly, the early ideals of Pentecostalism could not persist, and some churches drifted into authoritarian styles of leadership and exclusive positions on issues of gender, cultural propriety and even race (Mitchell, 2011, p. 156). Despite this, Martin argues that the intrinsic hybridity and flair for entrepreneurial improvisation has continued to characterize global Pentecostalism, giving it 'an amazing capacity to become indigenous, and adapt to local cultures' (2011, p. 69). This is well illustrated by Rob Warner's first-hand experience accounts of Pentecostal communities across five continents (2010, pp. 163–73). The stories he tells illustrate a remarkable capacity for mutations that correspond to contrasting cultural settings, from the favelas of Brazil, to the wealthy megachurches of South Korea, to the new churches sprouting up in the English cathedral city of York (see also Goodhew, in Goodhew (ed.), 2012, pp. 179–92).

In sum, 'global Pentecostalism is energized by a restlessly pragmatic impulse to experimental indigenization' and 'has demonstrated a confident adaptivity and a remarkable fluidity of acculturation' with the capacity to challenge the dominance of western patterns of secularization (Warner, 2010, p. 173). This is the case particularly in the guise of the emergent and independent churches developing in the former domains of Christendom in the West: their rise comes as secularization progressively weakens the hold of the older monopolistic churches. Despite this, Warner notes that the significant rise of the neo-Pentecostal new churches is still largely ignored by both media and much mainstream church commentary, and 'treated as if entirely subsumed within the polemical and distorting category of fundamentalism' (p. 180).

It is true that Pentecostalism often appeared fundamentalist in its official statements of faith, and the 'old-time religion' of classic Pentecostalism adopted a somewhat sectarian stance in the second half of the twentieth century. However, its emphasis in practice on 'fellowship in the Spirit', rather than doctrine, as the basis for association with other Christians, created a potential for ecumenical spread. A slow but steady growth of interest in Pentecostal practice by other evangelicals led to a cross-over that eventually manifested, to many surprisingly, in the charismatic movement, in the mainstream denominations from the 1960s. Not only the evangelical churches, but also both Anglican and Roman Catholicism, were affected by it from the 1970s onwards, taking it beyond being a purely evangelical phenomenon.

Over time, mainstream evangelicalism has become increasingly 'charismatic' in feel, though in a rather politer and more polished way than early Pentecostalism. The exercise of 'spiritual gifts' of the more spectacular kind appears somewhat to have receded, although the gift of tongues is often affirmed as a private devotional practice, effective in deepening intimacy with God and seen as being rooted in ancient tradition. Similarly, the rediscovery of the use of the body in worship has been linked back to pre-Reformation practice. There have been periodic revivals of dramatic and outlandish spiritual experiences, such as the 'Toronto Blessing' associated with the ministry of John Wimber (Percy, 1996); but for the most part today, the charismatic influence on evangelical spirituality has become most evident in a certain style of public worship. A music group with a worship leader will lead the congregation through a lengthy sequence of worship songs, carefully chosen to create changing devotional moods: loud and lively praise, worshipful intimacy, penitence, bold missionary proclamation. Nevertheless, it is probably true to say that at times all this can seem a far cry from the demanding call to holiness and Christian discipline of an earlier era of Pentecostal preaching.

The positive legacy of Pentecostalism is best rediscovered in elements that dig back deeper into its classic origins and early days, rather than in the contemporary worship style that has tended to define the 'charismatic' in the mainstream churches, and indeed often in the Pentecostal churches themselves. The 'new churches' form part of this movement of retrieval within the Pentecostal and charismatic traditions.

Tracing the legacies of Pentecostalism

The charismatic renewal has been more influential in moving congregations towards a new model of being church than the number of card-carrying 'charismatic' churches would suggest. In its earlier days some 50 years ago, this movement and its leaders were more explicitly indebted to the older 'classic' Pentecostal churches than charismatics more recently have tended to be. In this section I will look at this legacy under the headings of worship, fellowship and leadership. The phrase in the title of the chapter, 'distribution and difference', summarizes the key elements in words drawn from an insightful account by Don Cupitt, admittedly not the theologian most likely to come to mind in connection with Pentecostalism:

> A Pentecost-Christianity does not repudiate spiritual power, but it does seek to distribute it more evenly so that each layperson gains the courage to be creative and to be different. Difference is the real challenge: it is easy to be the same as others, one sheep in the flock, but hard to be different and to tolerate difference. (1989, p. 73)

The Pentecostal legacy in worship: communal narrative, testimony and celebration

Walter Hollenweger, the leading scholar of twentieth-century Pentecostalism, identified the distinctive features of Pentecostal spirituality and practice (1976 and 1986). In worship, there is an emphasis on an oral liturgy, with the expectation of spontaneity and communal expression of spiritual gifts. The term 'liturgy' continues to be applicable here because, in the absence of scripted, published and authorized texts, over time congregations evolve patterns, rhythms and communally owned and remembered oral traditions that recur recognizably in successive acts of worship. Theology is cast in narrative form, drawing on personal testimony, which itself forms a regular 'liturgical' ingredient of worship performance, provoking responses of praise among the congregation, and bolstering the sense of eventfulness and divine presence. Value is ascribed to individual experiences of visions and dreams in public, not just private spirituality, generally under the heading of 'prophecy'. Last, there is an emphasis on the close link between mind and body in expressions of spirituality (Hollenweger, 1986, pp. 551–2).

Jean-Jacques Suurmond characterizes the worship 'celebration' in the charismatic context in a way that demonstrates clear continuities with the Pentecostal tradition. The 'oral liturgy' means that worship is more easily 'accessible to people who have little or no literary training' (1994, p. 22). Although a recognized person presides over the celebration, it 'allows much room for spontaneous contributions and improvisations', especially through 'narrative theology and testimonies'. Teaching is less conceptual than in the inherited churches and instead draws attention to 'existential conviction', or 'what God has done for me' and 'what God can do for you'. The expectation that the gifts of the Spirit will operate in contexts of decision-making, as well as in worship, 'can lead to a community which is attentive to differences and is therefore reconciling' (p. 23). Last, there is a holistic view of the bodily and the spiritual, 'most clearly expressed in the celebration in the prayer for healing, which includes bodily ailments' (pp. 24–5). The celebration marks out church as 'different'. Suurmond writes:

> A celebration which is insufficiently 'different' cannot well proclaim the otherness of God's kingdom and thus the otherness of God … Celebration must again become what Harvey Cox described as a 'feast of fools', a playful protest that disturbs the social order and sets it moving with a view to its liberation and healing. (1994, p. 96)

Moltmann asks what it is about Pentecostal worship, and speaking with tongues in particular, that is so compelling. He reflects on 'services in the mainline Protestant churches', which 'offer a wealth of ideas in their sermons, and have wonderful chorales' (1997, p. 61). These services, however, seem 'poverty-stricken' in terms of the opportunity for personal expression, and 'offer no chance whatsoever for spontaneity'. By contrast, he finds that black Pentecostal congregations experience worship as an energizing and deeply personal articulation of who they are, with one another and with God. For example, he sees speaking with tongues as 'the beginning through which a powerful experience of the Spirit loosens the tongues of people who have been dumb, so that they can express what moves them so much'. It is an alternative culture, language and semiotics of worship to that which has shaped the historic churches of Christendom.

The breaking of the clerical (and professional) stranglehold releases confidence in people to be, and to become and to express, their true selves under God within Christ's Body. Their worship, so far from being an alienated and disconnected observance, becomes a vital telling of their story amid God's story in a way that dances with the uniquely distinctive life of every congregation. A vivid paragraph from Moltmann expresses it perfectly:

The awakening of personally experienced and personally expressed faith seems to me to be the charismatic experience today ... the charismatic experience begins with the new self-confidence which lets us say 'We are the church'. Before the mainline churches, the bishops and the synods quench the unfamiliar spirit of the charismatic movement, they should concede to God's Spirit the liberty to awaken men and women, to bring congregations to life, and to seek for forms of expression ... newer than the traditional liturgies. (1997, p. 62)

The Pentecostal legacy in fellowship: pneumatic unity in charismatic diversity

Pentecostalism offers insights into the understanding of church as fellowship or *koinonia* (communion), as analysed in some detail by Peter Hocken (1986, pp. 163 ff.). The key issue for Pentecostals is how 'unity in the Spirit' is worked out at the level of fellowship experience, including the corporateness of worship, more fundamentally than by way of doctrinal accord. Pentecostals are ultimately not 'conservative evangelicals', placing a premium upon the test of soundness by dogmatic orthodoxy. Contrary to this misconception, as Harvey Cox has put it, Pentecostal experientialism 'shatters the cognitive packaging' (1996, *Fire From Heaven*, cit. Warner, 2010, p. 180). As Hocken says, 'the fellowship experienced between the participants has not been primarily kinship of ideas, but knowledge of lives being touched by God in the same way' (1986, p. 178).

In an essay on the black-led Pentecostal Churches, Ian MacRobert identifies four functions of black Pentecostal congregations which add further weight to the case for affirming the full ministerial authenticity and giftedness of the local church (1989, pp. 128–9). First, such congregations promote healthy 'self-image' and 'ego gratification' (for an often originally disprivileged group), by providing a range of ministries and gifts which ordinary people can exercise. The gift of tongues, in particular, can be seen as symbolizing the authenticity of spiritual gifting without benefit of 'training' or special qualifications. Second, they provide a milieu for the development and expression of creativity and leadership, especially among people who may be deprived of this by their position in society at large. Third, they constitute a 'pneumatic community' in which power 'from beyond' can be accessed and applied. Fourth, they offer an encounter with God which is holistic in quality: spirit, mind and body are fully engaged. Together these offer a set of criteria for a church that is neither hierarchically nor clerically determined, but subsists in the assembly of the people, who are the primary locus of the divine presence and activity that is the dynamic heart of ecclesial life.

The Pentecostal legacy in leadership: personal authenticity and the challenge to elites

The pneumatological emphasis produces an approach to ministerial leadership that can be identified well beyond the boundaries of denominational Pentecostal theology. For example, Hans Küng makes a distinction between the institutional Church's practice of authorizing ministry and the unofficial but authentic gifting for ministry of lay people in local churches:

> there are institutions, and representatives of institutions, who are without anything charismatic ... and where there is no trace of the liberating Spirit of Christ ... there is no genuine ministry and no true leadership ... The man who has these gifts and uses them, on the other hand, is performing genuine service and leading, even when he possesses no institutional commission. (Küng, *Why Priests?*, 1972, cit. Harper, 1988, p. 251)

This crucial distinction between the existence of a charism for ministry and the institutional legitimation of it (office) is also made by Karl Rahner, who envisages a Church in which:

> office-holders in joyful humility allow for the fact that the charismatic element ... is just as necessary as office is to the Church: that office is never simply identical with the Spirit and can never replace him; that office too is really effectively credible ... only when the presence of the Spirit is evident and not merely when formal mission and authority are invoked, however legitimate these may be. (1977, p. 57)

This has long been the case within Pentecostalism, which has had an enduring tradition of expecting and affirming local and initially untutored gifting, even though the Pentecostal denominations have not been immune from the institutionalizations of ministry which have become routine elsewhere. Thus, Suurmond has warned against an understanding of church order that effectively sets the 'educated Word' against the 'untutored Spirit'. The 'word' in question is 'the word of the élite who have learnt to write, to preach and to discuss':

The word of dogma begins to justify the exclusion of those who think differently ... However, the Spirit is poured out uncontrollably 'on every living creature'. So all down history uneducated men and women began to prophesy. Those without a voice lifted up their voice without having undergone higher education sanctioned by the élite ... down through history attempts have been made to keep this dangerous spirit from people by caging it in the Word, in doctrine and structures. (1994, pp. 61–2)

The words 'sanctioned by the élite' through higher education fitly describes the model for leadership to which the churches are always tempted to return in the interests of professional credentials: this point will be taken up later, in Chapter 11.

Against the drift towards an institutionalization of ministry rendering it safer and more acceptable to the ruling classes, Paul Freston sees in the worldwide spread of Pentecostalism a grassroots movement from the underside of society that challenges and subverts familiar patterns of global domination by powerful institutions (2000, pp. 81 ff.). In this context, 'untutored' Christian leadership can be perceived by those in the more traditional churches as 'aggressive'. Freston quotes anthropologist David Lehmann's comment that what the established churches tended to criticize as 'aggression' among Pentecostals was in fact 'a challenge to the assumption of superiority'. Pentecostals are shocking because 'they are not submissive ... The white male from a rich country was put on the defensive by poor black women' (Lehmann, cit. Freston, 2000, p. 83).

Pentecostalism is often viewed with dismay 'because it rejects the traditional ... model of the religious field and popularises an alternative pluralist model' (Freston, 2000, p. 83): it enthusiastically welcomes maximal distribution and difference among churches and displays no deference towards inherited hierarchies. The established churches are prepared to 'embrace' and accommodate all manner of religious move-ments, so long as they themselves remain unchanged in their expectation of dominance. 'Indigenous ministry' becomes a threat when it challenges institutional power.

Lessons for the Church to come

In conclusion, we can say that inherited expectations of how ministry emerges, and what it looks like, are challenged by the Pentecostal legacy. Thompson and Thompson express it eloquently:

Ministry is primordially the *energy* of the Spirit in us, symbolized by the one Pentecostal fire distributed to each person, which leads us into *synergy* not only with God but with our *synergoi,* our fellow-workers, symbolized in the new wine of conviviality and the new tongues of communication. In this ancient context, ministry involves collaboration as *energy* involves *synergy*. (2012, p. 122)

Synergy, distribution, conviviality, collaboration: words like these return us to some of the themes of the previous chapter. A pneumatological approach to worship, fellowship and leadership has been guarded and transmitted by the global Pentecostal tradition, and generously distributed to the broader denominational spectrum. To conclude, I will briefly draw attention to aspects of this legacy likely to be especially relevant for the future Church.

First, Pentecostalism will not allow the subversive energy of the original flourishing of Christianity to be forgotten. In Chapter 2 we noted how the rejection of Montanism by the end of the second century dealt a severe blow to the encouragement of spiritual gifts, ecstatic experiences and ministries such as prophecy. Nevertheless, Origen, for example, despite offering a defence of hierarchy as necessary for church order, had an understanding of the Church that 'does not start from a constitution but from the concept of each congregation as a world of spiritual gifts in which every Christian can share even without the help of official mediators' (Melinsky, 1992, p. 40). It is clear that the 'pneumato-charismatic' and 'official-sacramental' approaches to ministry continued to coexist during the first few centuries of the Christian Church, and the Pentecostal impulse springs into new activity from time to time.

The charismatic movement that brought Pentecostalism into the mainstream has often been domesticated within the historic churches in the form of a cultural style, principally in worship. Classic Pentecostalism has also in many places become ossified into a rather backward-looking sectarian experience of church or, conversely, mutated into big business mega-church, often with an emphasis on a 'prosperity gospel' (Bowler, 2013). But the true legacies of Pentecostalism lie elsewhere; in its subversive energy. It dares to believe that there is no distinction of persons with regard to the Spirit's giftings: the first can be last, and the last first. God creates the Church by calling together a people and gifting them by the Spirit in a manner that cannot but release energy for collaboration. In this dynamic formation, people are empowered for gospel ministry and mission in ways that resonate with their own culture, rather than being expected to conform to some prescribed ecclesiastical design.

Second, the pneumatological orientation will remind the Church that the divine activity always supports an ecology of abundance. Where there are problems with collaborative ministry, these are the human problems of ordering and structuring that arise because we are all sinners who find it hard to cope with the simple truth of the generosity of God. This is recognized by Pickard when he describes the Church and its ministries as 'a challenge, not merely because of the complexity of church life but because, from a theological point of view, the greatest problem facing the Church is how to cope with the abundance of God's presence' (2009, pp. 165–6). Pentecostalism thrives in many places where people's economic experience of the world is scarcity, but their experience of God is of superabundance and plenty. Even if they are few, poor and powerless, they can change the world.

Third, the global, multicultural reach of Pentecostalism sets up a kind of firewall against imperialism, preventing the western churches of the Christendom era from falling back into the comforting illusions of their own superiority and the normative status of their traditions. For example, writing from the perspective of Black majority churches in the UK, David Shosanya suggests that Christians of African and Caribbean origin bring to the table an 'experience and interpretation of spirituality' that 'offers a very unique insight into the spiritual rhetoric that is increasingly becoming normative in Western culture' (Shosanya, cit. Standing, 2013, p. 71). Their tradition has 'inadvertently equipped them' to speak into the spiritual quests of a post-secular culture, and not least to question the complacent assumption of a liberal secular society that it can safely jettison religion while welcoming a free-for-all in spirituality.

As another example of the challenging of some western assumptions about the other-worldliness of spirituality and the secularity of the social world, Phyllis Tickle suggests that the pneumatological legacy of Pentecostalism has helped to reshape the understanding of Christian social action away from 'helping acts', 'done to' or 'for' people, and towards a much more holistic and participative 'kingdom' activity. This dynamic, interactive model has the serendipitous effect of making it possible to express theological ideas in the language of the world-wide web, which in turn can generate fresh, non-hierarchical metaphors for the Church.

> The kingdom is a lacework of inter-connected and equi-connected nodes or pods, like a spider's web that vibrates when any one of its strands is touched ... like the internet when any one of its sites makes contact with millions of other nodes, and reality is changed thereby. The kingdom is horizontal not hierarchical, and it is here, and it is now. (2012, p. 68)

None of these positive legacies for the contemporary quest for innovative, adaptive ministry require us to take a utopian view of early Pentecostalism. Mitchell accepts that the radicalism of the early twentieth century Pentecostal movements did not last for very long, as 'the deep-seated mindsets of the church–empire partnership proved extraordinarily resistant to change' (2013, p. 71; see also Mitchell, 2011, pp. 152–9). He regrets that counter-political Christian initiatives like Pentecostalism 'carried a propensity for accommodation to other people and cultures' (p. 74), owing to human sinfulness. However, sociologically speaking, accommodation to the times will always be one of the strategies on offer to enable churches and new movements to survive into the next generation. The social reality is a complex swinging of the pendulum between accommodation and fresh impulses of the latent subversiveness of the initial deposit of faith. The repeated revivification of the Pentecostal impulse sustains the hope that imperial Christianity will not triumph in the end.

Over the last 20 years or more, a further 'wave' of charismatic/Pentecostal influence has energized the emergence of a species of more radical, new, independent churches, some of which are carrying the unpredictability of the Spirit into areas that move them beyond their evangelical origins. Only recently beginning to be taken notice of by the mainstream churches, these self-consciously postmodern expressions of ecclesiality require a chapter to themselves. But first, we turn to a contemporary expression of ministry that is paradoxically very old, yet seemingly well adapted to flourish in the postmodern environment: chaplaincy.

7

Chaplaincy: A Very Ancient and Postmodern Ministry

Visible to the world, hidden by the Church: the public ministry of chaplaincy

In the course of my work teaching theology and ministry, I was asked to develop some academic programmes in chaplaincy. I built up a sizeable list of chaplaincy email contacts, sought advice from chaplains about what they felt they needed, and met with a small group to discuss ideas. Possibilities were also explored for collaboration with the well-established Centre for Chaplaincy Studies at the University of Cardiff. Over the following few years, three conferences were held, bringing together over 100 chaplains from across the sectors from healthcare and prisons to retail and leisure, and programmes in chaplaincy were validated at undergraduate and postgraduate levels. I learned a great deal about chaplaincy and was very impressed by its creative and often overlooked contribution to contemporary ministry.

There was relatively little published literature specifically about chaplaincy in the field of ministerial theology and practice prior to the volume edited by Giles Legood (1999), which contained thematic pieces on theological aspects of chaplaincy and a large number of short practice-related contributions from chaplains across all sectors. This format was repeated successfully 12 years later by Threlfall-Holmes and Newitt (2011). A number of studies of chaplaincy in particular contexts have been produced, for example hospitals (Swift, 2009, second edition 2014), industry (Torry, 2010), schools (Caperon, 2015) and the world of finance (Stewart-Darling, 2017). The year 2015 saw a major advance in chaplaincy publications with a significant research-based work setting out to develop a distinctive theology and missiology of chaplaincy (Slater, 2015), a well-regarded report by the Christian think tank Theos (Ryan, 2015), the title of which, *A Very Modern Ministry*, has been adapted for this chapter; and a substantial *Handbook of Chaplaincy Studies* (Swift, Cobb and Todd (eds), 2015). Throughout this period, a steady stream of research initiatives, reports, postgraduate dissertations and theses on chaplaincy came out of the Cardiff Centre for Chaplaincy Studies based at St Michael's College, Llandaff. More recently, fresh work has been published on the theology of chaplaincy (Caperon, Todd and Walters, 2018; Williams, R.C., 2018).

While this upsurge of interest in chaplaincy took place in an academic context, there was a lack of corresponding energy from the mainstream churches (with the honourable exception of the Methodist Church, which launched a project and website to promote news and resources, and provide basic training for chaplaincy, *Chaplaincy Everywhere*). The Church of England, devoting its new-found missionary zeal to pioneer ministries and fresh expressions, did not seem to regard its hundreds of chaplains as being relevant to these initiatives; a report by the Cardiff Centre had great difficulty even in getting reliable information from dioceses about the numbers of active chaplains within their boundaries (Todd, Slater and Dunlop, 2014). In an essay in Legood (1999), Keith Lamdin made an early plea, which bears repeating more than 20 years later, for the Church at large to pay more attention to what it might learn from its chaplains: because they find themselves in unfamiliar territory, they can illuminate knowledge of areas of life untouched by the parish, offer an experiment in a different way of doing ministry, and allow voices from the margins to be heard (1999, p. 148).

Chaplaincy is a growth area of ministry, and often an innovative one, yet at the same time under-resourced, under-recognized and, at least until recently, under-researched by the churches. It is even the case that sometimes the word 'chaplain' is used rather disparagingly. John Vincent used the term 'chaplaincy Christianity' to denote the 'basically culture-affirming' style of ministry in the institutional Church for which he had little time (1992, p. 65). Anthony Buckley, a school chaplain, tells of one parish priest who was told by her bishop, responding to her hope of going into chaplaincy: 'It is a shame you are thinking of leaving mainstream ministry' (2013, p. 114). Another would-be chaplain was referred to by his bishop as having been 'lured away' (p. 117). Yet another was asked by his archdeacon, 'How are you going to feel about not being in charge?' (p. 116). Buckley observes that someone becoming a chaplain may feel they are giving up 'being the vicar', with its job security, unquestioned authority, and 'knowing about everything that's going on' (pp. 115 ff.). Threlfall-Holmes confirms that 'many chaplains report that once they take a chaplaincy job they are perceived to have marginalized themselves' (2011, p. 138).

In a 'mission-shaped church', chaplaincy tends not to be seen as 'mission'; chaplains are not 'pioneer ministers' engaging in 'fresh expressions of church'. Even other non-parochial clergy can on occasion distinguish themselves from chaplains in a way that does chaplaincy no favours. For example, in his otherwise very helpful book on Self-supporting Ministry, John Lees (2018) at one point describes the chaplain's role as limited to 'pastoral engagement', unlike the more challenging presence of the Minister in Secular Employment who is actually doing the job alongside his or her fellow employees (p. 74). Yet many people who never encounter their local vicar may get to know a chaplain very well, even though the local church where that person lives when they are not in hospital, or at work, or in prison, may know nothing about this relationship. Grace Davie chooses chaplaincy as the subject of a case study; it is a sociologically significant form of ministry of 'presence' in a religiously plural society, in which most people do not practise faith within the context of organized institutional religion, but continue to seek a spiritual ministry at particular points in life (2015, pp. 114–20).

Chaplaincy demonstrates huge adaptivity, pushing at all the boundaries the Church constructs to categorize its ministries: chaplains can be ordained or lay, full or part-time, paid or unpaid, appointed by the Church or employed by the secular institution they serve. In some cases they may be ordained presbyters, yet have no church in which to preside, and so exercise a largely diaconal ministry. Others may be lay people who nevertheless are regarded by many within their institutional setting as though they were ordained ministers because they represent the Church. Many exercise their ministry without regard to parish or other territorial church boundaries, and may spend far more of their time with non-believers than with the practising Christian community. In this chapter we will explore some of the characteristics of chaplaincy that give it potential as a fresh and adaptive ministry for a post-church society.

Chaplaincy in context: background and models

Legood offers chaplaincy as a contemporary model of ministry capable of reconnecting the Church with a secularized society, arguing that it should form part of any wise strategy for ministry and mission. Making the assumption that chaplains are ordained (increasingly not the case since his work was originally published), he writes:

> Such clergy ... work largely with those who do not go to church (and therefore those whom the Church claims it most wants to reach). The experiences and voices of such clergy ... can both inform the Church

about the sectors worked in and inform the sectors about the Church. This is an exciting prospect as there is the possibility of real dialogue and mutual learning. (2000, pp. 127–8)

Ever since the origins of the territorial dioceses and parishes of the Church in England from the eighth century onwards, some clergy have been appointed to posts that were not set within this structure. These included the domestic chaplains employed by the nobility and by royal households to serve their private chapels; the colleges of Oxford and Cambridge and schools such as Eton; military garrisons; monastic communities, including those that set up hospitals; almshouses endowed by charitable foundations, and personal chaplains to bishops. Later, prisons began to employ chaplains whose duties were statutorily established. In all of these long-standing contexts of chaplaincy, the common thread is of ministry to people within 'closed' institutions, in the sense that they are not living day to day as part of the wider community, being prevented from so doing either by infirmity, imprisonment, voluntary seclusion or the requirements of employment.

One key difference about many of the chaplaincies that have arisen more recently is that they no longer meet this criterion, offering instead a ministry to people who regularly gather in, or pass through, particular locations where a need for some form of religious ministry has been recognized, such as airports, shopping malls and leisure centres. Management and church often work together to provide for chaplaincy in such contexts, as a focus of ministry for the people who use such facilities, or work there, that makes more sense than their residential base within the ambit of a parish or local church. In many cases, sometimes even in more traditional chaplaincies, it is no longer the Church, but the secular institution, that takes the decision to employ chaplains and to determine their job descriptions and terms and conditions of service, including their remuneration. The situation where the initiative to recruit a chaplain comes from the employing institution rather than the Church is a significant development for chaplaincy as mission.

Surveying the wide range of contemporary chaplaincies, Miranda Threlfall-Holmes has developed two sets of models of chaplaincy ministry, theological and secular. She employs this dual approach on the basis that to do justice to chaplaincy it is necessary to elicit from both the churches and the institutions employing chaplains what they respectively see as the roles, functions and significance of chaplaincy. The two sets of models can then be used to promote some fruitful dialogue, noticing the points of congruence and of divergence between them. In giving an overview of the models I will single out points of particular relevance to the quest for fresh, culturally adaptive expressions of ministry that is our principal concern here.

The theological model most readily understood and affirmed by secular employers is the pastoral: 'the role of the chaplain is primarily to care for people' (p. 120). It clearly aligns with pastoral care in the list of secular models, derived from what the employing institutions expect of chaplains. The pastoral model may be expressed in various ways, from the very informal 'listening ear' or companion, to the more professionalized therapist or counsellor, reflecting the debate in the wider Church about 'general practice' versus 'specialist' models of ministry. The model of pastoral care can often be 'de-theologized' by the secular institution into merely contributing to 'general well-being', or a role of 'damage limitation' when problems occur, or even being the 'professional nice guy' (2011, p. 123).

This secularization of pastoral care is mitigated by the accompanying secular model of spiritual care, which represents a more specific recognition on the part of the institution that 'chaplains are appointed to meet spiritual and religious needs as part of the duty of care offered by the employing organization' (p. 123). This is sometimes interpreted narrowly, with chaplains being expected to take responsibility largely where issues arise about organized religion, such as provision of space for prayer, dietary needs, or rituals around death and dying. The specialist focus on death is not necessarily a limiting factor for chaplaincy in healthcare contexts, since death is universal, yet all too infrequently spoken about candidly and in depth. The 'Death Cafe' initiative pioneered by some NHS Trust chaplaincies is a remarkable example of a ministry that opens up multiple horizons for spiritual and theological reflection ('No longer undone by death', *Church Times*, 5 May 2017).

Another theological model with a secular counterpart is the *incarnational/sacramental*, in which chaplains 'see their primary role as embodying something of God in the places where they minister' (p. 120). Here, rather as in the understanding of priesthood explored in *Praying for England* (Wells and Coakley (eds), 2008), the chaplain's ministry will often be said to be about 'presence', or '*being* more than *doing*'. One university college chaplain I knew described his work as 'hanging around creatively'. There is some resonance here with the secular *tradition/heritage* model, particularly in the case of long-established chaplaincies, such as those in the military or certain universities and public schools, where the chaplain performs a civic representational role that serves to sacralize the identity of the institution and maintain continuity of tradition (pp. 124–5). This links back to the *historical/parish* model, where chaplaincy aims to replicate local church ministry for people who are removed from the wider social context. The latter two models are a much better fit with traditional chaplaincies where congregational worship plays an important role, than with some newer forms of chaplaincy, such as in airports and retail, where this scarcely features at all.

The remaining models do not display such obvious correspondences across the two lists, theological and secular. The *missionary* model is the one that can most readily generate tensions with the secular environment: chaplains 'have been called or sent to a particular place, largely unchurched. Their task is to bring the gospel to the people there in whatever ways may suit the context' (Threlfall-Holmes, 2011, pp. 118–19). Some employers may be suspicious of chaplains who articulate their role in this way (typically, when 'mission' is interpreted as 'evangelism'). Chaplains exercise this mission in ways that vary enormously; a more developed discussion of chaplaincy and mission follows later in the chapter. The remaining model in the theological group is the *prophetic*, which might also be viewed as a variety of mission, of particular relevance to the post-church context: 'a whole cluster of models and metaphors for chaplaincy that have in common the theme of challenging the status quo and speaking prophetically into unjust or ungodly structures' (p. 122).

The prophetic model emphasizes the uncomfortable and marginalized dimensions of chaplaincy ministry, especially where chaplains feel they are occupying this position in relation both to the Church and the employing institution. Variations on themes of marginality and 'outsider' status are frequent in the chaplaincy literature as well as in the personal testimonies of chaplains. For example, Christopher Moody writes of the chaplain occupying 'other people's territory rather than your own', being a 'participant observer', in an environment 'without the usual flags and signposts' of parochial ministry; 'loitering on the edge of other people's lives' in the 'uncharted territory between clearly identified religious roles and language ... and the purely pragmatic concern of the institution' (1999, pp. 16–18). The sub-sections of his chapter vividly capture this portrayal of the chaplain's work: *wilderness ministry*, *in-between*, *shaman*, *watcher*, *resident alien*; and he warns chaplains against settling for something safer, a clearly defined 'job', such as student counsellor, or religious advisor.

In similar vein, Gerald Arbuckle describes chaplains as 'liminars', boundary figures who straddle the threshold between the two worlds to which they are answerable (1999, p. 158). They are outside the parochial structures, operating in secularized environments, concerned for people on the margins; they challenge organizational cultures, and engage ecumenically and often on an interfaith basis. Stephen Pattison sees these multiple marginalities as a strength for chaplaincy: it 'helps promote and preserve the common sacred, but it also keeps it in its place, on the edge of the main activities of the institution. If chaplains became less marginal, their work might be much more controversial, disputed and scrutinized' (2015, p. 24). Drawing on Mason (1992), Lamdin remarks that sector ministry (which includes chaplaincy) 'holds the energy of anti-structure in the church while the parochial and diocesan hold structure' (1999, p. 149). It is this tension between structure and anti-structure in the Church that is the matrix of the new and fruitful.

The remaining two models seem to shift chaplaincy in an unambiguously more secular direction. The *diversity* model sees the appointment of a chaplain largely in terms of ensuring that the requirements of the Equalities Act are being met. Chaplains will have a specific responsibility in relation to the protected characteristics of religion and belief, though pastorally they may also find themselves drawn into issues concerning others such as race, gender, disability and sexuality. Last, the chaplain as *specialist service provider* 'is there to provide certain professional services, whether as a pastoral carer, a spiritual carer, an expert in faith or faiths or as an expert practitioner and guardian of a cultural tradition' (Threlfall-Holmes, 2011, p. 125). Nevertheless, Threlfall-Holmes comments shrewdly that this last secular model might have its theological counterpart after all, as it comes rather close to the view of the churches most frequently taken by the non-churchgoing public, which 'may well clash with the theological models of ministry in which clergy are trained' (p. 126).

Chaplaincy: an alternative template for ministry

How then might the ministries exercised today by chaplains offer a template for an innovative ordering of ministry to meet changing social and cultural circumstances? In order to explore this, I will begin by offering three examples of writers on ministry who have deliberately used chaplaincy as a metaphor for the type of ministry they see as particularly apt for present needs.

The first comes from Timothy Jenkins, writing in a collection ambitiously entitled *Anglicanism: The Answer to Modernity* (Dormor et al. (eds), 2003; see also Jenkins, 2006, chapters 1, 2 and 14). Jenkins identifies two key characteristics of Anglican ministry as 'territorial embeddedness' and 'a conversational mode', and names chaplaincy as the model of ministry that captures this approach (2003, pp. 199–200). It seems to me that what chaplaincy can do is to demonstrate an equivalent to this idea of 'embeddedness' in *institutional* rather than territorial (i.e.

parochial) contexts. Chaplains usually have to negotiate their terms of engagement with the institution without the benefit of being 'in charge', so that the skills Jenkins identifies are crucial for their success in becoming 'embedded'. They have to 'engage conversationally, rather than authoritatively'; this involves 'being out and about, taking an interest, and "being used to think with"' (p. 200). This constitutes a considerable challenge for chaplaincies based on 'brief encounters' within transitional spaces like airports.

In the second example, Wesley Carr draws on chaplaincy to support a strong emphasis on the public representative nature of ordained ministry (1992, pp. 20 ff.). He sees parish clergy as engaging in a 'chaplaincy' mode of ministry when they seek access to local secular institutions, and suggests four reasons why this is often welcomed. First, the institution values 'the presence of someone who is in the system but not part of it' (p. 22), because they can listen and express concern without any vested interests in career prospects or power structures. Second, the chaplaincy role provides an 'honest broker' in situations where delicate issues involving conflict or requiring confidentiality arise, an empathetic but detached standpoint that Carr considers is precisely what ministry brings. Third, a chaplaincy presence can assist the institution in building its community links, improving its profile and guarding against isolationism. Fourth, chaplaincy enables ultimate concerns to be voiced that might otherwise go unspoken: as the Church represents 'values that transcend the immediate aims of the welcoming institution ... the presence of clergy allows people to acknowledge their ultimate dependence' (p. 23). Not all chaplains will be comfortable with Carr's interpretation of ministry, which relies to a significant extent on the model of 'set apartness' criticized earlier.

The third example of the use of 'chaplaincy' as a metaphor for apt ministry today is found in the work of Alan Billings, who does not make so much of the 'on the boundary' quality of the minister. He turns to chaplaincy after analysing the four 'historical models' of ministry as 'parson' (Anglican), 'minister' (Reformed), 'priest' (Catholic) and the 'utility' model (liberal), based on a professional specialism of some kind, such as 'counsellor' (2010, pp. 147–50). As the historical models have come under severe pressure in a secular environment, Billings sees chaplaincy as an appropriate model for the future. He argues that today ministry must continue to be 'offered to those who are not part of the Sunday congregation' (p. 148), because there continue to be occasions and contexts in which it is still the case that, so to speak, 'only chaplaincy will do'.

The aspect of ministry that Billings regards as appropriately expressed through the metaphor of chaplaincy arises when ministers must 'take into account the actual needs that the pastoral offices and occasional services are meeting' (p. 149), which may well be different from the Church's official teachings about them. For example, the Marriage Service is unlikely to be a perfect fit for couples who have lived together for many years, already have children, have been married before or indeed have little or no religious belief. Chaplains are accustomed to operating in the gap between the official language and practices of the Church and the inchoate hopes and fears of those who seek their ministry. This requires immersion in the situation, attentiveness, listening, observing, and 'faith seeking understanding' of what is going on in the context. Billings warns that 'unspoken terms and conditions' attach to the chaplaincy style of ministry: it can be 'justified in religious terms, as long as they do not discriminate against those who do not share their religion and do not seek to convert' (p. 150). He cites Timothy Jenkins to the effect that 'if religious professionals are too quick in "bringing God into a situation" then that will dictate the way a conversation goes – and important matters will be pushed to one side' (p. 159).

These examples indicate how chaplaincy can make a significant contribution to the process of reimagining ministry. In the rest of this chapter, this perspective will be developed in relation to four areas in which chaplaincy offers an alternative template for an adaptive ministry in a post-church society: theology, missiology, ecclesiology and culture.

Chaplaincy and theology

Over the course of the present century there has been a slow but steady advance in research-based exploration of the models and methods of theology that fit with the practice of chaplaincy and can be enriched and enhanced by reflection drawn from chaplaincy experience. Andrew Todd has pioneered this thinking, seen for example in his essays 'A Theology of the World' and 'An Invitation to Theology' (2018). The first distinctive contribution of chaplaincy is towards a theology that engages seriously with 'lived religion'. According to Meredith McGuire (2008), the religious conflicts of the fifteenth to the seventeenth centuries led to the separate churches each defining belief and practice more tightly in accordance with their denominational identities. This tended to obliterate the 'lived religion' of ordinary faith practitioners, who often retained earlier beliefs and practices. In a post-church age, it is important for theology to retrieve lived religion as a source of fresh theological reflection, as the gulf between 'folk' religion and 'official' faith widens. Todd argues that chaplains have a particular access to it:

Chaplains encounter those wrestling with what is sacred in their lives, and how to mark that in ritual ways, in acute settings such as healthcare, prisons and military operations ... Chaplains also embody, encounter and enable expressions of institutional religion ... but in settings outside religious domains. (2018, p. 162)

A second feature of this theology that emerges from practical reflection on chaplaincy is its crossing of boundaries because of the diversity of the contexts in which it must operate, including the multi-faith environment that characterizes much contemporary chaplaincy. Todd argues that 'chaplaincy occasions ... theology that ... crosses boundaries, and ... arises out of the dialogue, negotiation and even contestation between domains' (p. 159). Chaplaincy therefore proposes a 'relocation' of the enterprise of Christian theology, involving 'an understanding of religion, belief and spirituality that is not constrained by focusing solely on the institutional and on decline', and 'the stretching of theological perspectives beyond organisational boundaries' (p. 167).

Todd expects that this 'relocation' of theology by reflection on the practice of chaplaincy will be especially apparent in the fields of ecclesiology and missiology. His view is shared by Victoria Slater, who sees chaplaincy as essentially 'dialogical' (2015, pp. 5 ff.). This implies doing theology in a particular mode that is not always 'valued, validated or understood' by the Church at large (p. 6). She calls this a 'dislocation between the theology and concerns of the Church and those of chaplains who work within the social structures of society' (p. 7). It suggests that chaplaincy has been 'lost within the debate' between the enthusiasts for fresh expressions and the advocates of the continuing value of parish ministry (p. xvi), since both of these, while different in their expressions of ministry, remain more or less wedded to church-centred ways of doing theology. Slater therefore devotes a significant portion of her study to constructing an ecclesiology and missiology for chaplaincy.

Chaplaincy and missiology

Slater's missiology of chaplaincy draws on *missio Dei* theology (Bosch, 1992) and the concept of 'embeddedness', which we encountered earlier in Timothy Jenkins's work, to 'discern where God's Spirit may be at work in the world' (Slater, 2015, pp. 70 ff.). Among the signs of such work identified by Slater are what Stephen Spencer (2007, chapter 10) has called 'finding hope in local communities', witnessed in the presence of *shalom* and right relationships (Heywood, 2011, pp. 77–82), in which the Church sees itself as contributing alongside others to social flourishing, rather than achieving 'success' in itself (Morisy, 2009, p. 110). Slater cites places where her empirical interview data resonate with aspects of these missiologies, and goes on to develop from these 'three dimensions' that distinguish the mission of chaplaincy.

First, as an expression of *missio Dei*, chaplaincy 'needs to be substantially located in the structures of society', as it is primarily concerned with the world rather than the Church:

> [The] primary ministry of the chaplain is not to build up the existing empirical Church ... but to embody and express God's love and grace with and for those who gather in a particular institution, place or network, to express the values of the Kingdom of God and to witness as appropriate to the Christian Gospel. (2015, p. 89)

In this role, chaplains represent 'the dispersed Church, intentionally fulfilling its vocation as the community of people called and sent to serve and witness to the world' (pp. 89–90). Slater's other two 'dimensions' address the ministerial identity of the chaplain as 'a distinctive, representative and recognized presence' and, flowing from this, a 'professional integrity' marked by skill in working alongside those with different perspectives. She summarizes:

> The research evidence ... suggests that the theological integrity of chaplaincy can be found in its missional, incarnational and dominical character which focusses on the service of the *missio Dei*, the building up of the Kingdom of God and contributing to human and social flourishing. Chaplains go to where people are, rather than waiting for people to come to the Church, providing 'a very clear presence beyond the Church's walls'... a ministry in the public square. This means that chaplains are in a position to be practical theologians in public life, working out theology amidst the daily practicalities of life. (p. 91)

A similarly broad view of mission is offered by Fiona Stewart-Darling from her highly secular context of the financial sector at Canary Wharf: 'helping Christians to live their daily lives as integrated people, whose faith has an impact on their behaviour and relationships within their workplace' (2017, p. 99). In this understanding of mission, Stewart-Darling is ready to 'reflect on things from a Christian perspective', but only when invited to do so, rather as Billings warns against 'bringing God in too soon'. She identifies hospitality as the appropriate basis for mission through chaplaincy conceived in this way, because hospitality facilitates conversation (pp. 99–102). Alongside hospitality as 'a presence of welcoming in', there is scope for 'embassy' as 'a movement of going out' (pp. 105–6), as a model of mission typified by inter-faith dialogue: 'these twin poles ... are indivisible and mutually complementary, and our mission should practise both' (p. 107).

As an expression of *missio Dei*, then, a chaplaincy missiology is world-focused and embedded in the secular context, oriented to human flourishing as a sign of God's Kingdom, conversational and dialogical in method and generous in both its going out to meet the other and its welcoming in. Threlfall-Holmes has acknowledged that some find this an all too nuanced and indirect approach to meet the contemporary imperatives of mission, and remain suspicious of chaplaincy for the way that it can seem almost pathologically disinclined to evangelize. Bob Jackson, for example, proposed that the Church might well cut funding for chaplaincy as not meeting the priorities of the 'core business' of mission in the parishes (Jackson, B., *The Road to Growth*, cit. Threlfall-Holmes and Newitt, 2011, p. xv). Jackson's scepticism confirms that in the 'mission-shaped' ecclesiological climate, chaplains often present as a valuable and necessary irritant, with their insistence upon asking hard questions about what mission actually needs to mean if the wider cultural context is really to be taken seriously by the Church.

Chaplaincy and ecclesiology

Underlying the distinctive approaches of chaplaincy to theology and mission is an intractable issue about the relationship between the chaplain and the Church, and whether or not the 'parish priest' model is still appropriate for this ministry. This arises from the original understanding of chaplaincy as extending parish ministry into 'extra-parochial' contexts or 'closed communities' such as prisons, the military, hospitals and residential schools. As many of the more recently emerging chaplaincies do not fit this model, the question of its suitability has begun to reflect back upon some of the more established chaplaincy types as well, so that perhaps, rather belatedly, chaplaincy is now also posing ecclesiological questions to itself.

An example of this is John Caperon's contribution to a recent collection seeking to build up a distinctive theology for chaplaincy (Caperon, 2018). An Anglican priest with a long career in education who commissioned a report into school chaplaincy (see Caperon, 2015), Caperon senses an urgent need to address chaplaincy's challenge to inherited ecclesiology. He declines to go along with romantic ideals of 'priesthood', pointing out instead how the historical and sociological dimensions of the 'parson' have never been far away from issues of rule, governance and authority (pp. 121–2). Nor is he convinced by the nostalgic model of the communal ideal of the parish church ('a Christian presence in every community', as the strapline on the Church of England website has it), which he thinks often turns out to be something far more associational, that is, more a gathering of the likeminded than genuinely diverse and inclusive (p. 123). He notes that much of the in-house debate about the future of ministry has failed to take seriously the sociological dimensions, 'that varying models of church and ministry might reflect different social contexts' (p. 126). For these reasons, he thinks the focus on parish ministry as normative has not been much help to chaplaincy, which flourishes precisely because the 'parochial' ecclesiology is no longer adequate.

Caperon comments critically on the 'Reform and Renewal' (as it initially was) process, from Rowan Williams's three principles set out in 2010, to the House of Bishops' *Challenges for the New Quinquennium* (2011) and on to 'Renewal and Reform', as it now is (Caperon, 2018, pp. 127–8). He shows how the originally nuanced principles have steadily been reduced and simplified to an emphasis on achieving numerical church growth, which Martyn Percy alleges 'may now be the national church's main motivational impulse' (p. 128). His alternative vision agrees with Ballard (2009) to the effect that chaplaincy's distinctiveness and cutting edge depends on precisely *not* conceiving church as the gathered congregation, and mission as drawing people into it (p. 134; in stark contrast to the priorities of Bob Jackson referred to above). He commends Ann Morisy's view that chaplains operate 'a ministry of awakening, helping people become aware of the spiritual dimension and of the possibility of God ... using imagination and sensitivity to work alongside and with others' (p. 135). In this way, 'church' can be something that starts in an emergent network of relationships, encounters and insights, outside the bounds of 'church' as conventionally understood.

The idea of reconceptualizing 'church' by beginning from a question about what 'ecclesiality' might look like if all assumptions about 'the Church' – that is, church as we know it – could be put aside, merits closer attention in the light of the theme of 'adaptive ministry'. Slater suggests that chaplaincy ministry may aid the development of 'an ecclesiology that is dispersed, collaborative, ecumenical and actively involved with the whole of life' (2015, p. 91). She goes on to quote the allegation of one parish priest that chaplains too readily become 'comfortable being out in the world', and thus 'resistant to what the Church is for', living 'entirely on the margins' (p. 106). On the contrary, she responds by suggesting that 'a dispersed ecclesiology' could be hospitable to the idea that chaplaincy is not after all 'marginal', but central to the Church, when more ambitiously conceived (p. 107). In other words, it is not chaplaincy that needs to adjust and become more church-y, but the Church that needs to expand its horizons to embrace what it can learn from chaplaincy.

The priest quoted by Slater reflected an ecclesiology centred in the local church as a gathered congregation, which was effectively required to validate chaplaincy: in his team, which included some clergy with chaplaincy roles, 'we've given the incipient authority to the [chaplaincy] role by making them priests of incumbent status' (p. 107). Slater argues that this 'relational dynamic' between chaplaincy and church-based ministry only serves to perpetuate tensions between them. Others, however, want to preserve a more organic relationship between the chaplain and the local church. Rowan Clare Williams formulates the issue this way:

> Chaplains speak out for the place of faith in the public square, challenging its invisibility by their very presence ... In order to be nourished for their missionary task, they have to be fed and resourced by their own faith, *which means belonging to a supportive faith community* [emphasis mine]. They therefore have something distinctive to say about what a healthy ecclesiology might look like. (2018, p. 23)

Williams's insistence on 'belonging to a supportive faith community' raises the question of what a 'dispersed ecclesiology' might look like, and whether there can be any answers to it that move away from some minimal, foundational level of 'congregating'.

We cannot definitively answer this question at the present time. Slater's case studies suggest that most clergy were continuing to regard the parish setting as primary, and believed that chaplains needed to retain a commitment to this as one part of their ministry. However, if chaplains are to be fully embedded in the non-church contexts they serve, but are not to 'create an alternative church' in those contexts, how can they avoid becoming almost 'de-churched'? They seem to end up doubly marginalized, neither fully embedded in a traditional church setting, nor able to create one in their secular setting. However, if marginality has a positive value, it follows that rather than trying to develop an ecclesiology that would erase this aspect of chaplaincy, those engaging in mission and ministry outwith the borders of 'traditional church' are likely to be better off if they are authorized to establish a new kind of 'marginal church' in the context where they are operating. This drives us back to the issues about what 'church' and Christian faith *mean* in the contemporary cultural setting.

Chaplaincy and culture

Threlfall-Holmes believes that chaplaincy is often in the vanguard of issues about how the churches can communicate the Christian message in today's cultural environment:

> Chaplaincy may well be the canary in the mine for the churches' relationship to society. Chaplains seem often to be facing the rapidly arising and changing issues in contemporary society more sharply and more quickly than the rest of the Church ... Chaplains often have to formulate answers to questions the institutional churches have not yet begun to ask ... Models of ministry that arise from the chaplaincy experience may well be precisely those to which other clergy will need to adapt in years to come. (2011, p. xvii)

There can often be the risk of a 'siege mentality' within the churches, with Christians hunkering down with a fantasy of themselves as a persecuted minority. By contrast, the experience of chaplaincy, while very acutely aware of the tensions often generated by ministering in a secular environment, also tells a more positive story about the prospects for careful witness to the practical wisdom of faith within that same context. This is why Ann Morisy locates chaplaincy in what she calls the 'foundational domain' of Christian ministry: work in this domain aims 'to enable people to embrace *the possibility of God*', not yet to commit to faith (2004, p. 154). In this work it is *attitudes* to church that are being addressed, rather than lack of *knowledge*. This is where chaplains spend much of their time:

> Chaplains ... have to develop the skill of code switching ... listening to the sentiment being expressed however inadequately or unorthodoxly, and then being willing to *meet* that sentiment respectfully and to resist the urge to shape or force that sentiment to fit with Christian orthodoxy ... The chaplain works at the level of the imagination. (pp. 152–3)

Morisy develops the example of churches that run community projects (adult education, drop-ins, counselling, food banks and so on) from the church premises through the week, while a congregation continue to meet there for Sunday worship. In a cultural climate where many people are almost entirely unacquainted with the conventional practices of organized religion, she observes that these can appear to unchurched users as if the church has closed down and the premises have become a community centre instead. If the church wants to maintain a fruitful link between its community work and its worship, serious 'foundational domain' work needs to be done, something she thinks is unlikely if the only description on offer of what the church is doing beyond the community centre is 'Sunday services'. Accordingly, she recommends the appointment of lay volunteer 'community chaplains' as liaison persons between the project and the church (pp. 187 ff.): they need to be skilled in 'naming' the ways that God is at work in the project, but to do this in ways that are appropriate to the foundational domain.

Morisy provides a list of chaplaincy skills, including creating warm and trusting relations, speaking from a faith that is both secure and questioning, recognizing vulnerability, and providing opportunity for corporate reflection on current issues from a faith perspective (p. 196). This is where her concept of 'apt liturgy' comes in (pp. 156 ff.), where chaplains are skilled in designing simple and accessible acts of worship that connect with the everyday experiences and concerns of non-church people, in language and imagery that do not rely heavily on features drawn from conventional religious observance. She insists that the 'lack of orthodoxy' of people's religious ideas and experiences must be 'accepted rather than dismissed or shaped by the formularies of the institutionalized church' (p. 171).

Stephen Pattison also commends a chaplaincy ministry that reaches out to all those who are uncomfortable with the dogmatic requirements of conventional religion, in a context where the traditional churches appear to have turned aside from 'notions of broad inclusion in the whole population and low-key pastoral presence and care in favour of a stance based on clear commitment, active membership and mission' (2015, p. 13). For this ministry, 'being perceived as marginal' may well be a strength, both for the unchurched people among whom the chaplains minister, liable to be put off by a person who seemed very much a representative of institutional religion, and for their secular institutions, which might equally be cagey about too much apparent endorsement of religious orthodoxy. Hence Pattison concludes:

> Part of the continuing acceptability of chaplaincy may depend on its perceived powerlessness and dispensability ... Furthermore, this expression of religion comes to the customer rather than requiring the customer to go to church and be forced to shape their needs and spirituality to that of a religious organization. (2015, p. 24)

Pattison maintains that it is precisely under cover of what he calls 'vague "uselessness" and a certain perpetual liminality' that chaplains can continue to get on with offering something different from the prevailing instrumental values within their institutional context.

In a comparable way to Pattison, Billings outlines aspects of social and cultural change that have proved hospitable to the rise of chaplaincy (2015, pp. 32 ff.). He notes that 'chaplains learned to reflect in their practice a non-judgmental approach', which he contrasts with the perceptions people tend to hold of the attitudes of clergy in general (p. 33). Although Billings is less favourably disposed than Pattison to what he refers to as 'formless religiosity flowing through numerous non-traditional channels' (p. 34), he nevertheless notes that 'chaplains learned not to dismiss these new expressions of spirituality'. In both cases, chaplaincy is seen as a response to cultural change in tension with some aspects of the response preferred by an increasingly evangelically influenced Church. Chaplaincy has learned to function within public institutions amid 'a complex kaleidoscope of traditional religion, new spiritualities, many faiths, non-believers and aggressive secularists' (p. 34) in a way that should be invaluable to the Church at large in search of viable models of ministry and mission for the future:

> Ministering to people who could come from any of these backgrounds might seem like mission impossible, but over the years chaplaincy has evolved to do exactly that ... in this way, chaplaincy has become a distinctive form of ministry, though the implications of this were not always understood by those whose ministries centred on the churches. (Billings, 2015, p. 35)

Conclusion

At the end of his account of the history of workplace chaplaincy, Malcolm Torry concludes that 'in a society ... in which religion is increasingly privatised and commodified, industrial mission [as workplace chaplaincy was formerly known] has stood for religion as fellowship, as reconciliation ... and as finding God active in the world and in its institutions' (2010, p. 180). Torry considers this a worthwhile kind of 'secularization' of religion itself, since, as Legood warns, 'there is a danger of the Church becoming unhealthily self-regarding and self-serving unless it is confronted by more than the experiences of its worshipping congregations' (2000, p. 140). Threlfall-Holmes concludes that 'chaplaincy should be viewed as a normative and valuable part of the mission of the Church ... in which different modes of ministry are used strategically to reach different sections of the population that we exist to serve' (2011, p. 139). What then in summary does chaplaincy bring to the table?

Theologically, it can make a valuable contribution to stimulating contextual and dialogical reflection that can access and validate the 'lived religion' of non-church people for the enrichment of Church and society alike. Missiologically, its 'conversational style' offers non-church-based opportunities to create openings for reflection on the profound questions of life and faith 'without strings attached', especially with those who style themselves 'not religious'. Ecclesiologically, its non-territorial form of 'embeddedness' makes it flexibly responsive to how people relate in configurations other than territorial communities, and contributes valuable resources for envisaging how 'church' can come into being beyond the boundaries of the historical institution. Culturally, its go-between character on the threshold of both Church and society enables it to minister within secular environments in terms accessible and understandable to them, and to reflect secular culture back to the Church. Grace Davie commends a list devised by Mathew Guest, which captures well the benefits brought by chaplaincies: 'places of spiritual exploration; centres of ecumenical endeavour; ... safe havens for many faiths and none; leading exponents of multi-faith awareness; and servants of the whole community' (Davie, 2015, p. 120).

Chaplaincy has emerged in recent decades as an 'adaptive ministry' par excellence. It refuses to conform. It never quite fits into the formal theological categories. It frequently operates 'under the radar' and consequently gets away with things that play fast and loose with the ecclesiological rules. But in the perception of the Church at large, chaplaincy has not been the principal focus, or usually even one of the recognized examples, of innovative ministry strategies: in the mainstream denominational churches at least, this honour rightly or wrongly belongs to Fresh Expressions, to which we now turn.

8

Fresh Expressions: Hope for the Mainstream Denominations?

This chapter picks up the threads of the narratives of decline and the challenges of social and cultural change that were examined in Chapter 1. To prepare for this, it was necessary to journey into Church history to make a case for regarding ministerial orders and structures as always adaptive to changing circumstances (Chapter 2). This was developed in relation to the inherited model of a 'threefold ministry' of bishops, priests and deacons (Chapter 3), and the theological and practical meaning of 'ordination' itself (Chapter 4). Chapters 5 to 7 examined three areas of development in ministry that contribute to the search for an adaptive response to the contemporary context: initiatives in lay, shared and collaborative ministry, the influence of Pentecostalism through the charismatic movement, and the growth of chaplaincy as an innovative model for a world-facing ministry. A fourth development, however, has attracted the greatest attention and financial investment, from the mainstream churches over the last 15 years. The churches (especially the Church of England and the Methodist Church) have placed their hopes in 'Fresh Expressions'. The form with upper case is used to denote the official national Church initiative that now has its own organizational structure. When referring more generally to examples of this type of ecclesial innovation, 'fresh expressions', lower case, is used, although it is not always easy to maintain the distinction.

The Fresh Expressions initiative set up in the wake of the influential *Mission-shaped Church* report (Archbishops' Council of the Church of England, 2004) offers this definition:

A fresh expression is a form of church for our changing culture established primarily for the benefit of people who are not yet members of any church.
* It will come into being through principles of listening, service, incarnational mission and making disciples.

- It will have the potential to become a mature expression of church shaped by the gospel and the enduring marks of the church and for its cultural context. (Croft, 2008b, p. 10)

This is a carefully articulated and instructive statement that raises several important issues for ecclesiology and the relationship between church and context. First, 'a form of church for our changing culture': to what extent is a fresh expression of church at liberty to *endorse* aspects of contemporary culture, such as mistrust of institutions and dogmas? For example, can it encourage people to construct their own personal spirituality, religious beliefs and values? Second, 'principles of listening, service, incarnational mission and making disciples': to what extent does 'listening' imply that the listeners themselves may be changed, including theologically, by what they hear? To what extent is 'incarnational mission' a two-way process, that is, while a new form of church is incarnated in the cultural context, does the culture equally come to 'fresh expression' in the new ecclesial reality? Third, 'with the potential to become a mature expression of church': is the objective that 'unchurched' people in due course will become fully 'churched' via their participation in the fresh expression alone? If so, must the 'mature expression' entail the embrace of the full panoply of beliefs, practices and cultural and institutional heritage of the historical churches?

The range of new ecclesial expressions that have been pioneered is certainly impressive: churches meeting in schools, pubs, leisure centres and gyms; on every different day of the week at all hours of the day; fashioning their gatherings in cafe style, or with a nightclub or dance culture ethos, or shaped around an activity such as a skater park, football team, bikers' meeting, or outdoor family events like a hike, a barbecue or a nature trail. To proceed with the exploration in this chapter, I will provide a broader setting by locating the Fresh Expressions movement alongside other models and strategies for the renewal of the local church in response to contemporary social and cultural change.

Evaluating strategies for renewing the local church

Some years ago, I proposed six types of potential future shapes of the Church, drawn from a survey of literature on strategies for the renewal of church and ministry, arranged according to the degree of their engagement with the 'popular postmodernity diagnosis' (Williams, 2011). I defined this as the view that a postmodern society is characterized by decentralization, fluid networks, shifting allegiances and pick-and-mix lifestyles, and rejects the constraints of dominant meta-narratives and institutions (see, for example, Riddell, 1998, chapter 7; Gibbs and Coffey, 2001, pp. 83 ff.; Ward, 2002, chapter 10; Archbishops' Council, 2004, chapter 1). The article investigated the adequacy of this diagnosis and raised some critical questions for the churches in the way they deploy it in order to develop strategies for renewal. In the table below, the six types should be read clockwise, from 1 to 6, as two groups of three.

1. Retrieving the Tradition (Platten, 2007; Avis, 2005, Billings, 2010 and 2013)	2. Local Ministry (PGreenwood, 2002 and 2009; Bowden and West, 2000; Bowden, 2003)	3. Mission-shaped Church (Archbishops' Council of the Church of England, 2004; Bayes and Sledge, eds, 2006; Croft, ed., 2008)
6. Emerging Church (Gibbs and Bolger, 2006; Rollins, 2006; Moynagh, 2012 and 2017)	5. Post-Christendom (Murray, 2004; Bartley, 2006; MacLaren, 2004)	4. Fresh Expressions (Mobsby, 2007; Goodhew, Roberts and Volland, 2012; Shier-Jones, 2009)

Broadly speaking, the top row, 1 to 3, yield prescriptions for the churches that remain comfortably within modernity (or in the case of Retrieving the Tradition, in some respects even pre-modernity), whereas on the bottom row, types 4 to 6 assume a context of postmodernity while drawing different conclusions for the future shapes of the Church. Each approach is characterized by family resemblances rather than exclusive features, so there is room for overlap between them. Approaches 3 and 4 are closely connected, as both stem from the *Mission-shaped Church* report, but differ in their evaluation of the extent to which popular postmodernity erodes the effectiveness of the traditional parish way of doing things. The difference is reflected in Robin Gamble and Michael Moynagh's respective contributions to a collection of essays on *The Future of the Parish System* (Croft, 2006): one recommends 'doing traditional church really well', but the other argues that 'good practice is not what it used to be'. The types may be summarized as follows:

- *Retrieving the Tradition* resists the analysis of popular postmodernity and retains an optimism that sufficient vestiges remain of a resilient

Christian culture for churches that show imagination and initiative to be able to reactivate a rich latent Christian potential.

- *Local Ministry* seeks renewal of local church life by mobilizing the gifts of the whole church and fostering patterns of collaborative ministry. It endorses a postmodern view only in questioning hierarchies and encouraging greater diversity at local level.
- *Mission-shaped Church* challenges the churches to engage with, and embody, a mission agenda in all their activities rather than focusing on alternative patterns; to do what they have always been doing, but giving their activities a deliberate 'mission' twist.
- *Fresh Expressions* (together with the allied concept of 'pioneer ministries') puts the emphasis upon setting up new patterns of church life alongside and within more traditional expressions.
- *Post-Christendom* advocates a radical 'stripping down' of structures to embrace something akin to a 'primitive' Christian model, with the Church as a small minority group within society embodying an alternative lifestyle and countercultural values.
- *Emerging Church* communities are sceptical of 'inherited' models of church, advocating the need to 'start again' in a new place. They resist being seen as a 'movement', as this suggests something centrally planned and coordinated.

The analysis can be taken further by reading the table vertically rather than horizontally, with the six types treated as three pairs, 1 and 6, 2 and 5, 3 and 4, to produce a complementary set of insights. Reading this way reveals how each pair of types depends on underlying shared assumptions about what makes churches 'attractive', or what the fundamental human needs are to which churches seek to appeal, even when the types are making a different judgement about the 'modern/postmodern' setting. Thus, both types 1 and 6 look to an innate religiosity and appetite for the spiritual. Although in sharply contrasting ways, they both place the focus for developing a strategy for the renewal of church life on 'cultural engagement': how the church will represent that spiritual dimension in a relevant and attractive way; for example, in its worship and forms of 'presence'. Types 2 and 5 prioritize the need for a sense of belonging and communal participation. Again, in different ways, they focus on 'ecclesial enrichment', the quality of church life and what it looks like as a community of disciples of Jesus Christ. Finally, types 3 and 4 tend to value purposeful and productive action: hence predominant attention is given to 'missional endeavour', generating activities most likely to facilitate growth and serve the fundamental purposes of the Church.

	Focus on culture: 'cultural engagement'	Focus on people: 'ecclesial enrichment'	Focus on activities: 'missional endeavour'
Cultural analysis weighted towards *[pre]* modernity	**1. Retrieving the Tradition** (Platten, 2007; Avis, 2005, Billings, 2010 and 2013)	**2. Local Ministry** (Greenwood, 2002 and 2009; Bowden and West, 2000; Bowden, 2003)	**3. Mission-shaped Church** (Archbishops' Council of the Church of England, 2004; Bayes and Sledge, eds, 2006; Croft, ed., 2008)
Cultural analysis weighted towards postmodernity	**6. Emerging Church** (Gibbs and Bolger, 2006; Rollins, 2006; Moynagh, 2012 and 2017)	**5. Post-Christendom** (Murray, 2004; Bartley, 2006; MacLaren, 2004)	**4. Fresh Expressions** (Mobsby, 2007; Goodhew, Roberts and Volland, 2012; Shier-Jones, 2009)

In the context of this typology, 'Fresh Expressions' appears as the most moderate of the strategies that express a commitment to the 'popular postmodernity' diagnosis, with a primarily activity-based approach as 'missional endeavour'. They offer a way in which the inherited denominational churches can experiment in a relatively 'safe' fashion, mandating a degree of 'ecclesiological irregularity' against the secure backdrop of 'traditional church'. This designs into the strategy a number of tensions that are starting to come to notice as fresh expressions projects develop beyond the initial stages and consider their future as authentic 'church' (Mobsby, 2007).

The focus on 'missional endeavour' can mask unresolved questions about how this relates to the inherited Church that still acts as the guarantor and guardian of the fresh expression project: there can be a lack of attention to the domain of 'ecclesial enrichment'. In terms of 'cultural engagement', activities are typically designed to appeal to particular client groups, such as young families, pub-goers, sports enthusiasts, single people or the widowed. The most widespread Fresh Expression of all, 'Messy Church', is not so very different from many long-standing church activities for parents and children. Over time, it will be vital to avoid resting content with superficial answers to the profound cultural challenges to conventional religious faith and practice that the traditional churches are struggling to meet.

To examine the issues further, we will look at two contrasting treatments of the Fresh Expressions initiative, both published with admirable even-handedness by SCM Press: Goodhew, Roberts and Volland (2012), and Davison and Milbank (2010; for a detailed critique of their arguments from a strongly pro-Fresh Expressions standpoint, see Cray, 2010). The problem with both books, despite their diametrically opposed stance towards Fresh Expressions, is that they combine ecclesiological idealism with sociological scepticism.

Fresh Expressions in ecclesiological and sociological perspective

'Fresh!' (not stale)

Goodhew and colleagues follow closely the ecclesiology for a missionary church previously set out by the authors of the *Mission-shaped Church* report (Archbishops' Council of the Church of England, 2004, pp. 84–103). Here, the watchword is that 'God is on the move and the Church is always catching up with him' (p. 86). There is a clear conviction that 'churches are created by God to grow' (p. 93). The language of 'pioneer missional leaders' (pp. 132–5) and 'bishops in mission' (pp. 135–6) is established. Goodhew and colleagues maintain this tone of urgency and activism. The narrative of the Acts of the Apostles is interpreted in terms of a clear, intentional and planned mission strategy on the part of the early Church (2012, pp. 2–19). God as Trinity is presented as the original pioneer of fresh expressions: 'The Father, Son and Holy Spirit bring into being that which is fresh, not stale. Freshness is the hallmark of what they do' (p. 24). The Christian tradition itself is seen as 'a long series of fresh expressions'; and 'God the Holy Trinity shows that the essence of God is creating new forms of Church and longing to see the Church grow' (p. 37).

The upbeat feel of this language, with its air of confidence about God's priorities, leaves little room for the authors to respond to others who may have doubts about it. For example, they acknowledge that Alan Smith (2008) criticizes a theology of mission that focuses on the action of God and the Church much more than on the mystery of God's being (Goodhew et al., 2012, pp. 107–8). Nevertheless, their response (p. 108) continues to stress God's *actions*, and how the churches need to emulate them. Later on, addressing various stereotypes of 'pioneers' ('predominantly young, white, male, middle-class, well-educated, sporty, charismatic … intent on planting large, lively churches peopled by those who are rather like themselves', p. 136), their defence is to insist that 'one thing is for sure: pioneers *act*', perpetuating the sense that overall this is a very *activist* book. Writing about 'mission entrepreneurs' (pp. 143 ff.), they include a 'comment feed' of views, some of which are markedly less positive about the use of this term in relation to Christian ministry (Howson, pp. 146–7; Sutton, pp. 147–8; Warren and Bell, p. 149). These include important reservations about the free-market capitalism connotations of entrepreneurs and some of the personal characteristics often associated with them, but the authors make no response to the objections.

The authors' theological assurance allows them to sidestep the critique of the churches' condition and prospects brought by a *sociological* perspective. Although they acknowledge the need for contemporary Christians to be 'sociologically savvy', they allow this sociological awareness only a very limited role, in ensuring 'realism as to the cost of engaging in the most challenging contexts' (pp. 66–7). This is a throwback to the so-called 'religious sociology' of the 1950s and 1960s, that used sociological analysis largely as a tool for the Church to identify its most and least fruitful likely mission fields (e.g. Boulard, 1960). But, since then, both sociologists and theologians have proposed a deeper, more mutual relationship between ecclesiology and sociology, in that it is impossible to do justice to the reality of 'church' without combining theological and sociological perspectives (Martin, 1996; Percy, 2005; Gill, 2012; Ward, 2017).

Goodhew also demonstrates his reservations about sociology in the introduction to a volume of research essays (Goodhew (ed.), 2012), arguing that in Britain too many theologians and church leaders 'have consciously or unconsciously internalized … the secularization thesis and its eschatology of decline'. This has led to 'the assumption that church growth is impossible', encouraging the mindset in which 'shrinking congregations are considered unproblematic' (pp. 18–19). In this way the prognosis of inevitable decline has become a self-fulfilling prophecy, but it can be reversed once the churches get out of this mindset. Yet secularization theory does *not* exclude the possibility of church growth; it does, however, shed some light on the *types* of church growth that are more likely to occur, and raise pertinent questions about their long-term viability (Beckford, 1989; Warner, 2010; Davie, 2015).

'For the parish' (not against it)

Davison and Milbank share with the authors of *Fresh!* a disinclination to allow sociological analysis to influence their ecclesiology. Initially, it seems their position might be otherwise, as they begin by making the important point that the social expression of a doctrine (in this case, ecclesiology) cannot be changed without also changing the doctrine itself in some way (chapter 1). They recognize that 'fresh expressions of church' cannot just be about churches doing new and different things, or old things in different ways, but will issue a challenge to the doctrine of the Church. However, the way they go on to apply their argument is problematic, owing to their determination to separate theology entirely from sociology. As a result, they present their case against Fresh Expressions as a head-on collision of ecclesiology; but the trouble is that ecclesiologies that refuse to allow themselves to be influenced by sociology are liable to idealism and abstraction.

An intolerance of arguments citing sociological grounds for particular choices made by churches in the sphere of ministry and mission is a feature of the book. For example, the authors criticize the view of Sally Gaze that in small rural churches it is sometimes necessary to settle for a degree of segregation if you want to get a new initiative off the ground, because there are sociological factors that impede the creation of truly mixed worshipping communities (Gaze, 2006, p. 48, cit. Davison and Milbank, 2010, p. 71). Their judgement is that it is 'surely the calling of the Church to rise above such secular futilities'. Likewise, they attack the creation of churches for distinct social and cultural groups on the basis that 'unwillingness or inability to integrate within a wider community is a mark of insecurity or of psychological disturbance' (p. 79), betraying a seeming lack of recognition of just how *alien* most church cultures are to most people. Quoting a passage from the MSC Report which argues that the attempt to bring two cultures together typically results in the dominance of those with educational and economic power, they comment: 'This passage is an extraordinary abdication of any sense that the Church has a supernatural identity and mission. Sociology is allowed to triumph over theology' (p. 80).

This strong objection to what the authors see as the 'triumph' of sociology over theology affects all of their judgements not only about Fresh Expressions, but about contextual-practical approaches to ecclesiology and theology as a whole. They are sceptical about the approach to doing theology as reflection on practice (p. 128), arguing that 'we need the whole of Christian tradition ... to judge the cultural productions of our own day' (p. 130). In their view, theological tradition is a one-way traffic that sets the template for social and contextual expression. There are many examples of this, such as the assertion that in worship 'the gathered people of God share through Christ and the Spirit in the divine liturgy of heaven' (p. 133). But do we have any empirical means of examining what it might mean for this to be happening, and whether it is happening in any particular church service? What sociological and cultural criteria might come into play in assessing this? What happens if 'real churches' sometimes don't seem to be like this? Without a methodology of practical theological reflection, such a statement about what is happening in worship risks looking like theological abstraction.

Davison and Milbank's rejection of sociological perspectives and reliance on a decontextualized theological basis for their ecclesiology has the effect of concealing the truth that their view is really that fresh expressions are un-Anglican, rather than ecclesiologically unsound in any absolute sense. For example, for them the problem of a 'mixed economy' Church of both traditional and fresh expressions side by side is that it gives 'permission to ignore church structures and depart from the liturgical norms required by the canons' (p. 74). In a footnote, they comment that it is 'difficult to see what is distinctively Anglican' about Steven Croft's published work on ministry, as all of it 'could apply to the Methodist Church' (p. 74). They allege that those who are the driving force behind Fresh Expressions may not be 'entirely comfortable with what it means to be an Anglican' (p. 95), and for them 'the Church of England may as well be another radical Protestant movement'. Yet Anglicanism can be socially construed as a Church defined by internal difference and dialogue; thus 'being not entirely comfortable' may be a very honourable state for an Anglican to be in.

Despite their opposing evaluations of Fresh Expressions, these works share a reliance on 'pure theology' and a disparagement of sociological perspectives in articulating their ecclesiology and its implications for contemporary practice. As a result, while Goodhew and colleagues celebrate 'freshness', and Davison and Milbank prefer a somewhat rose-tinted view of traditional Church, neither are really able to address the key critical questions raised by the Fresh Expressions movement, and in particular the ongoing relationship between a fresh expression and the inherited church that sponsors it.

Fresh Expressions and the inherited church

Employing a more sociologically astute approach, Martyn Percy (2008) argues that fresh expressions, while remaining dependent on the 'host body' of the parish church, serve to weaken it by draining away energies into what he calls 'dispersed intensity'. This involves multiple 'outlets' in the form of highly associational small groups based on developing personal faith practice around a common interest, at the expense of 'utility-extensive models of service' that require time and commitment. Fresh expressions collude uncritically with cultural trends by endorsing 'therapeutic religion', promoting individualism and focusing overly on 'brand' and 'image'. Whatever truth there may be in these charges (and I think there is), in Percy, as with Davison and Milbank, the recommendation of the parochial model as able to overcome these drawbacks appears more than a little nostalgic.

Others want to see a much cleaner break between new forms of church and the traditional denominations. Pete Rollins (2008b) suspects the institutional Church is seeking to 'domesticate' the Fresh Expressions movement by 'clearing a space' for it, tolerating it as an 'alternative' in a 'mixed economy church'. He wants 'emergent communities' to remain *outside* the institutional churches, so that they can more effectively challenge them. In the same volume, Louise Nelstrop raises the question whether those such as Ian Mobsby and Pete Ward, who imply that 'fresh' or 'emergent' churches must ultimately replace inherited ones, will prove to be right (Nelstrop, 2008, pp. 191–2). For Mobsby, most fresh expressions are not 'postmodern' enough, because unlike the 'emerging' churches that are characterized by utilizing a postmodern contextual understanding, they fundamentally 'appear to hold a more Christendom mindset' (2007, p. 31). He believes that the mainstream denominational churches will not be able to sustain renewal via fresh expressions unless they are willing to learn from the more radical non-denominational emerging communities.

[Good for essay 2 — handwritten margin note]

This view has been supported in research undertaken by Beth Keith (2014), who found that the great majority of pioneers operating within traditional church structures felt that greater distance from these would help them. They found they could begin to 'dismantle', but in trying to 'reconstruct' they could only get so far before opposition set in: 'as pioneers engaged with the mission context, new experiences conflicted with existing ideas and beliefs' (2014, p. 129). Keith recommends that these pioneers need to be allowed greater flexibility to be more radical: those who were pioneering outside existing structures were happier. But they need to guard against a drift away from the structures and resources they may require if their sustainability is not to be threatened, and they also need to be 'in the fold' sufficiently to be able to exercise influence on the sponsoring or parent church.

Critics like Mobsby and Keith are putting their finger on the essential question about how thorough and far-reaching are the sociological and theological analyses underpinning the practical proposals of the Fresh Expressions initiative. Sutcliffe considers that the question why theology is important to pioneers has been 'given relatively little exposure in the literature generated out of the Mission-shaped Church movement' (2014, p. 159). He calls for a 'pioneering', 'disruptive theology', noting how, through new theologies 'notions of divine gender have been challenged ... assumptions of western (white) christologies have been shown to be deficient ... and there has been a resurgence in pneumatology from the southern hemisphere where *spirit* is a personal and communal reality' (p. 173). In the same way, ministerial theology cannot be immune: in response to the FE Report statement that it will be one mark of a 'mature' fresh expression to have an 'authorized ministry', Sutcliffe asks pointedly how exactly this is to be defined.

As these questions multiply, the Fresh Expressions initiative is at risk of becoming stranded between the imperatives of change and innovation and the exigencies of inherited Church, between postmodern instincts and modern/pre-modern ecclesial realities, a halfway house between security and risk, unsure whether to cast loose into adult independence or remain tied to the apron-strings of its ecclesiological patronage. In the final part of the chapter, we search beyond the Fresh Expressions literature for other contributions that can enrich and develop the quest for culturally appropriate new models of church.

Nuancing Fresh Expressions: some complementary approaches

Pete Ward offers an example of an approach that attempts to visualize how inherited Church might evolve under changing socio-cultural conditions. If, as we were exploring in Chapter 1, identity and community are becoming more 'liquid' as late modernity evolves, the Church cannot expect to withstand these developments. According to Ward, the inherited 'solid church' is prone to 'mutation' in three ways. For some, 'heritage site' is a viable option, particularly in rural commuter villages to which people move because they imagine they may find there a survival of an earlier form of community, or seek to create it, centred around the church. For others, church as 'refuge' may allow a community of need to develop in a safe space, protected from the stressful downside of postmodern living. Elsewhere, a 'nostalgic community' can offer a place where people retire to long for the good old days and exchange stories of the glorious past (2002, pp. 22–30). These may sound defeatist options, but they are an attempt to envisage liveable outcomes for the remaining lifespan of churches that, in the long run, may well be heading for extinction. It may be that such churches can provide much needed spiritual solace, support and sustenance for what Ann Morisy (2009) has called 'bothered and bewildered' people in 'troubled times'.

Morisy is one of a number of writers and thinkers on the contemporary Church who introduce a more nuanced note into the way they reflect on ecclesiology, with the aid of some thoughtfully applied social and cultural analysis. This is not merely in the sense of a missionary Church being under an imperative to respond to the culture 'out there' but, beyond this to discern what might be required of a culturally attuned and sensitive post-Christendom Church, amid the shifting and fluid patterns of late modernity. Morisy observes that the Church has a plausibility crisis that means that hope 'cannot just be proclaimed or asserted' (2009, p. 26):

> Although the formulas of our Christian faith have been hard won, they are unconvincing to bothered and bewildered people because they are self-referential and self-validating ... Rather than bring confidence, the formularies of our faith that have been honed over centuries, in a troubled, postmodern world, only serve to confirm the clannishness of the church process, where people speak in riddles that are understandable and *plausible* only to a few. (p. 28)

Morisy argues that so far, 'reflection on *how* people embrace faith ... has not percolated the evangelistic efforts associated with ... "Fresh Expressions" or "Mission-shaped Church"' (p. 49). Her concern is for the articulation and demonstration of a healthy 'lived religion' by a Church that 'shifts the balance from investment in "belief" to acknowledging the everyday relevance and cathartic and energising nature of the story of Jesus who shows us how to live' (p. 116). Rather than grand schemes to increase the size of congregations, she places the emphasis on 'micro-actions' that demonstrate the meaning of theological assertions in an earthed, practical way, sensitive to the conditions of personal social and cultural contexts.

Duncan MacLaren is another thoughtful contributor who recognizes the churches' crisis of plausibility and the necessity of careful social and cultural analysis for addressing it. He suggests that churches need to build 'plausibility shelters', defined as 'makeshift structures which provide a degree of protection for beliefs, while being realistic about the fact that competing definitions of reality will clash in our everyday experience' (2004, p. 125). Although MacLaren calls his preferred model of church a 'benign sectarianism' (p. 127), his recommendations also seem appropriate for more outward-looking, open-ended types of church: nurturing relationships and forming community; engaging with competing ideologies rather than retreating into a church sub-culture; drawing on communal spiritual practices from a variety of contexts past and present; cultivating attentiveness for the 're-enchantment of everyday life', and developing a shared vision of life in the Kingdom of God (pp. 127–31).

Doug Gay offers some insightful, honest personal reflections on the frustrations of pioneering within inflexible structures. Gay's declining traditional church in Glasgow required a 'compromise' deal: 'evolution in the morning, revolution in the evening. Continuity in the morning, pioneering in the evening. Nurturing the existing congregation in the morning, planting a new one in the evening' (2014, p. 42). The 'evening revolution' comprised a monthly cycle of gatherings known as 'peacetime', church for peace and reconciliation, in a context where sectarian division has been rife; 'healthservice', church engaging with suffering, healing and wholeness; 'commontable', church practising table hospitality; and 'still life', church, creative art and silence (pp. 49 ff.). Gay (2011) called this the 'remixed' church, retrieving and unbundling fundamental Christian themes from the historical conventions with which they have become entangled, and repristinating them as a contextualized theological praxis for today.

A further example of an approach rooted in an empirically based theology is found in Mobsby, who identifies five areas of 'becoming' in which churches are developing a Christ-centred identity: community, belonging, forgiveness, justice and hope (2012, pp. 145–52). He summarizes: 'Once people find hope, forgiveness, openness, belonging and community, *it is hoped they will have had personal experience of the love of God*' (p. 151, emphasis mine). Some within the Church will identify experiences of this kind as experiences of God, but it always remains possible for 'spiritual tourists' or seekers to experience the same things without this resulting in personal faith. This is preferable to a dogmatic approach that closes off all experience of God to any who decline to embrace orthodoxy.

Conclusion

In this chapter I have sought to broaden the approach to fresh expressions within the mainstream denominations by way of a more nuanced approach to sociological currents and theological implications than an activities-focused approach often allows. I have pointed to examples of alternative church practitioners who are building in theological reflection, in ways that recognize how the cultural setting will require not only innovation in activity and style, but also theological change as a key element of ecclesiological renewal. Another such contributor, Kim Hartshorne (2014), quotes the words of John Caputo as a theological rationale for these critical adaptations of church:

> My idea is to stop thinking about God as a massive ontological power line that provides power to the world, instead thinking of something that short circuits such power and provides a provocation to the world that is otherwise than power. (Caputo, 2006, p. 13)

We shall focus attention on Caputo in the next chapter, where the need for this more careful, considered approach will be further developed in relation to the role of faith in society and how the churches can make a distinctive contribution in the future.

9

Signals of the Impossible: Reimagining the Role of Christian Faith

The preceding four chapters have explored some of the principal streams that have contributed over the last 50 years or so to the efforts of the churches to renew their life and ministry, in response to the kinds of social and cultural change that were examined in the Introduction and Chapter 1. Collaborative ministry, charismatic renewal, chaplaincy and fresh expressions have all sought to offer alternatives to hierarchies and inflexible institutions, to promote greater diversity in models and styles of ministry and to enhance the role of lay people and reduce clericalism. Some developments, such as Local Ministry Schemes and Fresh Expressions, have enjoyed significant backing from central Church organizations; in others, typically the charismatic movement and the rise of chaplaincy, new directions have emerged and evolved with relatively little leadership 'from the top', and sometimes with a degree of suspicion.

As we have seen in Chapter 8, the Fresh Expressions movement has attained a pre-eminence, in the Church of England and the Methodist Church especially, probably not seen in any previous initiative. It has become the strategy of choice for a 'mixed economy Church', backed by bishops, resourced and funded, and accompanied by new training programmes for 'pioneer ministers', and the legal provision of 'Bishops' Mission Orders' to enable experimentation across parish boundaries. The previous chapter argued that fresh expressions represent a moderate accommodation to some aspects of social and cultural change in late modernity, chiefly by means of activities offered as an alternative to traditional 'Sunday church'. It is doubtful whether this relatively contained and controlled measure of experimentation will prove sufficient, especially in light of growing evidence of a much deeper alienation from the traditional churches among younger people.

The next stage of our exploration therefore probes further: just how radically different might an adaptive ministry need to be, and what is the distinctive contribution to society of the Church that such a ministry is there to serve? The chapter begins with an enquiry into the broad framework of 'popular postmodernity', focusing on the increasing subjection of religion and spirituality to marketization and consumerist pressures, leading to the diversification of spiritual products, goods and services to meet individual tastes and preferences, according to individual consumer choice. The second part sets out to construct a more authentic reimagining of the role of the Christian religion, its practices, lifestyles and communities, within contemporary post-Christian contexts, drawing on a deconstructive framework. The proposal to be expounded is that the Christian Church performs an indispensable role for the good of society, as both a sign and an expression of things that are impossible. This is a role that can potentially be performed by *all* types of church; the proposal is not merely about the abolition of inherited models and their replacement by more radically postmodern alternatives.

Religion and consumerism

Varieties of spirituality

In Chapter 1 we considered Mathew Guest's proposal for 'spiritual capital' as a potentially fruitful way of identifying and regenerating residual religious culture. Guest's position can be both complemented by and contrasted with the findings of Heelas and Woodhead (2005), based on a research project in the Cumbrian town of Kendal. They found the general public engaging in a plethora of practices that fitted within their broad definition of 'spirituality', an arena of activity they named the 'holistic milieu'. In their critique of the Kendal project Voas and Bruce summarize these practices as embracing 'anything from earnest introspection to beauty treatments, martial arts to support groups, complementary medicine to palm reading', reflecting the concern of participants for an overall personal well-being (2007, p. 44).

The holistic milieu embodies what Heelas and Woodhead call a 'subjective-life' spirituality, that is, it is all about who you are in your truest, innermost self. Conversely, the 'congregational domain' of conventional church-based religious practice enshrines a 'life-as' spirituality, constituting the attempt to live 'life as' a Christian, subject to the requirements of an authoritative institution:

Life-as forms of the sacred, which emphasise a transcendent source of significance and authority to which individuals must conform at the expense of the cultivation of their unique subjective-lives, are most likely to be in decline; subjective-life forms of the sacred, which emphasize

inner sources of significance and authority and the cultivation or sacral-
isation of unique subjective-lives, are most likely to be growing. (2005,
p. 6)

There is a notable imbalance between the way these two are presented,
with 'life-as' being described rather negatively in terms of enforced conformity and the suppression of personal uniqueness, whereas 'subjective
life' is given a much more positive treatment.

The problem with Heelas and Woodhead's unfavourable portrayal of
'life-as' spirituality emerges in a passage where the authors summarize
the benefits of life in the congregational domain for those who prefer it:

> ... praising God rather than delving into the self; 'doing your duty'
> rather than 'doing your own thing'... becoming, for example, a better
> mother, a more devoted disciple, a more godly father, a more obedient
> child, a Christian more closely conformed to Christ, or more selflessly
> devoted to the task of serving humankind. (2005, p. 111)

The authors claim that this domain is in decline 'because many people
are simply no longer willing to submit to the roles, duties, rituals, traditions, offices and expectations which these institutions impose' (p. 112).
However, even if there is truth in this assertion, conventional Christian
practice as 'life-as' spirituality is not necessarily neglectful of 'selfhood'
in a harmful way. People may be drawing on the spiritual capital accrued
by immersion in Christian liturgy, prayer and preaching over many years:
for such a faith, an authentic 'subjective-life' is best attained precisely
through the cultivation of a particular 'life-as' pattern, following Jesus,
being united with Christ, or 'losing's one's own life in order to find it'
(Matthew 16.25).

Voas and Bruce criticize Heelas and Woodhead for over-valuing the
potential of 'subjective life' activities for producing genuinely lasting
and authentic spiritual capital. With their individualism and therapeutic
mentality, they connote less of an alternative to the secular lifestyle
than a superficially 'spiritualized' version of it (2007, p. 59). Although
Heelas and Woodhead commend such 'spirituality' for being 'without
the baggage' associated with 'religion' (2005, p. 90), for Voas and Bruce
this can amount to 'another way of saying that it is not very religious'
(2007, p. 59). In a later book (2008), in which Heelas comes out as something of an enthusiast for the 'holistic milieu', he quotes Graham Ward
castigating so-called alternative spiritualities as producing

forms of hyper-individualism, self-help as grooming, custom-made eclecticism that proffer a pop transcendence and pamper to the need for 'good vibrations' ... a collection of religious people ... who will be unable to tell the difference between orgasm, an adrenalin rush and an encounter with God. (Ward, 2006, cit. Heelas, 2008, p. 84)

Although Heelas rejects Ward's view that spiritualities of life are little more than gratification and narcissism, the result of a capitalist marketing strategy, the problems of allergy to commitment, and an excessive focus on self-regard, continue to call into question their capacity to create and sustain spiritual capital in the way that 'life-as' spirituality has done in the past.

Spirituality is therefore an area where a too ready accommodation to contemporary market trends is unlikely to serve the churches well in the long run. The next section investigates religion, consumerism and marketization in more detail.

Lifestyle and branding in the religious market

The emerging phenomenon of a consumer society was examined over a century ago by the sociologist Thorstein Veblen (2009, orig. pub. 1899). Veblen argued that when the level of wealth in a society means that the better-off can afford to purchase more goods than they actually need to live on, a 'leisure class' develops, that engages in what he called 'conspicuous consumption'. Certain commodities become associated with high economic status, and are readily displayed by those who possess them, regardless of whether the elites who determine cultural 'taste' would approve of them; as a contemporary example, Gordon Lynch cites the quantities of 'bling', or ostentatious jewellery, favoured by hip-hop artists (2005, p. 61). Drawing on the work of Karl Marx, the French thinker Jean Baudrillard argues that this represents a shift from measuring the value of a commodity by its utility to its market value, in respect of its worth both in monetary terms and the prestige enjoyed by its owner. Some decades after Veblen, Theodore Adorno of the Frankfurt School of 'critical theory' condemned this form of consumption as 'substitute gratification', a false promise of 'happiness' designed to work, rather like Marx's view of religion as the opium of the people, as a placebo to dull the senses and deflect people from paying attention to serious questions (Adorno, 2001). In the title of a well-known work, the cultural critic Neil Postman (1985) dubbed this *Amusing Ourselves to Death*. This is a serious challenge to the churches, which have seen themselves as dealing with the big questions of life and death but without employing eye-catching marketing methods in order to do so. The sociologist Stephen Hunt argues that the churches have now inevitably found themselves drawn into this consumer culture:

> It is not unreasonable to suggest that the decline in religion in the West ... has meant that churches are now forced to see themselves as units in a market competing for the time, loyalty and money of a limited clientele. In this situation, they largely behave as secular, commercial units operating in their markets with an eye to mass appeal, advertising, showing a sensitivity to competition and 'profit' innovation, and so on. (2004, pp. 32–3)

The consumer culture leads to the value of branding as an indicator of lifestyle: where there is a commodity that basically everyone needs, added value has to be achieved by the distinctive features of the brand that delivers a culturally positive message about the person who visibly displays or consumes it; not just any old jeans or trainers will do (Lynch, 2005, pp. 58–64). This is the case with the Alpha course, or more recently the emergence of Messy Church as a brand: these convey lifestyle messages about 'church' expressly targeted to people who would not ordinarily think that church was for people like them. As Carrette and King put it in their forceful critique of marketized religion, 'spirituality is appropriated for the market instead of offering a countervailing social force to the ethos and values of the business world' (2005, p. 126).

The churches' negotiation of the perils of consumerism and marketization has been uneven and sometimes contradictory. Richard Roberts (2002) argues that although the churches responded critically to the Thatcherite enterprise culture of the 1980s at the level of social ethics (notably in the *Faith in the City* report), they did not pay attention to the implications for religion itself. Accordingly, they have since adopted many of its features, such as valuing clear ideological commitment over fuzzier consensus, seeing religion as a consumer choice, and modelling the Church as a managed subsection of society, controlling its output and regulating its practitioners (Roberts, 2002, pp. 53–4). The result is schemes such as Alpha, dubbed by Roberts 'the Tupperware Party solution to the threat of secularisation'; whereas what is actually needed is 'ruthless self-appraisal, a commitment to reflexive socio-cultural analysis and a willingness to venture out in a newly defined enterprise of faith' (p. 187).

Roberts's critique echoes the earlier judgement of Adorno in rejecting marketized solutions as a distraction from engagement with the big questions. However, too often the churches have misdirected their criticisms, not attacking the trivialization of faith inherent in many consumerist initiatives, but instead deploring the lapse of taste involved in the embrace of popular cultural styles. These are two very different issues. Pete Ward notes how in Victorian times Matthew Arnold treated 'culture' as what keeps the barbarians at bay and prevents the delicate ecology of civilized society from falling into chaos, or anarchy (Ward, 2008, p. 155). Debates about 'taste' in the contemporary worship and practice of the Church of England often display something of this attitude of highbrow versus lowbrow or popular culture (pp. 154 ff.). As an example, Ward cites a put-down by Richard Holloway, describing modern evangelical worship as demonstrating 'a sort of aesthetic contraction and banality in which liturgy is fast food rather than haute cuisine' (cit. p. 155).

The critique of consumerism in religion and spirituality should therefore not be confused with making judgements based on cultural tastes. Ward argues that the opening up of the religious marketplace to a wider range of cultural expressions, for example in the field of church music, has enabled popular culture to shape the Church and help it become more 'liquid' (pp. 150–1). Rather than being lulled into submission by mass popular culture, as Adorno thought, people on the social margins can sometimes find there culturally effective resources for challenging and subverting the process of their co-option by the powerful (pp. 162–3). A contemporary Christian example would be the positive impact of the work of the grime artist Stormzy on young black urban working-class males, in which rap is only the starting point for a range of social and educational projects.

Gathering up the threads of this discussion, we can say that the churches need to exercise great care and discretion when experimenting with the branding and marketing of new religious 'products' in response to cultural change. Cultivating entrepreneurial flair in presentation cannot be a substitute for deeper socio-cultural analysis and a serious quest for radically unfamiliar forms of church and ministry. Engaging with popular culture is valuable, but only if it is permitted to penetrate and interrogate inherited ecclesial praxis beyond the appearance of being more contemporary. The allure of the 'spirituality in preference to religion' route is hazardous, as so many of the commodities on offer gain their appeal from the absence of precisely the qualities that make genuine religion so challenging, profound and potentially transformative. Fresh expressions risk reducing church to a lifestyle option in which whatever takes place must at least be entertaining, which is why it is often a forlorn hope that they will form a 'bridge' into 'mainstream church'. Sadly, the consumer may feel that Sunday church lacks the brand values that characterize the fresh expression, symbolizes a lifestyle the non-church person does not find attractive, and offers a product that does not entertain.

We will come back to the alternative possibilities for 'church' in the next chapter, but at this point the question is this: what is there in Christianity that is arresting, different and distinctive? In a culture of deregulated religion, how shall Christianity position itself within the marketplace? It takes more than repackaging: changing the style, the form, the mode of delivery, but insisting that the thing in itself remains the same. Cultural engagement necessitates addressing theology, not just reinventing church: as Rob Warner concludes from his study of new churches in York, in due course 'ecclesial experimentation' will lead to 'doctrinal reformulation' (2007, p. 196). The rest of this chapter offers a proposal about what Christianity distinctively brings to the table. This will not be in the guise of a marketable commodity, but a challenging and potentially transformative mindset, attitudes, and individual and collective practices that may not have mass appeal, but will stand out from the crowd.

Christian distinctiveness: a de/constructive proposal

It is important to stress that in this section I am not proposing a theory of religion, but offering an account of what might be distinctive about Christianity for a post-church society. Historians and sociologists know that generalizing, global definitions of religion are a contested minefield, and have been ever since Schleiermacher defined religion in terms of the 'feeling of absolute dependence'. While philosophical sources, including Caputo (2001), tend to present their proposals as being about 'religion', the reality is often that they are basing them on a Christian template, and it remains an open question to what extent their ideas can be applied to other faiths. Christianity is the only faith I know 'from the inside', and the view of it presented here seems plausible to me: I cannot claim any more than this.

The American philosopher John (Jack) Caputo, from an Italian Catholic background, is a leading exponent of an approach to theology based on the philosophy of deconstruction. His influential study *The Prayers and Tears of Jacques Derrida: Religion without Religion* (1997) pioneered an unconventional religious reading of the French-Algerian Jewish postmodernist thinker usually regarded as an atheist. Since then, Caputo's work has become more explicitly theological; one reviewer wrote of his *The Weakness of God: A Theology of the Event* (2006) that he 'comes out of the closet as a theologian'. This was followed by the more popular and accessible *What Would Jesus Deconstruct? The Good News of Postmod-*

ernism for the Church (2007), the most directly relevant of his works for ecclesiology. His *The Insistence of God: A Theology of Perhaps* (2013) continued the theological trend, along with *The Folly of God: A Theology of the Unconditional* (2016) and the part-autobiographical *Hoping Against Hope: Confessions of a Postmodern Pilgrim* (2015).

Deconstruction and the limits of language

Caputo's work on Derrida is the starting point for understanding his theology, which means that my 'constructive proposal' is actually a deconstructive proposal. The technique of deconstruction originates in the field of linguistics (de Saussure, 1959; see Grenz, 1996, pp. 114–17; on Derrida, see Grenz, pp. 138–50; for an introduction to deconstruction, see O'Donnell, 2003, pp. 46–63), with the notion that language does not work by assembling building blocks of fixed units of meaning, but is an altogether more flexible and fluid medium in which meanings are strongly contextual and often contested. Deconstruction exercises suspicion about accepting concepts and meanings as they are: 'texts are never simply unitary but include resources that run counter to their assertions' (Appignanesi and Garratt, 2004, p. 80).

Caputo offers a typically humorous definition in popular style, based on the idea that nothing can ever be expressed properly 'in a nutshell':

> Whenever deconstruction finds a nutshell – a secure axiom or a pithy maxim – the very idea is to crack it open and disturb this tranquillity ... that is a good rule of thumb in deconstruction ... One might even say that cracking nutshells is what deconstruction *is*. 'In a nutshell' ... Have we not run up against a paradox and an aporia*? ... The impossibility of an aporia is just what impels deconstruction, what rouses it out of bed in the morning. (1996, p. 32. *'Aporia' is the gap in an argument that prevents it from arriving at a neat and tidy conclusion)

The 'aporia' within language is captured by Derrida in what he calls *différance*, a play on words that only works in French, where the effect is to create a term that means both 'difference' and 'deferral'. That is, to use language is not to 'fix' meanings but to make distinctions of the type 'this is not that', with the effect that *final* meaning is always 'deferred', put off, not yet attained. 'Any meaning ... is provisional and relative, because it is never *exhaustive* ... it can always be traced back to a prior network of differences' (Appignanesi and Garratt, 2004, p. 79; for an account of Derrida's deconstruction in a theological context, see Smith, 2006, chapter 2).

This indicates why Caputo sees deconstruction as good news for the Church, because it corresponds well with the activity of doing theology, which is about God; and God is never finally known (and can certainly not be summed up in a nutshell). In the domain of theology, a comparable linguistic strategy is employed by postmodern Ulster theologian Peter Rollins in the title of his book, *How (Not) to Speak of God* (2006). A deconstructive approach therefore rules out assent to authoritative dogma as the foundational requirement of faith profession and practice; and this elimination applies also to ecclesiology and ministry. Don Cupitt writes that

> the incurable plurality and endlessness of interpretation makes the very notion of a single publicly-established, authoritative, permanent and compulsory orthodoxy impossible either in society at large or in the church in particular. Truth cannot be determined once-for-all and objectively, but only evolved provisionally and *ad hoc* ... Meaning and truth are like mushrooms; they have to keep springing up afresh all over the place. (1989, p. 15)

Cupitt argues that the era of Christendom with its all-embracing cultural dominance of the churches and their imperial power fitted well with a dogmatic and enforceable mode of faith within a monarchical structure: 'as a result, to this day our value-judgments tend to favour unity, self-sameness, agreement, discipline, order, leadership and patriarchal control' (p. 17). In post-Christendom, post-liberal, postmodern mode, such values are superseded by fluidity, diversity, unpredictability, collectivity and anarchy. 'Truth is not the position you hold but the path you tread ... truth must be forever a running argument and a continuing process of production, and it can never become a settled conclusion' (p. 60). It will be creative; and it must affirm 'contingency and dispersal' (p. 61).

The titles of Caputo's self-declared works of theology bring the point home. *The Weakness of God* (2006) promotes the desirability of a 'weak theology' over one predicated upon certainty and unchangingness. 'Strong theology' insists on bipolar 'categories of theism and atheism, belief and unbelief, existence and non-existence'. Such binaries are exactly the linguistic forms Derrida wishes to disrupt (Woods, 2009, pp. 18–19). 'Weak theology' on the other hand 'is content with a little adverb like "perhaps" ... introducing modalities, conditions, degrees, and exceptions'. 'God' denotes 'a call rather than a causality', and names 'an event transpiring in being's restless heart' (Caputo, 2006, pp. 8–9). *The Insistence of God* (2013) substitutes 'insistence' for 'existence' and celebrates the domain of 'perhaps', where the 'might' in 'God Almighty' is not 'power', but 'turns out to be the subjunctive might of "maybe" or "might be"'

(p. 9). To resource this deconstructed, non-dogmatic reappraisal of theology, Caputo draws on Derrida's motifs of impossibility and madness.

Christian calling, madness and the impossible

For Caputo, 'the impossible is a defining religious category' (2001, p. 10). Religion enacts the longing for a future: not the 'relative future' we all have to make prudential plans for from day to day, but the 'absolute future' with which 'we are pushed to the limits of the possible, fully extended, at our wits' end' (p. 8). There are New Testament precedents, in the disciples asking Jesus who can be saved, and Jesus replying that 'for [mortals] this is impossible' (Mark 10.27); or St Paul telling the Corinthians that he is writing about something that 'no eye has seen ... no ear has heard, and ... no human mind has conceived' (1 Cor. 2.9).

The embrace of the impossible signals that religion is a form of madness. How so? Caputo says that the Aristotelian virtues (courage, temperance, honour, liberality) are the so-called 'cardinal' virtues, from the Latin for 'hinge', because all the other virtues hinge upon them. They are moderate, balanced and rational. By contrast, the (Christian) theological virtues of faith, hope and charity 'unhinge' us. They pitch us into the madness of impossible things: loving our enemies (pp. 13–14), 'unfolding the power of the impossible beyond the possible' (p. 15). This is why Caputo entitles his main exposition of this approach to Christian theology 'A Prayer for the Impossible' (Caputo, 2007, chapter 3). Deconstructive theological language is 'the affirmation of the impossible' (p. 124); to enter language in the cause of theology is to step defiantly into radical uncertainty in the pursuit of a vision of what might be.

Theological language is not first and foremost a statement of what is the case, but is vocative in style, the mode of language in which an address is made to a person, a call that invites a response: '*John*, have you got a minute?' '*Saul*, why do you persecute me?' Caputo observes that the purest form of call is the one where it is not certain who is calling, because the response is then not a calculative one (as when the phone rings and you can choose whether to answer because the caller number is displayed), but an act of faith (as picking up the phone used to be in the days when the number was not displayed!). The language, beliefs, practices, institutions and communities of Christian faith are a medium for the cultural exchange and embodiment of these engagements with radical uncertainty and the call to embrace the impossible. Caputo helps us to explore some of these (im)possibilities in more depth.

The first example is the Christian praxis of grace, given expression through the language of 'gift' and 'forgiveness'. Derrida's deconstructive method reveals the impossibility of the gift, because as soon as someone gives to another, however freely and graciously, an obligation of reciprocity is created. The recipient of the gift incurs what we call a 'debt of gratitude', whereas the giver experiences a sense of satisfaction: thus the giving 'adds value' to the giver but impoverishes the recipient, who now owes a debt – quite the opposite result of that intended by the original giver. Christianity, by contrast, is there to make what Caputo calls the 'madness' of the gift into a real possibility, because when the giver is God, the gift cannot be anything other than sheer gratuity, and the response cannot be to reciprocate, because in respect to God we are always already indebted to an impossible degree. We are called by the notion of divine gift to embrace this madness ourselves, and to give unconditionally because this is the only way that the cycle of giving can be a virtuous one. St Paul's vision of the Church is a place where mutual generosity marks the presence of the God of Jesus Christ: 'Thanks be to God for his indescribable gift!' (2 Cor. 9.15).

In a similar way, in a calculative context 'forgiveness' is another impossibility. True forgiveness has to engage with the actuality of the debt while willingly cancelling it and its long-term harmful effects. This is not the way of the world: as Caputo points out, 'banks do not make gifts, and when they do, we know they are up to something, trying to sell us some new service ... Nor do they forgive anything. They are business people and strict in their accounting' (2007, p. 73). Genuine forgiveness is possible only on the basis of those who are forgiven not meeting the conditions for forgiveness, otherwise the act of forgiveness would set up a further relationship of obligations. The forgiveness of God cannot be a matter of squaring the accounts, but is recklessly extravagant because it signals a new order, a summons or call to a new being. If this were not so, then the response of the elder brother in the parable of the prodigal son ought to be commended for its prudence (p. 75).

Prudential considerations likewise influence the interpretation of another theological concept, that of hospitality. Caputo reminds us of the contradictory meanings of the cluster of related words that include 'host', 'hospitality', 'hostel' and 'hostile'. The tension arises because the word *hostis* in Latin means 'stranger', and the stranger can be seen either as the 'alien' who threatens to be seen as the enemy, leading to a prudential strategy of 'playing safe'; or the 'guest' who enjoys the unexpected generosity and welcome of the 'host', as in George Herbert's classic poem 'Love'. Christianity calls people towards the unreasonableness of the inclusive, all-embracing meaning of hospitality, the welcome for the unloved, the outcast and those who are subject to suspicion.

Another example of 'the impossible', not discussed by Caputo, but highly relevant to the Church, is the notion of decision-making by consensus, so that 'decisions are delayed until agreement is reached' (Viola, 2008, p. 195). In this ecclesiology, the leaders (elders) do not decide things: only the whole Church does this, and not even by majority voting. There must be agreement, consensus, and never 'for and against'. Viola admits that 'to be sure, consensus is *humanly* impossible': but immediately he adds, 'but so is salvation' (p. 196). The aspiration to 'being of one mind' can *only* make sense within the context of an expectation of the working of the 'indwelling Spirit', as practised for example by the Quakers. Someone might object that 'it would be madness' to try to run the Church in this way: but that is precisely the point.

None of these concepts, of vocation, gift, forgiveness, hospitality, consensus, and indeed also of love itself, is *specifically* or exclusively theological, and this gives them a potential reach well beyond the bounds of conventional organized religion. Writing in *The Guardian* (13 April 2019), Oliver Burkeman, who describes himself as 'not religious', commends Christian writer David Zahl's book *Seculosity* (2019). The title is a conflation of 'secularity' with 'religiosity', and the book is a critique of 'performancism', a way of life devoted to the continual effort to do *enough*, in every domain: in your job, family life, sport, in politically correct attitudes, a healthy diet and ecological awareness. This is today's religion, because 'deep down, we're using these things to try to achieve salvation'. Remarkably, Burkeman finds himself warming to Zahl's case that the Christian religion can resolve this dilemma, because it 'is suffused by forgiveness and what Christians call grace: the sense that enoughness is bestowed, not achieved, and that you needn't reach any particular standard of performance or virtue in order to qualify'.

All these things have to be recognized as madness and impossibility before the necessity of God breaks through. Put another way, 'the real is what we are trying to make come true, even when it resists our comprehension, our grasp or grip' (Caputo, 2007, p. 79). For Derrida, what is 'really real' is *ce qui arrive*: another French play on words, meaning either 'that which happens' or 'that which is coming'. Turning what happens into what is yet to come is a profoundly Christian idea. Keeping alive the hope that we have never 'arrived' but that God's future is always 'arriving' is a vital cultural function of communities of Christian faith. Living in the unsettling uncertainty and instability of the interim is central to the experience of life, a reality that can be temporarily staved off by multiple strategies of displacement and evasion, but demands the implausible madness of faith to meet head-on, subvert and undermine it.

Conclusion: faith for a post-church society

The approach to Christian distinctiveness offered here is not exclusively the preserve of those steeped in the mindset of French postmodernists. Others too are engaging with the impossibility of God, and employing a kind of deconstructive method to seek ways of entering into the feel, the texture or innermost quality of faith. To cite just one example, in her work on the 'new atheists', Tina Beattie regrets how a (largely male) form of modernistic reason has often rejected the divine as that which is not empirically available. But she wants to recover the 'non-availability' of God as the very *raison d'être* of creative faith: 'We are those who choose to remain in the mystery of the unfinished story, inhabitants of the "immensity of waiting" which is Saturday' (2007, pp. 170–1). To dwell in Holy Saturday is to know only too well the experience of Good Friday, but not yet as one fully in the grasp of the hope of Easter.

It lies outside the scope of this book to develop the deconstructive pattern of Christian faith any further. But where contemporary ministry and mission are concerned, it offers a way in which open and questioning Christians, humane and generous atheists, and all the varieties of agnostic in between, might make common cause. What is needed is a Church that can handle such an approach. That is why Caputo turns the question 'What would Jesus do?' into 'What would Jesus deconstruct?', and the answer is 'the Church'. 'The church is a provisional construction, and whatever is constructed is deconstructible, while the kingdom of God is that in virtue of which the church is deconstructible' (2007, p. 35).

The strategies for renewal upon which the mainstream denominational churches are relying often fall short in this regard. 'Fresh expressions' offer revamped presentation, but deliberately seek not to alter the product, and risk theological vacuity. New forms of spirituality seem tempting, but play into the contemporary tendency towards self-obsession and the prevalence of style over substance. Market solutions risk emptying Christian faith of the capacity for social transformation. It is more crucial for the Church to represent something *distinctive* than to rebrand the same product in fresh packaging. What is distinctive in Christianity for today is that it deals with the impossible, without which hope for the future cannot be sustained and no one can be saved. The next chapter pursues the implications for the future shapes of church of such an approach to the role of Christian faith.

10

'Ecclesianarchy': A Blueprint for Adaptive Ministry

In the Introduction, I proposed that in a post-church society, the praxis of ministry needs to be conducted on an *adaptive* basis. The early chapters looked for evidence of such adaptivity in the ebb and flow of ministerial theology and practice through the course of Church history. The middle chapters evaluated selected contemporary examples of renewal in ministry as expressions of a more adaptive approach. The preceding chapter offered an alternative picture of the role of a distinctive Christian faith presence in society under the conditions of postmodernity, and set out an agenda: the Church has to be perpetually deconstructed, for the sake of the Kingdom of God. This chapter builds on the deconstructive impulse by looking at the more radical, experimental expressions of church as symbol, site and enactment of the impossible, in a society struggling to gain a positive sense of what it might mean to be 'post-secular'. The concept around which these ideas gather is 'ecclesianarchy' (earlier versions of parts of this chapter were published in Williams, 2016 and 2018).

Hierarchy and anarchy in the Church

Roger Haydon Mitchell (2013) expounds how the Church embraced, and further developed and enforced, the model of 'sovereignty' as it moved from being a movement for peace to an institution of power in the partnership of Church with empire. 'Empire' entails sovereign power (i.e. monarchy, see pp. 24–5), sovereign law and sovereign payment. Christian doctrines of salvation became bound up with these models; for example, Christ's death came to be seen as due payment for our sins, or for God's offended honour. For Eusebius (p. 25), only a monarchical order can guarantee or preserve 'peace': there is absolutely no place for pluralism. So, peace is 'enforced' – the oxymoron is striking – and maintained through hierarchy (the monarch at the top, but only under God) in a 'priestly theocracy' (p. 26).

The formalization of the Creeds contributed to this objective, guaranteeing unity of belief to serve and complement monarchical power. Further, since God as monarch rules by way of laws that safeguard his honour (masculine pronouns for God are retained intentionally here), a system of offerings is required to placate him when these laws are broken. This transactional relationship is no longer one of love, gift, forgiveness and outrageous hospitality, but a radical reversal of the gospel in which 'the only way to bring about peace and prosperity is by the operation of sovereign power, appeased by money and enforced by war' (p. 28). In the imperial model, 'the people' have to be understood as symbolized and embodied in the 'sovereign state', a position Mitchell sees as ideological, because it does not properly represent 'the essentially loving, egalitarian nature of divine-human relationships' (p. 82).

The radical alternative offered by Christianity is one in which 'faith embraces a relational encounter based on love, not sovereign power' (p. 83). Thus 'the interminable transformations of the church-empire partnership can at last give way to an incarnational rhythm of revolutionary activism and life-laying-down submissive love' (p. 85). Mitchell acknowledges a 'counterpolitical' stream of 'kenarchy', the 'emptying out' of sovereign power, that bore witness to the radical alternative throughout the history of ecclesial sovereignty and empire. He cites such figures as Irenaeus (who was 'eirenic'), St Francis, and William Penn and the 'Diggers', who challenged the sovereign claim to private ownership of land in favour of a communitarian approach for the benefit of the expropriated poor (pp. 55-6).

Drawing on Hardt and Negri's study *Empire*, Jennifer Buck makes a comparable point: 'Early Christians were generally an anti-imperial force and created a movement to oppose or escape from power. Christianity today can serve similarly to protest ... Their challenge is for the church to better understand love as a political concept' (2016, p. 8). In a similar manner, Graham Ward argues that 'discipleship is political because it is implicated in a messianic reversal of established values and in a challenge to received authorities and principalities' (2009, p. 284). The links between the political, ecclesial and spiritual domains in Christian movements that have manifested elements of the counter-political vision are brought out by Troxell (2012, p. 5) who names numerous historical examples including the early Franciscans, the Radical Reformation, the Catholic Worker movement, Thomas Merton's social criticism, liberation theology, the peace protests of the Berrigan brothers, and the role of Christian theology in the Civil Rights Movement.

Political reflections like these underpin the idea of the Church as an 'institutional an-archy' (G. Hasenhüttl, cit. Jeanrond, 1999, p. 95).

Historically, however, anarchy as a political (or anti-political) movement tended to be atheistic. The Russian anarchist Mikhail Bakunin
(1814–1876) despised Christianity as the most absolute manifestation
of religion as *archē* (Greek αρχή), in the sense of rule, governance, or
authority (Guérin, ed., 2005). Since classical Christian theology has
relied heavily on the notion of the *archē* as the fundamental source and
origin and the guarantor of order, the denial of *archē* in the atheistic
assertion of anarchy can well be understood. Bakunin saw the Church
as the instrument of institutional maintenance of Christian domination,
culpable of tyranny and oppression, stifling human flourishing and keeping people in infantile dependency through its assertion of Lordship.

Nevertheless, traditions of Christian anarchism grew up alongside the
atheistic movements, most notably perhaps in the work of Leo Tolstoy
(1828–1910). Not surprisingly, Christian anarchists largely rejected the
institutional Church as an authoritarian corruption of the original message
of Jesus. They saw in his teachings the seeds of an anarchist stance in the
Christian faith, that is, a rejection of all earthly governments in favour
of the radical new order of the Kingdom of God (Christoyannopoulos,
2010). Jacques Ellul writes that 'for Christian anarchists, the goal of anarchy is "theonomy", the rule, the ordering, the αρχή of God' (2011, p. 78).
Christoyannopoulos argues that Christian anarchism commutes the
political ideology of anarchism into an ecclesial one: although Christian
anarchists are highly critical of the state as empire, they 'do not favour
any overthrow of the government ... simply living in ... a decentralized
community is a political statement ... the very existence of the church
is, in itself, a political statement' (2010, pp. 207, 225). In an extensive
treatment of both political and theological anarchism, Hugh Rock (2014,
chapters 10 and 11) refers to 'the Christian practice of the authority of
no authority', which is quite close to the notion of 'ecclesianarchy', and
which he illustrates from the practice of the Quakers (2014, pp. 303–12).

In the postmodern environment, the conditions are more hospitable to
a new rapprochement between anarchism and the Church: I have coined
the term 'ecclesianarchy' to denote this emergent ecclesiality. It remains
a massive question whether the churches can forsake their reliance on
models of power, authority and social organization derived from the
secular institutional and political structures within which they have
evolved, and under which they have enjoyed influence and prestige in
both pre-modern and modern times. This requires a courageous hospitality towards dissent; as Gerald Arbuckle puts it:

> Organisations, the Church included, are built to administer, maintain
> and protect from harm that which already exists; in contrast, creative

or dissenting people are designed to give birth to that which has never been in existence before. Thus dissenters threaten the well-oiled structures ... The alternatives they propose are seen as chaotic, something to be avoided by those taking comfort in the predictable and safe ways of tradition. (1993, p. 1)

Conventionally, 'chaos' equals 'something to be avoided'; whereas under the conditions of anarchic church, chaos needs to be retrieved as a moment of creative possibility. In the rest of this chapter, we will take some soundings in the literature of postmodern church to explore this question further. The task will be to identify some of the elements of ecclesial praxis in which such non-imperial aspirations might be enacted, focusing on what I have called dispossessive [anti]structures, dispersed leadership, decentred worship, and dis-illusioned ecclesiality.

Deconstructive church

Dispossessive [anti]structures

According to the biographical detail at the front of his *How (Not) to Speak of God* (Rollins, 2006), the Ikon community in Belfast describes itself as 'apocalyptic, heretical, emerging and failing'. Here is how Rollins depicts what takes place at Ikon's regular events:

I am referring to the formation of passionate, provocative gatherings, operating on the fringes of religious life, that offer *anarchic* [emphasis mine] experiments in theodrama that re-imagine the distinction between Christian and non-Christian, priest and prophet, doubt and certainty, the sacred and the secular – gatherings that employ a rich cocktail of music, poetry, prose, imagery, soundscapes, theatre, ritual, and reflection: gatherings that provide a place that is open to all, is colonized by none, and that celebrates diversity. (2008a, p. 176)

This is not so much 'a church' as an experiment in 'ecclesiality'; it is 'church' deconstructed into a never-twice-alike 'Happening' (p. 184). I am not suggesting that the future lies in all churches becoming like Ikon, but that something is captured here from which the inherited denominational churches need to learn. As Caputo puts it:

An institution modelled *after* deconstruction would be auto-deconstructive, self-correcting, removed as far as possible from the power games and rigid inflexibility of institutional life, where a minimal institutional architecture pushes to some optimal point, near but not all the way to *anarchy* [emphasis mine], some point of creative 'chaosmos'. (2007, p. 137)

I have indicated in these passages where Rollins and Caputo both introduce the concept of 'anarchy' in relation to church. Caputo's *chaosmos* is a typically postmodern piece of word-play that insists on putting the opposites together, and it foregrounds something vital for a postmodern ecclesiality and an adaptive ministry. Church always lives from and negotiates the 'edge of chaos', as Moynagh (2017) has it. Terms like 'anarchy', 'auto-deconstructive' and 'chaosmos' signal a kind of centrifugal pushing back of control away from the supposed 'centre' in order to make room for the unpredictable and the spontaneous. The postmodern ecclesiality is 'dispossessive', as 'possession' of the praxis of church is consistently rebutted to deny hierarchy and centralization, so that 'structure' gives way to 'anti-structure'.

Gibbs and Coffey (2001) describe the emerging Church as realized through networks rather than hierarchies, leading to flattened organizational structures and authority based on relationships rather than status. There is a culture of permission-giving rather than 'rules and regulations' that inhibit imaginative action: 'permission-givers … are prepared to give unlikely ideas a try and allow individuals to take responsibility for their implementation' (p. 87). People are practically equipped and personally empowered for their roles and responsibilities, within which 'each team has its own social dynamic, a "chemistry" that not only makes it work but creates a fulfilling and joyful experience for the participants' (p. 90).

For the Anabaptist writer Stuart Murray, whose work we drew upon in the Introduction, the deconstruction of the Church at the very least means simplification: the centuries of Christendom have made church woefully complicated. 'The transition from institution to movement, from the centre to the margins, means discarding baggage and retaining only what we need to sustain worshipping missionary communities' (2004, p. 275). The reimagined Church will be reinterpreted along the lines of a 'monastic missionary order' (p. 279) and a 'safe place to take risks' (p. 280), travelling light enough to be able to cope with experiments that don't succeed, and the facility to change tack at short notice. Abandoning the clergy/laity divide will help the Church to recover friendship: 'non-hierarchical, holistic, relaxed and dynamic' (p. 275). 'Membership' will be a problematic concept; 'companions', 'fellow travellers', 'pilgrims' or, as the Quakers have it, 'a society of friends' might be closer to the mark. And if there is a touchstone for authenticity or even 'orthodoxy' and 'orthopraxis' it will be simple: just Jesus.

Dispersed leadership

In conversation with Phyllis Tickle, the American commentator on 'emerging church', Peter Rollins has some striking things to say about 'church' ('Phyllis Tickle and Peter Rollins discuss Emergence Christianity', www. youtube.com/watch?v=9sRsOhy_WWA, accessed 28/02/20). He advocates a 'doughnut' model, that is, there is a hole at the centre, constituted by what he calls a form of leadership that 'refuses to be a leader'. With characteristic provocation, he insists that the responsibility of church leadership in his community is to say 'we don't care about you': because the person who needs to care is the person alongside the one in need. Where the church is a non-hierarchical community, people are to care for each other. There is no option of running to the leadership with the cry, '*You* must care for me!'

The characteristics of leadership in emerging churches are identified in Gibbs and Bolger's research (2006), particularly in chapter 10, entitled 'Leading as a Body'. Ian Mobsby of London's 'Moot' community is quoted on the theological foundations of his position:

> It starts with an understanding of the Trinity ... There is no hierarchy. We are attempting to model this Trinitarian understanding by having an active community approach that empowers all to have a voice, to help make decisions, and also a fluid community that people are free to leave or join. (Gibbs and Bolger, 2006, p. 194; see also Mobsby, 2007)

Mobsby's leadership is not exercised in taking services, which are 'run by different people every time' (p. 194), nor in making decisions, which is a collective task. He sees his leadership roles as 'to help keep the community healthy, to be a pastor for prayer and pastoral needs, to be a mediator when things go wrong, and to be custodian to a vision to keep the group journeying together' (p. 212). Karen Ward of the Church of the Apostles in Seattle explains that 'we have no up-front leader ... no presiding priest, no big pastor'; her role is more that of 'a curator' (as in a gallery or exhibition) than 'the moderator of an assembly' (pp. 164–5).

Gibbs and Coffey observe that 'leadership in a network is precarious because the authority of the leader can be challenged at any time' (2001, p. 85). There is a decentralization away from the focus always being on the designated leaders, coupled with a mutual accountability: 'healthy networks are concerned not with control but with empowerment' (pp. 91–2). Although in many places, leadership models have moved on from 'one-man band' to 'conductor of the orchestra', this can still risk becoming 'a controlling model of leadership'. Gibbs and Coffey think that a more radical analogy would be the leader of a jazz band:

The skill of the conductor is in the area of creative interpretation [i.e. of the score], while that of the jazz-band leader is in facilitating creative improvisation by every member of the group. Each performance is different, creating a serendipitous experience as each performer makes a free-spirited contribution, while at the same time being at one with others in the group. (2001, pp. 110–11)

The jazz analogy is also employed by Buschart and Eilers (2015, pp. 233 ff.), who see improvisational performance in jazz as a model for holding the 'tension between transformation and identity' required of contemporary Christian performance of the faith: 'The inherent dynamism in jazz improvisation allows performers the freedom to supplement, develop and even transform a piece of music, but always within the constraints that maintain the piece's identity' (p. 236). They apply the analogy to John Milbank's concept of renarrating Christianity through the ongoing performances of the Church through ever new iterations ('non-identical repetition', as Catherine Pickstock puts it). The idea of performance leads us directly to the consideration of worship in this perspective.

Decentred worship

It is apt that Jonny Baker of London's Grace Community entitles his book *Curating Worship*, since the book itself is a noteworthy example of 'curating' by Baker, being a collection of interviews and conversations with 'alternative worship' practitioners that together create a rich tapestry of insights into the 'curator' approach to worship design:

If it has been done well, it is a space that can be navigated seamlessly and visitors can immerse themselves in it without giving a second thought to the curator ... A worship curator makes a context and a frame for worship, arranging elements in it. The content is provided by other people. (2010, pp. xiii–xiv; for a host of examples, see also Pierson, 2012)

The challenges of 'curatorship' of worship in a contemporary environment, especially where the congregation is increasingly drawn from the 'post-church' generations, are not restricted to the more radically experimental alternative worship communities. They are faced acutely by the denominational churches within the Fresh Expressions movement, and indeed in the context of traditional local churches too, where ministers are working hard to introduce a new generation of unchurched households to the life and worship of the Church.

As we saw in Chapter 5, the Anglican liturgist Mark Earey has addressed these issues (Earey, 2013). His pastoral experience has convinced him that what he calls the 'operating system' of the Church (the framework of canon law for the regulation of worship) is now unsuited to the new 'software' (the more flexible approach that was intended to be brought in by the Church's *Common Worship* suite of liturgies at the beginning of the twenty-first century), and militates against getting the best out of the resources available. Accordingly, Earey argues for a radical change from a law-based 'bounded set' approach that prescribes what is permissible and polices the boundaries, to a 'centred set' approach setting out core liturgical principles, guidelines and benchmark texts, leaving churches and ministers (with the benefit of a good liturgical education) free to order worship as they will, within this broad framework. The new system would entail 'letting go of the idea of liturgical conformity as a core part of what makes a church or an act of worship Anglican', and replace a rules-based approach with one based on relationships, trust and account-ability (p. 140).

An approach to 'decentred worship' that both complements and extends the curatorship model is proposed by Pete Ward in the context of what he calls the 'liquid church' (2002, chapter 10), demonstrating affinities with the testimony of several of the leaders in Gibbs and Bolger's work. His examples include a labyrinth in St Paul's Cathedral, a multi-activity act of worship at Greenbelt and an experience of Greek Orthodox worship while on holiday. Ward's vision of worship also extends to the decentral-ized 'network' church that fosters a multiplicity of nodes of connectivity that join people together, not only by acts of worship, but also by commit-ment to particular forms of social action, social media communications, special interest groups, creative activities and so on. He illustrates:

> Community would evolve around what people find interesting, attrac-tive or compelling. A good example would be a spirituality based on the environment. Liquid church might begin to explore the idea of prayer walks or spiritual journeys. Groups might begin to find ways to connect prayer life to walking activities. It might be possible to take people on activities that combine meditation and mountain climbing. Another, less athletic, idea might be a guided stroll along a river or stream with places to stop, pray and read the Bible. (2002, pp. 89–90)

I had a surprising encounter with something like Ward's 'liquid' model a few years ago when visiting an ancient and beautiful abbey, entering the building to discover a broad and expansive, flexible space: at the centre a labyrinth, with people making their way around, lighting candles and meditating at stations along the way; at one end a cafe with comfy sofas and armchairs and a supply of devotional books and magazines; at one side a row of pews, in which three men were seated, two with their arms around the shoulders of the third with whom they were quietly praying. Provisionality and impermanence often characterize such worship: for Kester Brewin, 'worship and liturgy are acts of "spiritual cartography", a process of mapmaking which should be dispensed with when the map no longer marks the cultural landscape' (Steele, 2017, p. 160). Brewin terminated the alternative church Vaux in 2008, in preference for the idea of 'pop-up churches', more able to respond swiftly to circumstances (Moody, 2015, p. 22).

At the most radical end of the spectrum, Pete Rollins describes gatherings for worship as 'transformance art', performances that are designed to unmask and deconstruct any residues of purely conventional, inherited religious belief and practice in favour of a profound disorientation, 'spaces that make sense to *nobody* … that rupture everyone and cause us all to rethink' (2008a, p. 174). Transformance art is performed within a 'theo-dramatic space' that Rollins describes as 'immersive', able to facilitate profound collective reflection. Here 'individuals can lay aside political, religious and social identities' in 'creative, ritualistic acts' that are able to conjure up the spirit of 'the event housed within the religion without religion that is Christianity' (p. 176). Authentic Christianity is 'housed within' the accumulated layers of its outer institutional forms, and this 'event' is *not* 'religion' as conventionally understood. Here we come closest to the deconstructive model that resonates with Caputo's approach to theology discussed in Chapter 9, and to worship as a symbolic enactment of the impossible. This brings us finally to the impossibility that lies at the heart of ecclesiality itself.

Dis-illusioned ecclesiality

Caputo offers a portrait of what he calls a 'working church' *in extremis*, drawn from the *Diary of a City Priest* by Catholic priest John McNamee, ministering in a run-down ghetto area of Philadelphia (Caputo, 2007, chapter 6). The situation is repeatedly described as 'impossible': both the neighbourhood itself and the condition of McNamee's life within it. Ministry there is almost devoid of the trappings of 'conventional' church, even down to the absence of any viable Catholic congregation. McNamee sees a grotesque disconnect between what 'church' means as traditionally understood, and what actually goes on in his parish. There is the 'big Church', the 'bureaucratic Church', or hierarchy; and there is his 'working church', making it up as it goes along, managing crises, picking up life's rejects, enduring constant disappointment, confronting institutional inertia, salvaging urban wreckage.

McNamee's is still 'inherited Church': a Catholic parish, albeit one that rational calculation would provide the authorities with absolutely no reason not to close down. Faced with such an impossible situation, McNamee reminds himself that 'the gospel is not a set of doctrines but a way of life ... the one where truth means *facere veritatem*, making the truth happen' (Caputo, 2007, p. 124). Amid the ever-present reality of doubt there are moments of profound love, a moral passion that generates awe; he sees it in the devotion of a little Irish nun in the slums, 'the unspeakable, unintelligible cruelty of existence along with some pulsating event of love and mercy ... What must be believed cannot be believed – that is the mystery we call God' (p. 123). In this church, the typical prayer is that of the dying Jesus: *eloi, eloi, lama sabachthani*: 'a perfectly auto-deconstructing prayer: it is addressed to God – which presupposes our faith that we are not abandoned – and asks why God has abandoned us'.

Such experiences of ministry do things to the minister's intimations of God, as Peter Owen-Jones confesses: 'the God I now know is quite different from the one I started with. I'm not quite sure who has changed ... The God I have met has forced me to confront my own pain' (1996, p. 187). There is a message here for many a declining, depressed and ageing church, and for clergy who may respond to bright ideas about transformative new expressions of church with a weary sigh, an ironic smile or a muttered expletive. In becoming increasingly 'disillusioned', or disappointed with the Church as it is, there is a potential to be 'dis-illusioned', that is, to be divested of all illusion about 'ideal churches' that others might promote as the benchmarks of a successful ministry. Caputo says that the least promising environment for the Church gives a special priority to the Feast of St Thomas the Doubter: 'in a situation like this, faith is impossible, *the* impossible: one is called on to have faith in a world in which it is impossible to believe anything' (2007, p. 121). In this context, a surplus of 'official ecclesiology' would be a burden too far, just too much to make oneself believe in.

By contrast, Rollins's Ikon Community in Belfast is far more self-consciously a radical experiment in postmodernity: 'a concrete, community-based, practical, and para-liturgical undertaking, less interested in theology than in "theo-drama"' (Caputo, 2007, p. 131). Its multi-media, avant-garde liturgical/ritual happenings are designed to subvert all attempts to subsume Ikon within the category of ecclesiality understood as institution, guardian of orthodoxy, moral authority or ministerial order. But it creates *intentionally* what McNamee comes to by the sheer force of what *happens* to him: the realization that 'theology is idolatry if it means what we say about God instead of letting ourselves be addressed by what God has to say to us ... Faith is idolatrous if it is rigidly self-certain but not if it is softened in the waters of "doubt"' (p. 131).

Ecclesial reconstruction

It is in the interests of the cause of Jesus and the Kingdom of God that we must be disabused of our notions of church in order to be able to see what is required in a new era. Such deconstruction does not ruin and destroy but strips back to the foundations and retrieves valuable elements from the long history of the Church for co-option into eclectic new forms. This in essence is the approach of Doug Gay (2011) in his constructive proposal for 'remixing' the Church. The 'remix' is a familiar part of today's popular music culture, creating new versions of familiar songs by importing samples from other works, adding alternative beats and rhythms, repeating some passages and reducing others to only a word, a phrase or a few bars. For Gay, 'remixing' is the final stage of a process in which the 'emerging church' is engaged.

It begins with 'auditing', taking stock of where we are now as church, our strengths and weaknesses, opportunities and challenges. The next step is 'retrieving', scouring the inherited traditions to see what we need to rediscover from times past to help resource contemporary renewal. This requires 'unbundling', the complex process by which we attempt to disentangle what we actually need from the ecclesiastical parapher-nalia with which it has become bound up over time. We then add new contributions drawn from a wide range of cultural sources in an act of 'supplementing'; and finally, in what Gay calls 'bringing it all back home', a distinctive 'remixing' of church takes place.

Gay offers six indicators of authentic church practice for emergent ecclesialities, or what he terms 'Church Pragmatics' (2011, pp. 108–20). The emerging Church will be a pilgrim Church of disciples: the heart of church is never anything other than 'following Jesus', walking in the Way, which implies generosity of spirit, inclusive hospitality and breadth of vision. It will be a richly storied, richly memoried Church: not appro-priating one particular historical period as normative, but celebrating the deep wisdom of the saints through the ages for our benefit. It will be a Church apostolic and catholic: not insisting on a narrowly denominational definition of church order, but validating all that bears the marks of mission and fundamental ecclesial character. It will be a liturgically ver-satile Church: forsaking the stranglehold of churchmanship traditions and cultural prejudices for a creative mixing of musical styles and media, genres and voices, images and stories. It will also be a mission-shaped Church: not 'confronting' the world, but embracing a 'narrative practice' of the gospel in 'worship, preaching, evangelism, pastoral care and prophetic action' (p. 117); and a political-prophetic Church: in the 'unbundling' of Christendom, rediscovering and resourcing the counter-cultural dynamic of Christianity (p. 119).

This is 'ecclesianarchy' brought within a creative, critical and reflective framework that restrains the flight to the extreme and co-opts diversity to the cause of a new, post-denominational type of 'born-again ecumenism' (Gay, 2011, p. 107). Ecclesial reconstruction cannot only be the domain of the outlandish and the experimental, of the churches that style themselves 'emerging' or 'emergent' and (certainly in the case of Rollins) want to maintain a very clear distance indeed from 'inherited Church'. Nevertheless, without the willingness to embrace a measure of ecclesianarchy, remixing cannot be done, and once this step is taken, there is no going back to the securities of before. I will end therefore by pointing to some examples of alternative approaches to church that belong neither to the 'emerging churches' movement, nor to the Fresh Expressions initiative within the denominational churches.

The first is Chris Baker's concept of the 'hybrid church' that develops from his engagement with 'third space' theory. We have already drawn on his work in Chapter 1 as a stimulating example of fresh thinking in the context of emerging postmodernity, and here we return to it as an expression of church as ecclesianarchy. Baker sees the church operating across a number of liminal spaces between boundaries:

> ... between the local and the global ... the explicit and the implicit ... the solid and the liquid. This blurring of the boundaries emerges from a growing recognition of the need to adopt flexible, multi-disciplinary and partnership-based approaches within increasingly contested, rapidly changing and polarized spaces, and to achieve solutions that work in the absence of overarching methodologies or ideologies. (2009, p. 132)

Baker's model is about (principally urban) churches reconnecting with localities and communities in ways that *begin* from analyses of local economic, social and political configurations rather than from a 'given' gospel that waits to be better communicated. Such churches seek to embody an emergent 'third space theology', which Baker (chapter 7) suggests will involve at least six main strands.

First, 'a theology of blurred encounters': the church facilitates engagement with 'the Other', but in ways that raise questions for the churches, faced with a radical uncertainty, as much as they provide 'answers' to those seeking a deeper meaning to daily practicalities and challenges. In a similar way, a 'risky hospitality' (one of the 'impossible' things derived from Derrida that were explored in Chapter 9) may enable everyone to 'eat well', but also place the host in danger of 'being eaten'. Less controversially perhaps, 'catholicity' will be understood in terms of 'inculturation' (see Heard, 2013) and Christology will draw on post-colonial insights (Lartey, 2013). There will be a theology of creation that underpins a social ethic drawing on post-liberal, multi-disciplinary perspectives, and 'a Pentecostal theology that stresses the importance of difference and diversity as signs of the kingdom' (p. 137). Each of these interwoven strands carries implications for the knowledge bases, skill sets and personal qualities required by ministers, and points to a recognition of the need for specialisms.

As a second example rooted in practice, the contributors to a collection of essays on social regeneration and the role of the churches in the 'Greenwich peninsula' area of south London (Torry, ed., 2007) furnish a wealth of fascinating, occasionally depressing, often hopeful and sometimes moving insights into local communities and churches that have been battered and bruised by urban decline. They have suffered the stop-start pattern of changing political initiatives, funding crises, failed projects and local factional in-fighting, and yet have retained the imagination and determination to fashion a more hopeful future. Jeremy Fraser writes pungently of the frustrations of local politics and the mistrust of local people in Peckham, concluding that although 'regeneration might be a buzz word created by lazy bureaucrats', the churches 'can make it into something good for our communities' (p. 18). Martin Clark describes how a run-down parish church, marooned amid a sea of demolition and squalor as an entire estate was pulled down and rebuilt around it, has now been transformed and refurbished in an act of 'redeeming sacred space' (pp. 93–103). Sue Hutson gives an account of her work with churches in Southwark to establish projects that serve the local community: 'where regeneration brings in massive housing developments, large offices and the like, the church may be the only organization that offers opportunity and space for the human needs of a community. A touching place' (p. 153).

Finally, Kester Brewin (2000) proposes an ecclesiology of 'Temporary Autonomous Zones' that has affinities with the notions of 'adaptive ministry' and 'ecclesianarchy' promoted in this book. These zones are a kind of 'pop-up church' occupying a particular space in a locality for a time, where new ideas can be explored in a free, open and non-judging way, similar to Rollins's 'suspended space' (Marti and Ganiel, 2014, p. 154). Elsewhere, Brewin has used the images of 'pirates' (as 'heretics') and 'carnival' (a liminal space) to symbolize the subversion of normal rules of social engagement in the interests of achieving a glimpse of a kind of utopia. He writes of a 'nomadic ecclesiology', always on the move, with no permanent resting place, which differs from a 'pilgrim church' model, where the journey is shaped by a known destination (Steele, 2017, p. 162). Katharine Sarah Moody cites Brewin's striking idea of 'church' as a place where people can 'do their dirt[y] work', engaging the idea of 'decay', 'practices in which belief and identity are broken down in order to "open them up for re-use"' (Moody, 2017, pp. 206–7). The model of 'church' as an agency to reconnect people with the transformative reality of death and decay seems yet another guise of the 'impossible'.

Marti and Ganiel capture well the dilemma built into the position of innovators like Brewin: 'emerging Christians are somewhat unique institutional entrepreneurs, in that one of their primary purposes is to resist the institutionalization of their faith rather than to reform or create new institutions' (Marti and Ganiel, 2014, p. 8). Therefore, emerging churches are *relatively coherent* yet *haphazardly organised*; they are 'deliberately *messy*' (p. 30; all emphases in original). Brewin issues a warning directed at initiatives like Fresh Expressions that unleash radical possibilities but stop short of pursuing their implications:

> My problem with many of these 'Emerging Church' projects is that they are still attempting to bring church up to date by 'trainspotting' some aspects of culture and making church fit it. I want to argue that in the 'Emerging Church' the emphasis will be on being the train, rather than trainspotting; rather than trying to import culture into the church and making it 'cool', we need instead to become 'wombs of the divine' and completely rebirth the Church into a host culture. (Brewin, 2004, *The Complex Christ*, cit. Mobsby, 2007, p. 28)

It is easy to be critical of these experimental forms of church from an inherited ecclesiological perspective; but the fragility, risk and susceptibility to wrong turns that such temporary ecclesial arrangements may suffer from are arguably compelling features of 'authentic church'. 'Ecclesianarchy' is not tidy; but genuine innovation rarely is.

From a sociological perspective, David Martin offers an assessment of new movements 'from the margins' which should offer those struggling with the ungainliness and unpredictability of a new church project some encouragement:

> The dialectic continues … it relates to the Christian repertoire and the adaptation of its images to new worldly contexts, above all power.

The key elements in that repertoire concern the radical reversals of the kingdom, the identification of the divine with powerlessness in the Incarnation, and the reversal of Babel in the universal speech of Pentecost. All of these encounter the inherent character of human society, necessarily based on authority and power, as well as based on a solidarity against 'the other'. So the *logic* of Christianity, exemplified in its repertoire of images, encounters the *logic* of social organization. It simultaneously adapts to it and infiltrates it with contrary imaginations. (2005, p. 11)

For Martin, the disruptive and subversive impulses of Christianity repeatedly butt up against the social constructs of power, resulting in an apparent capitulation in which the latent revolutionary potential of the faith lies dormant. It awaits the time when the processes of social and cultural change once more open up channels through which the transformative Spirit can flow; but when this occurs, Christianity may well need to shed accoutrements and adornments seen by many as sacred and changeless. As Peter Rollins (2008a) insists, 'betrayal' is a necessary movement of Christian fidelity, and this applies as much to ecclesiology as to any other branch of Christian theology and practice. An 'ecclesianarchy' represents the necessary betrayal of the Church of Christendom for the sake of the Church of the future, which faces an impossible situation, as it always must if it is to retain its Gospel authenticity.

Conclusion

This chapter has argued for de/reconstructive church as an ecclesianarchy that abandons models based on empire, hierarchy and control in favour of a radical emptying of institutional presence and a dispersal (or retrieval) of spiritual energies through and among the people who constitute its reality. The inner logic of all of the strategies for renewal examined in this book points in this direction: collaborative ministry deconstructs hierarchical ministerial order and challenges the lay/clergy divide; Pentecostal influence elevates the unpredictable spontaneity of the Spirit above official authority and formal structure; chaplaincy in a less conspicuous way subtly pushes at all the boundaries within which inherited local church ministries are confined; and fresh expressions at their most vital produce new wine that struggles to be contained within the old wineskins of traditional priestly ministry, parish and diocese.

At the same time, an ecclesianarchy is emphatically *not* in itself one variety of avant-garde, alternative church in the manner of Rollins's Ikon collective. This book is not arguing for the replacement of the Church of England, or any denominational church, by some other more fashionable model. Rather, what matters is the recognition by the historic churches that they do not have a monopoly on 'correct' ecclesiology. They cannot therefore continue to see themselves as a 'norm' to which temporary experimental ecclesial communities will eventually have to conform. Using just worship as an example: by all means let there be cathedrals with choirs, Anglo-Catholic shrines with incense and Benediction, neo-Puritan conventicles prioritizing solemn biblical preaching, charismatic celebrations with singing in tongues and prayers for healing, lively family Eucharists with traditional hymns for the old and action songs for the children, early morning devotional communions according to the Book of Common Prayer, stripped-down chaotic informal gatherings on unchurched estates and much else besides. The models, structures and expressions of ministry pertinent to each of these will look very different, and the churches will need to recognize, affirm and embrace the adaptability this demands, unfettered by a surfeit of dysfunctional ecclesiology and ministerial theology.

The remaining two chapters will consider some of the implications of all this for the training and support of those in forms of publicly recognized or authorized ministry.

11

Stirring Up the Gift: On Being Formed for Christian Ministry

In these final two chapters, attention turns to how the training and ongoing support of ministers might facilitate the more flexible, adaptive approach demanded by the emerging new types of church. This chapter focuses on ministerial education, and in keeping with the historical approach to the contested nature of ministerial order and theology taken in Chapter 2, appropriate models and methods for the present social and cultural climate are set in the broader context of those from earlier times. Earlier versions of some of the material in this chapter were previously published in Williams (2010) and Williams (2013).

Historical models for ministerial formation

The primitive Church: charisma, apprenticeship and catechesis

In the earliest days of the Church, ministry flowed from charisma and could be validated in a simple act of recognition: as Paul is represented as advising his young protégé Timothy, 'stir up the gift of God that is within you through the laying on of my hands' (2 Tim. 1.6). The relationship between Paul and Timothy suggests an 'apprenticeship' model in which a junior Christian would 'sit at the feet of', and learn to imitate, a senior practitioner. This pattern, common in the philosophical schools of antiquity, is not so very far removed from the model of Anglican curacy into relatively recent times. The format of recognition of charisma, plus apprenticeship, is perhaps most closely replicated today in the new and independent Pentecostal communities that reject more formalized processes of 'ordination' in favour of a strong reliance upon the role modelling of charismatic leaders (see Viola, 2008, chapter 12 and the Appendix).

Intellectually, education for ministry in the early centuries was driven by the ongoing battles against heresies within the Church, and the demands of mission to other faiths beyond it, both signalling the need for sound catechetical instruction of converts (Rowdon, 1971). Catechists needed to be able to draw on the tradition, using selected texts from the Fathers, in order to demonstrate how issues facing the Church, including debates about belief, had been settled earlier. This approach guards against a 'democratization' of belief in local churches, where influential lay people might promote beliefs that do not accord with orthodox teaching, because they are not sufficiently immersed in the tradition. This is essentially the model still preferred by conservative commentators such as Edward Norman:

> The guiding principle of preparation for ordination should be the acquisition of a known body of Christian teaching, in order to transmit it faithfully; and not a process of self-discovery in the course of which merely human sensation will direct priorities and substances. Priests are not called upon to determine the veracity of the doctrines upheld by the Church, but to teach them. (2002, p. 131)

Doubtless with this kind of position in mind, Percy observes that 'many who teach in the church ... are trained and formed in an environment that assumes that the task of education is to implant (correct) knowledge in those contexts where they minister' (2005, p. 90). Although this may make sense in an environment where 'revealed' and 'eternal' truth, or even the 'infallibility' of the teaching office or the Scriptures, are upheld, under the conditions of late modernity this currency is devalued, and ill-suited for preparing ministers to engage with it.

The Middle Ages: a monastic model and a classical education

In the so-called 'Dark Ages' that followed the fall of the Roman Empire, it was 'hardly surprising that Christian instruction and training found refuge in the seclusion and relative safety of the monasteries' (Rowdon, 1971, p. 77). A monastic template for ministerial education has been enormously influential ever since, continuing to the present day in the disciplines of life practised and encouraged by residential theological colleges and seminaries. But the development across Europe of the universities, starting in Bologna in 1088, offered the Church a more prestigious alternative to monastic education. Universities aimed to provide a classical education to prepare men for the professions, within which theology took a central and foundational role alongside such disciplines as law and medicine. As an academic subject, theology would cultivate *phronesis*, the 'practical wisdom for living' that Aristotle saw as the ultimate goal of education (Toulmin, 1996, p. 395).

The significance of this Renaissance university model for today is that in an era when rationalistic assumptions are giving way to the more indeterminate (quantum) logic of postmodernity, the discipline of theology can sustain 'critical being', a more holistic concept than the Enlightenment rationalist model of 'critical thinking' (Barnett, 1997, p. 48). Theology asks questions about the 'interrelatedness of things', and seeks to hold together disciplines the later development of scientific method has split apart (Toulmin, 1996, p. 403). The combination of the classical and the monastic in ministerial formation, emphasizing the virtues of character, sound knowledge and holy wisdom, is a model that enjoys renewed advocacy at the present time, for example in the work of Jeremy Worthen (2012) on Christian formation.

Worthen proposes a threefold framework of 'primary', 'reflective' and 'academic' theology. 'Primary' theology corresponds to the implicit or 'inhabited' theology that comes from sustained practice, and is the normal mode of theology for most lay people most of the time. However, many will shift from primary theology into 'reflective' mode when circumstances give rise to questions that their primary theology seems inadequate to address. A small minority will engage directly with academic theology, especially those training for ministry. While prioritizing the study of academic theology, they need to anchor this in a practice of theological reflection that leads back to the enrichment of their 'primary' theology (Worthen, 2012, pp. 134–5). Significantly, for all, 'formation in understanding ... requires us to welcome companionship and collaboration' (p. 140).

In an increasingly post-church environment, the place of academic theology within Worthen's framework will require some adjustment, as more candidates for authorized ministries come forward from unchurched backgrounds, often lacking even a rudimentary knowledge of the Christian past and the main contours of its theological traditions. In this situation, students will need to explore their personal, implicit theologies, and develop the skills of practical, contextual reflection prior to being plunged into formal academic theology. In this way, they will learn how they are already actually *doing* theology, and how it is relevant to their experience, before they discover how to use the historical archive as a resource. As we shall see, the relationship between academic theological education and practical ministerial training has been a source of (not always creative) tension in modern times.

The post-Reformation era: a graduate gentleman or a biblical teacher

The post-Reformation era saw theological and ministerial education for the established churches devolved almost entirely to the universities (in England this meant only Oxford and Cambridge). However, the education acquired was by no means theologically substantial, or ministerially specific. The French historian Halévy wrote in his *England in 1815*:

> England was probably the sole country in Christendom where no proof of theological knowledge was required from candidates for ordination ... at Oxford, theology was reduced to one single question asked of all candidates for examination. At Cambridge no theology whatsoever entered into any of the examinations for a degree. The entrance examination once passed ... students who were not the eldest sons of gentle families, and did not possess sufficient industry or capacity to face more difficult examinations, could proceed without further delay to the clerical status. (Halévy, cit. Rowdon, 1971, p. 82)

The profile of this model is readily recognizable in the clergy who appear in the novels of Jane Austen. Judith Maltby has noted that the university culture had little to do with theological education, and everything to do with forming the clergy as properly groomed members of the gentlemanly classes: 'a graduate priesthood was presented by the authorities as a favourable contrast to the poorly educated, or so it was thought, dissenting clergy' (2005, p. 12). The 'gentlemanly amateur' quality of the Anglican clergy, at ease in society and untroubled by abstruse theological niceties, had still not entirely disappeared as recently as the late twentieth century. As a Clergy Training Officer in the early 1990s, I visited most of the clergy in my 'patch', covering a large part of the Yorkshire Wolds and coast. A surprising number of villages still retained their own parsonage and resident incumbent, a few of whom had been in post for a very long time and continued to embody exactly this model of ministry.

The alternative offered by those churches that emerged from the Reformation in the cause of non-conformity was to develop a form of theological education that placed enormous emphasis on the *teaching* role of ministers, and specifically on the exposition of the Bible. Denominational colleges were set up that could create their own curriculum to facilitate this, a model adopted later by the Evangelical movement within the Church of England. Referring to the 'Reform' group within the Church, Martyn Percy depicts its character as 'a kind of clear, plain, morally certain and pedagogically cerebral Christianity' with 'little scope for ambiguity or difference, for the Bible is held to be clear on all matters of importance ... "Trust and Obey" – there is no other way' (2005, p. 186).

The practical theologian Johannes van der Ven considers that this Protestant 'kerygmatic' model of Christian pedagogy proved unsuitable for an emerging modern era (1998, p. 46), in retaining the ideological construct of a dominant Church, based on a medieval template (p. 89). A new model, rooted in processes of practical theological reflection, would be required; but before getting to that, there is more of the story to tell.

Revival and the return of charisma: the Wesleyan model

The programme for training lay preachers initiated by John Wesley harked back to the more primitive 'charismatic' models. It pioneered a form of 'on the job' training, designed to recognize personal call and gifting, even in untutored men who could never have gone to university. They were enabled to fulfil their ministerial potential through a combination of itinerant preaching and demanding prescribed study, allowing the one to resource and reflect back upon the other. Wesley was deeply influenced by the continental Pietist tradition he encountered in the Moravian community at Aldersgate Street, with its model of academic learning as facilitating *Wiedergeburt*, 'new birth'. Learning is *convertative*, a good *in itself*; in terms of educational method, this requires friendship, collegiality and a conversational mode.

The Pietist/Wesleyan model commits to mutuality in the learning and teaching process: 'honest, constructive feedback given in love to assist one another in the "pursuit of perfection" is to be welcomed' (Nevins, 2015, p. 59). In more recent times, it has regained influence in innovative programmes of lay ministerial education (including in some places for evangelists), as well as in church-based programmes of Ordained Local Ministry training, where the practical/contextual and 'on the job' elements have been the distinguishing features. A mixed economy has developed, of residential theological colleges and these more practice-based, locally designed and delivered courses. Academic quality has been guaranteed by partnerships with the universities: but they have changed radically since their medieval origins, and this has led to a host of new challenges about the relationship between the academic and the formative dimensions of ministerial education.

Post-Enlightenment reactions: Athens and Berlin, scholarship and seminary

The foundation of the Humboldt University of Berlin in 1809 introduced a new concept of the 'Enlightenment university', dedicated to the advancement of knowledge through the testing and publication of scientific research. Whereas the medieval ('Athens') paradigm for the university drew on the ideals of a classical education from antiquity, the new 'Berlin' paradigm of *Wissenschaft* (scientific knowledge) 'accepts no authority other than that of autonomous reason and seeks the truth unhindered by dogma, tradition or institutional hierarchy' (Thiemann, 1991, p. 164; see also Kelsey, 1993). This created a problematic climate for theology, dethroned from its position as 'Queen of the sciences'; the Lutheran theologian Friedrich Schleiermacher, teaching at Berlin, addressed this in his new programme of theological education for ministry. He proposed a threefold curriculum dealing respectively with the philosophical foundations of belief, historical developments in doctrine, and the practical application of theology in Christian ministry. Later developments in ministerial education continue to owe much to the benefits and weaknesses of this formula.

In Britain in the nineteenth century, negotiations between bishops and the universities (Oxford and Cambridge were joined by Durham in 1832) succeeded in strengthening the academic theological requirements for ministerial education. However, as 'the study of theology at the older universities became more serious and scholarly ... it also became more academic and theoretical' (Rowdon, 1971, p. 82). The churches' response was to set up residential colleges that allowed Church institutions to assert control over the training of their ministers according to perceived needs, rather than in conformity to an academic paradigm. The colleges tended to be established on 'party' or denominational lines (Anglo-Catholic and Evangelical for Anglicans, Congregationalist or Presbyterian for non-conformity), and their ethos drew on the earlier monastic models for formation.

For a long time, the theological colleges were deeply suspect to Church authorities who feared they would destroy the character of the English parson: colleges would produce a type of priest 'who won't drink his glass of wine, and talk of his college, and put off for a few happy hours the sacred stiffness of the profession and simply become an English gentleman' (Trollope, *Clergymen of the Church of England*, cit. Maltby, 2005, p. 217). The Bishop of Oxford, Samuel Wilberforce, founded Ripon College, Cuddesdon in 1854 in part because he deplored in his clergy 'the want of clerical tone and of religious habits' (Hoyle, 2016, pp. 104–5).

He believed that a college for the formation of ministers would remedy these deficiencies. But before long he was dismayed to find that with their other-worldliness, ascetic devotional practices and distaste for earthly pleasures, the clergy it was producing were far too 'holy'.

In other words, theological colleges were suspected of promoting a 'hothouse' variety of rigorous spiritual training that would cast the clergy into a mould that would preclude the real human being from showing through. Melinsky claims that the colleges, while having 'the appearance of providing a liberal education', actually 'powerfully reinforced trad-itional attitudes and played down innovation' (1992, p. 254). The model produced 'an alien type of leadership', turning ministers into 'a profes-sional elite' and implicitly underscoring the alliance of the Church with the privileged classes (p. 255). In particular, the separation of academic learning from practical ministerial training by subcontracting the former to the universities was 'powerfully dissuasive of any systematic thinking about the practice of ministry and training appropriate to it'. In the present century, an attempt to remedy these deficiencies has been made by means of a fresh approach to the partnership with the universities and the rela-tionship between the academic and formational dimensions of learning.

Current theological models for ministerial education

Learning, habitus and communities of practice

The theologian Edward Farley proposed that theological education should be structured around three 'dimensions of redemption': *ecclesia*, the context in which it occurs; gospel, its origins and background, including its historical basis and philosophical substance; and faith, the mode of practice, including ethics, in which it is lived out (1988, pp. 137–8). Farley's threefold model is reminiscent of Schleiermacher, but more sophisticated in its treatment of practice, departing from the pattern in which theory is first learned and then applied. This reflects his concept of theology as *habitus*, defined as 'a state or disposition of the soul which has the character of knowledge' (Farley, 1983, p. 13); 'theology is a prac-tical, not theoretical, habit, having the primary character of wisdom' (Farley, 2003, p. 19). Theological education is properly structured as neither theory nor practice viewed as the poles of a dialectic, but better described as 'inhabited wisdom' that shapes and sustains the character of the person of faith.

This point may be amplified in the concept of performativity as devel-oped, for example, in the work of Stanley Hauerwas (2004). Any ultimate 'learning outcome' of Christian theological education must have to do with the formation of 'communities of practice' that more effectively perform the faith visibly and distinctively amid the world. The concept of communities of practice was developed by Wenger (1998), and demonstrates how learning takes place in the intersection of community (belonging), practice (doing), identity (becoming) and meaning (experience). For learning 'belongs to the realm of experience and practice. It follows the negotiation of meaning; it moves on its own terms. It slips through the cracks, and creates its own cracks. Learning happens, design or no design' (p. 225).

Contemporary theological education therefore requires the constructive provision of appropriate contexts for both individual and collective practical reflection. Doctrines are no longer the starting-point of theological learning, but emerge as the always provisional end point of a critical, experiential and participative reflection on faith praxis. This is why Edward Norman's lofty dismissal that it 'does not require group sessions in self-discovery to grasp doctrines which were known to the ancients' (2002, p. 131) is the exact opposite of the truth, which is well articulated by Jeff Astley:

> Theology is essentially reflective religious discourse: i.e. the rational, self-critical, coherent and systematic articulation of beliefs about religious entities ... But such scholarly pursuits are parasitic on *somebody* having his or her own theology: *doing theology* for themselves ... Doing theology for oneself may be encouraged, even evoked, by discovering what others think ... it may be argued that theology only really begins for people when they begin to face the questions 'What do *you* think? Who do *you* say that I am?' (1996, pp. 68–9)

Wherever academically accredited qualifications for authorized ministry are required, this model of theological education will raise questions about the choice of Higher Education partners, the design of the curriculum and its pedagogical methods, modes of assessment and academic oversight and support.

The Church and the academy

The kinds of issues discussed above influenced the Hind Report (Archbishops' Council of the Church of England, GS 1496, 2003) on ministerial formation in the Church of England, but its preoccupation with 'structure and funding' meant that educational models were not very extensively considered. This deficiency was addressed in the subsequent joint Church of England/Methodist/United Reformed Church report, *Shaping the Future: New Patterns of Training for Lay and Ordained* (Archbishops' Council of the Church of England, 2006), with a welcome broader remit including 'Education for Discipleship' for lay adults, Reader and lay preacher training, and Continuing Ministerial Education for clergy. Unfortunately, by this time it was too late to create a unified approach including the pre-ordination phase of Initial Ministerial Education as well, and these churches continue to suffer from a lack of coherence of training in this respect.

Under 'Training Specifications' (p. 38), the Reader/Local Preacher task group propose a threefold division of domains of learning, similar to 'Bloom's taxonomy' (Bloom, 1956, revised Anderson and Krathwohl, 2001) of 'cognitive', 'affective' and 'psycho-motor' skills, in the form of 'knowledge and understanding', 'conviction (spirituality)' and 'competence (skills)'. In 'Shaping the Curriculum' (p. 76), the Curriculum group proposes a different type of model, closer to the approach of Schleier-macher, based on dividing up the subject matter into the three fields of church, mission and practice; doctrine, history and tradition; and Scripture, hermeneutics and homiletics. Both models acknowledge that ministerial education is a complex entity in which (though differently expressed) there are at least three strands that need to be interwoven for learning to be effective, and both avoid cordoning off 'academic' learning into a protected enclave of its own.

Considerable controversy was unleashed in 2015 when the Church of England's report *Resourcing Ministerial Education* proposed to devolve decisions about training pathways for those recommended for ordination, together with the funding for them, to the dioceses (*Church Times*, 27 March 2015). Many academic theologians feared that this would result in a damaging deterioration in the theological quality of the clergy, as bishops would decide that many of those to be ordained did not need much formal academic theology for the practical purposes of ministry. Conversely, others (for example, David Heywood, in a letter to the *Church Times*, 2 April 2015) believed that the academics were merely defending their corner, and it was high time that a better way was found of integrating the theological dimension into ministerial formation on a model based on practical theological reflection within communities of practice.

To some extent, debates about the relationship between Church and academy were overtaken by the churches' Common Awards programme, introduced in 2014, which relies on a sole partnership with the University of Durham for its academic accreditation and quality oversight, with the

Church institutions (colleges and non-residential courses) responsible for delivery. Apart from Oxford and Cambridge, for which perhaps not surprisingly the Church made an exception in the case of the training of 'academically gifted' ordinands, despite evidence that the theological curriculum and pedagogies remained very traditional in those institutions, most other universities no longer have any direct investment in ministerial education. Whatever the undoubted merits of Common Awards, the challenges of a post-Christendom age mean that the churches must guard against slipping back into a methodology of furnishing students with a fund of academic theology combined with a separate toolkit of pastoral and missional skills. Ministerial education must maintain its integrity in drawing its commitment to *habitus* from the Athens model, and its dedication to criticality from Berlin, in a critical and creative interpenetration of academic theological education and practical learning.

The rest of this chapter points to some characteristics of such a theological education that can be seen as particularly relevant to the adaptive ministry argued for in this book.

Theological education for adaptive ministry

Theological education for adaptive ministry will draw on classical (*phronesis*), monastic, charismatic, pietist (small group) and liberationist (practical/critical reflection) models, together with a deconstructive approach that incorporates a more fluid, contextual and adaptive style. Particular attention needs to be paid to the habits, customs and beliefs of churches, in order to identify what it is they value and espouse. Kathryn Tanner has a vivid description of the work of the contemporary theologian who operates within these parameters:

> The basic operations that theologians perform have a twofold character. First, theologians show an artisanlike inventiveness in the way they work on a variety of materials that do not dictate of themselves what theologians should do with them. Second, theologians exhibit a tactical cleverness with respect to other interpretations and organisations of such materials that are already on the ground ... They do not construct their theological positions by applying generalities to particular cases, or emend them by trying to reproduce the same clear meanings in terms of a new day ... Instead, they operate by tying things together. (1997, pp. 87 ff.)

These techniques of 'artisanlike inventiveness', 'tactical cleverness' and 'tying things together' are exactly the skills required for ministers as practical theologians in an environment of ecclesial experimentation and adaptive ministry.

Drawing on their experience of pioneering 'new monastic' communities, Mobsby and Berry (2014) commend a seven-point approach to Christian formation that is designed for 'never-churched people who are wanting to dig deeper with the Christian faith', but is very much adaptable to the needs of ministerial education. They describe it as 'a focus on learning through intentional community and belonging, with different expectations of levels of commitment regarding a rhythm of life, spiritual practices, virtues and postures' (pp. 143–4). Because of the context of new monasticism, there is a strong emphasis on familiar practices such as the use of spiritual directors, contemplative experience and prayerfulness. But they contextualize these with an affirmation of discipleship as 'not about choice as consumptive gratification ... but rather ... following Christ as the passionate life ... that celebrates all that is good in life, but ... also ... leads to the cross, pain and suffering' (p. 144). This is a reminder that the practice of Christian faith goes against the grain of the times.

Mobsby and Berry draw several examples from the formational programmes of a variety of new ecclesial communities. The '24/7 Boiler Rooms' work to 'a learning philosophy that develops mind, body and spirit in the context of practical action as well as more formal "classroom" settings' (p. 146). Students learn in three interlocking contexts. The 'Living Room' entails periods of communal residential living to develop Christian character. The 'Boiler Room' is a group of about 12 to which they are allocated for the duration of their time on the programme to experience 'a rhythm of work, rest and prayer' (p. 147), in Benedictine manner but with an outward-facing missional focus on social projects in contexts of need. In the 'Classroom', they are exposed to a wide variety of teacher/practitioners to promote in-depth engagement with faith and the Bible (p. 149).

The Contemplative Fire communities (p. 153; see also Roderick, 2008) offer a threefold structure of 'Learning Journey: equipping, exploring and accompanying others', 'Still Waters: encountering the present moment in quietness', and 'Across the Threshold: engaging with wisdom on the boundaries'. The last of these is especially significant for the post-church context, as wisdom is not seen as limited to what can be mined from within Christian tradition. In Telford, the 'safespace' community uses a more open-ended process of theological cultural interpretation, where people 'talk about the difficult issues of life such as relationships, justice ... sexuality, addiction, suffering and spiritual practices', participating in a cycle of reflective Christian responses through daily, weekly, seasonal and annual gatherings (p. 155).

All of these innovative models begin with praxis and context, as 'hermeneutically primary': Christian experience itself is the breeding ground for theological formulation (Graham, 1996, cit. Percy, 2005, pp. 138–9). Theological education is situated within a reflexive interrogation of the norms and values that shape the practices and ethos of the Church, through which 'the community enacts its identity' (Graham, 1996, p. 109). This requires what Graham calls 'attention to *alterity*': a contextual formation for ministry will engage with both the blessings and the challenges of 'the other', with diversity and inclusion, and where honesty demands, confronting exclusion too. Only with the embrace of such self-critical disclosure will theological education have the capacity to be truly transformative.

Learning for unknowing

In the culture of postmodernity, churches engage with Christianity as a faith that symbolizes and enacts the impossible. Theological education must therefore inculcate those values and attitudes of mind that can live with nescience, uncertainty and unpredictability. In characteristic postmodern manner, this impacts on the ways in which ministers exercise power through powerlessness, involving 'voluntary self-limitation of capacity and even effect', as Martyn Percy has argued (1998, pp. 46–7). He sees the leader as 'choosing to appeal for consent rather than to demand ... submission', and 'preferring to be rejected and so to suffer than to impose and get one's own way' (p. 49). Theological education needs to embrace the reality that there is no place for compulsion in Christian leadership, and models of ministry that exercise power in forcible ways distort the gospel itself. The Christian way must be genuine and not manipulative, and so personal self-examination and supervision are essential to forestall the danger of leadership giving way to authoritarian abuse.

Percy goes on to employ the metaphor of 'mothering' as an image for theological education (in the following material in this section I am indebted to Percy's essay 'Mother Church' in Percy, 2005, pp. 111–32; these ideas are much more fully developed in Emma Percy, 2018). This is a 'cluster metaphor' that can draw several disparate ideas together, such as intimacy of relationship with the need to 'let go' and allow independence to develop. It signals something learned principally through example and intuition, and gives a priority to passion and immediacy over 'cool detachment'. It embodies a process pervaded with mystery and ambiguity, and an enterprise whose very 'success' entails a 'giving up', even a painful loss.

Feminist theologians can play a significant part in negotiating the transition into a pattern of theological education for adaptive ministry, because they have worked from a standpoint of the discriminations suffered by women within a hierarchically ordered patriarchal Church, and have explored alternative, non-hierarchical models of theological learning and of the exercise of power and leadership. In the words of Rebecca Chopp, feminist theology 'deconstructs and reorders values, norms and structures' (1995, p. 96). It is like quilting, a craft that works with 'hundreds of scraps of material of all different sizes, textures, colours and shapes', and 'represents the piecing together of our everyday experience in a communal act of love and the acceptance of all people and life experiences'.

For Mary Grey, a similar attitude is displayed in a strong emphasis on relationality as the fundamental basis of ontology for God, humankind and the world. As an educational model, it can encourage 'refusal of the victim situation, recovery of self-image, the process of coming to self-knowledge and the discovery of layers of connectedness' (1989, p. 26). She acknowledges that in some quarters such a model of mutuality in education may 'seem merely a soft option, accused of lacking intellectual rigour', an allegation that has certainly been levelled at some of the more imaginative programmes for theological education, for example in Local Ministry. But the emphasis here on deconstruction, relationality and difference coheres well with the approach to the social role of the churches and Christian practice proposed in earlier chapters.

Conclusion: the threefold framework

Gathering up the ideas elicited from the historical survey and ensuing discussion, we can say that theological education for ministry can best be designed according to a threefold pattern. The three interwoven strands are theology formed through spiritual character, theology formed through ecclesial practice, and theology formed through intellectual knowledge. They are distinct in that each one issues from a different starting point, but none can stand alone: all three strands are reflective in character, all three are theological, and all three can be enriched from academic resources. It is not the case that only the first is 'spiritual', the second 'practical', or the third 'academic'.

A theology formed through spiritual character, sometimes called 'wisdom theology', develops around the kernel of an inhabited tradition. People build up a fund of theological experience through the habits of prayer, worship and discipleship that comprise the Christian life, lived in companionship with others. A theology formed through ecclesial practice comes about through exposure to the context, and creative engagement with the critical issues it raises for church life. This is worked out in a collaborative manner involving projects and fieldwork, together with ongoing reflection on practice. A theology formed through intellectual knowledge develops around sustained engagement with structured re-sourcing from the tradition, and opens up a spirit of seeking in which the positive value of questioning and exploration is owned, endorsed and commended to others. The role of a minister requires a well-stocked mind capable of standing in a critical, discerning relation to the traditions in which spiritual wisdom and practical ministries are being formed.

In this model, all ministerial education is theological education. It is emphatically not the case that the 'theological' component is what the academy provides, while the Church takes care of the rest. As Mark McIntosh observes, 'Christian communities themselves believe that *theology comes to birth because of their ongoing encounter with God*' (2008, p. 13, emphasis in original). Theology is embodied in 'a way of life, a pattern of existence under the steady shaping motion of one's encounter with the really real', and its authenticity is subjected to the test of prac-tice (p. 50). The character, the virtues and performances that are shaped and nurtured over time through the lived study of theology, constitute in themselves one kind of encounter with the so-called 'object' of study – the divine – that can only ever be the active subject. The student of theology has to be open to being changed by it – and many are.

However, change and transformation do not cease at the point of transition into authorized ministry. Today, more than ever, serious atten-tion needs to be paid to the support and guidance of ministers in the uncertain and often perplexing territory into which Christian ministry will take them. A deconstructive ministry for a context of 'ecclesianarchy' is very unlike the secure pastoral living enjoyed by ministers within the Christendom inheritance of the age of the Church. The handling of ministerial roles while preserving a vital humanity is the subject of the final chapter.

12

Identity Crisis: Negotiating Role and Person in Ministry

In an interesting piece of research funded by the Church of England, the organizational psychologist Jane Sturges interviewed 36 clergy and asked them what they would consider as 'success' in their ministry (Sturges, 2013). Many younger clergy, especially of the Catholic tradition, said 'being a good priest'. Two responses, 'making a difference to people's lives' and 'enabling others', were especially prevalent among women clergy. Male clergy, particularly of the Evangelical tradition, often mentioned 'church growth'. 'Having influence', either in the community or on the policy and behaviour of the Church, was often identified by those who had held senior positions in previous careers. Long-serving clergy were apt to choose 'leadership', for example in 'running a large church' or 'being a community figurehead', and 'professional development'. 'Work/life balance' tended to be mentioned by younger clergy and those in their first post (perhaps the older clergy never expected to enjoy this, or had long since given up on it). Finally, 'recognition' was important, from parishioners, for those early in their career, and from senior diocesan personnel, for those with more years of experience.

The respondents felt that the achievement of these measures of success was helped by support from their Church organization at career, personal and spiritual level, good training, and developmental provision. However, there were some significant obstacles to 'career success': personal attributes ('if your face doesn't fit'; or, often, gender issues); a lack of support from senior personnel; unmanageable workload; and, especially, the poor quality of people management in the institution generally. It is clear that to a large extent the obstacles identified are working against the very things that the clergy felt would enhance their sense of achievement in ministry. The indicators of 'success' are a mixture of the personal and relational (making a difference, enabling others, having influence, recognition) and more institutional or role-based criteria (achieving church growth, exercising leadership, being a community figurehead), while 'being a good priest' might well be interpreted in either of these ways.

In the context of the inherited institutional Church, there is always a tension in ministry between 'role' and 'person'. Some clergy resign themselves to this by conceding that as far as the ministerial task is concerned, 'role' effectively trumps 'person', which may be corralled into private life and leisure time only. Others, however, kick against the tension and make the continual battle for supremacy between role and person a distinguishing feature of their ministry. As Hoyle rather ruefully puts it, 'a priest may spend a few months acquiring a bit of inherited behaviour and then decades struggling out of what was always a borrowed skin' (2016, p. 102). In the context of adaptive ministry for a post-church society, this tension will not disappear, but its contours will alter. The expectation that authorized and publicly recognized ministers will retain, display and operate from their distinctive humanity will be greater, while the roles they may occupy from time to time become more fluid.

For example, this is already being experienced by clergy in communities where they are still asked to perform large numbers of baptisms. The family occasion of a christening is bigger than ever, and freighted more and more with meanings that deviate significantly from 'official' Church teaching. The minister therefore needs to think very deeply about what his or her role is, and how they can express this in an authentic, personal way that at the same time conveys something of the theological significance of the rite that is likely to be very far from the minds of most of those present. What will *not* do is to retreat into the institutionally prescribed role, bolstered by the official liturgy, in a manner that communicates 'this is how the Church does it, and you have opted to come to the Church, so take it or leave it'. We need therefore to delve further into the challenges and dilemmas of the role – person relationship.

Ministry, character and goodness

A life in ministry can be experienced as lonely and futile, or even as a source of existential dread (for a heartfelt account, see Clitherow, 2004). There is a ministry that is, on the surface, orthodox, faithful to the Church, firmly remaining in role; and there is a ministry that turns the believer inside out, demanding the facing of pain and the expulsion of self-deception, in order to serve God with authenticity. In her series of novels chronicling the careers of several clerical families through the twentieth century, Susan Howatch comes back again and again to Christian ministry entailing *getting the measure of our pain*. All of Howatch's leading clerical characters can testify in two ways. One testimony stays with the roles, the appearances; the other reveals how hard-won, and at what personal and spiritual cost, the ability to sustain those roles and appearances authentically is.

In the first novel, *Glittering Images* (1987), we encounter Jon Darrow as the brilliant spiritual director, dismantling and reassembling with surgical precision the spiritual life-story of the young theologian Charles Ashworth in his time of crisis. Darrow, an Anglo-Catholic monk, exemplifies austerity, discipline and tough compassion, with a dash of mystery and glamour about his charismatic gifts of discernment and psychic insight. Ashworth is impressed by his unshockable serenity, his steadiness in the presence of emotional upheaval, his unerring instinct to know what to do. But in the second novel, *Glamorous Powers* (1988), it is the turn of Darrow himself to be exposed in weakness and crisis, and to confront the damage and pain of his own past, to exorcize his personal demons. We enter the pain of a man endowed with extraordinary gifts that make 'ordinary life' next to impossible for him, gifts he might rather not have had, 'glamorous powers' that constitute a constant source of temptation and a point of vulnerability. Of course, they are the self-same gifts that are also the source of his striking ability to help others in crisis.

The point is that *both* testimonies are true. Darrow *is* the brilliant, disciplined, gifted spiritual director; this is not hypocrisy. But in order to be that person, Darrow is also the tortured soul wrestling with his demons and getting the measure of his pain, bearing witness to a God whose call can in no way be met by remaining safely within the parameters of orthodox language and churchly tradition. If we are able to own this reality, we are reaching a critical starting point for fresh reflection on what ministry might mean. As Magdalen Smith puts it:

> [Priests] can keep other people at emotional arm's length; they feel they cannot come with their own questions of anxiety or theological doubt. The same principle applies if we continuously give the impression that we are shiny, sorted-out people ... vulnerability as a priest means working at not allowing others to pressurize us into being who they believe we should be ... if our exposed humanity can provide the rich soil from which our leading originates, then this becomes a brave and unorthodox model for those who look to us for spiritual, theological and emotional progress. (2014, p. 121)

Smith's phrase about 'keeping people at arm's length' echoes the words of Franz Kafka, who portrays a chaplain saying to Josef K: 'I had to speak to you first from a distance. Otherwise I am too easily influenced and tend to forget my duty' (Kafka, *The Trial*, cit. Harper, 1988, p. 35). Eddie Gibbs comments that often the minister 'never fully identifies with his [*sic*] people, preferring to distance himself. Such aloofness was actively encouraged in theological college training. Ministerial students were advised not to make their friends within the parish!' (1981, p. 268). When I stood down from a parish post to take up a full-time diocesan role, the bishop gave me permission to continue to live in the same parish, but only after agonizing over the question for some time. Some members of his staff felt this was a break with convention that could go badly wrong if 'friends in the parish' saw me as a rallying point to stir up opposition to things a new incumbent was doing that they didn't like.

The peril of the priest who speaks only 'from a distance' in order to maintain his 'duty' is wittily depicted in the popular best-seller *Chocolat* by Joanne Harris (2000; some details are changed in the film version). The novel dramatizes the showdown in a provincial French village between the life-denying, buttoned-up religion of the local church and its repressed young priest Father Reynaud, and newly arrived *chocolatier* Vianne Rocher, with her exotic and mysterious past life of restless travelling and a hint of paganism and witchcraft. Reynaud touches the lives of the villagers with the hand of death and denial, producing only lovelessness and bigotry. Vianne, on the other hand, brings release, courage, warmth and passion. An abused wife finds the strength to leave her husband and discover her potential; a lonely old man with his dog escapes his shyness and begins to socialize; a mollycoddled schoolboy cuts loose of his mother's apron strings and starts to live.

The story unfolds during the course of Lent: for the Church, the traditional season of self-denial and abstinence, marked by Fr Reynaud's cold, scolding sermons and a campaign for the eviction of the river gypsies who have moored their houseboats on the village waterfront. But for Vianne, Lent carries its pre-Christian meaning: the overture of springtime, of thaw and green shoots, of hope reborn, all symbolized in the grand, alluring and sensual Festival of Chocolate she plans to coincide with Easter. In a hugely comic denouement, the priest succumbs to temptation, breaks into the *chocolaterie* on Easter Eve, gorges himself upon chocolate and falls asleep, to awaken on Easter morning in the shop window before the astonished gaze of the parishioners. He is disgraced and fallen, but humanized – rising to his new life of sensual indulgence on Easter Day. This is not merely the story of a simplistic opposition between the cold formality of conventional religion and the glamorous allure of an idealized paganism. Rather, the narrative reveals that what is actually *happening* in people's lives through their contact with the *chocolaterie* and its mysterious proprietor tells a story of the intrinsic meaning of God-language in a way that the externals of village religion do not.

'True religion' is also a thread running through Nick Hornby's *How to be Good* (2001), which offers a wry and astute commentary on the relationship between religion and goodness. The narrator, Katie Carr, is a GP with a career stuck in a rut and a marriage running out of steam: her self-image is of a 'good person', which she thinks she *must* be because she is a doctor, whose sole business is doing good to the suffering. Why then, she asks herself, is she committing adultery, and why is she finding the opinionated rants of her husband David, a newspaper columnist writing under the tag 'the angriest man in Holloway', so intolerable? One day, David encounters an eccentric faith healer called GoodNews and experiences some kind of religious conversion that transforms him into a person of unflappable serenity, full of the milk of human kindness. He begins to commit acts of reckless generosity, giving away their son's computer to a women's refuge and donating their Christmas dinner to the homeless. He invites all the neighbours round and unveils a plan for them to take in homeless people in their surplus capacity spare rooms. But Katie resents it all, seething at her own hypocrisy as a self-styled 'good person' who can't cope with generosity, selflessness and sacrifice.

In desperation, she goes to church one Sunday. The congregation is sparse, and seems only minimally interested in what is taking place. The crazy vicar launches into a chorus of 'Getting to know you' from *The King and I* during her sermon. Katie is struck by this part of the message, when the vicar declares that God can't 'get to know you' if you insist on pretending to be good. Sometime later, the eccentric vicar turns up in Katie's surgery and confides that she is having a faith crisis and wonders if it's all worth it. Meanwhile, GoodNews reveals his true colours in the utter failure of his hippie-ish message of love and peace to enable him to be reconciled with his estranged sister, either by telephone or positive psychic energy. Collapsing in a foul-mouthed yell of frustration, he is gone from their lives. It's the breaking of the spell. For both Katie and David, married life can get back to normal; nothing heroic, nothing unreal, but just possibly some scope for an *ordinary* goodness that sits alongside folly and failure. Somehow, the cranky vicar whose faith was so fragile has also been a catalyst for getting things back into perspective.

Research among Anglican clergy by Yvonne Warren identified the pressure to live up to an expectation of exemplary goodness as a particular strain: 'Guilt is often a major preoccupation for clergy. They feel that they have "let God down", and others also, and that they can "never get it right" or do enough' (2002, cit. Lewis-Anthony, 2009, p. 54). As Sara Savage notes, ministers can fall prey to 'erroneous beliefs': 'I must be successful in everything I do .... If I make a mistake I am a total failure ... My value as a person depends on how other people view me' (2006, p. 27). The experiences of Jon Darrow, Father Reynaud and Nick

Hornby's eccentric vicar all testify to the absurd but liberating truth that as Christianity is impossible, so is any ideal of ministry as being an exemplary Christian. In a post-church society, the subversive strategy of Christian presence is a communion of the broken and a fellowship of the failed, a shaft of divine illumination in a frantic world where motivating yourself to succeed is frequently the sole, but bogus, recipe for happiness on offer.

Role management and personal development in ministry

In his honest and often uproarious account of training for ordained ministry, Peter Owen-Jones begins by noting the minister that the public sees, and the one they don't:

> What they don't see is the priest having breakfast in the morning, driving alone to the funeral. They don't hear the prayers that are inspired by their tears. They cannot know the conflicts that crackle inside us and the nature of the journeys we have made to reach them. They are not allowed to sense any doubt or any of the questions that pour out of our hearts; these are out of bounds ... the public are presented with the prepared: the approved and pristine version of the church, the 'here's the one I made earlier'. (1996, p. 5)

Owen-Jones wryly observes that one way this was revealed was in the way that, once ordained, he often sensed 'negative vibes' from people who discovered for the first time that his wife did not go to church. It 'seems to send all sorts of shivers down Evangelical spines' (pp. 103–4); even though 'the church does not pay my wife, it pays me: voluntary work is voluntary and that also implies that it is not unreasonable if my wife volunteers not to do it'. His refreshing conclusion is that if the congregation want a devout, committed Christian couple to run the show together, that is not what they are going to get, and they need to get over it.

The curse of Herbertism

How then shall the often-conflicting demands of roles and responsibilities be handled? Lewis-Anthony starts from the premise that Anglican ministry has been bewitched for almost 400 years under the spell of the work of George Herbert as supposedly depicting the ideal parish priest. To demonstrate that this model has survived at least into the latter part of the twentieth century, he quotes Sir Humphrey Mynors, then deputy governor of the Bank of England, addressing a diocesan conference in 1968 on 'What I look for in my parish priest':

> My parish priest enters completely into whatever activity he is engaged on at the moment, and *is felt by others to be doing so*: and yet he remains in a sense withdrawn, uncommitted. He can go from a funeral to a football match, from a committee to a confirmation class, *giving to each all he has*, as though their concerns were the only thing that mattered to him. He can switch from one wavelength to another, as it were, at the turn of a knob. (Lewis-Anthony, 2009, p. 47)

Lewis-Anthony comments tartly, 'in Herbertism, the parish priest is no more than a particularly well-worked transistor radio'. Broadcasting on different channels with different formats and music policies at different times convincingly, 'giving to each all you have', is not a recipe for personal integrity, nor is such omnicompetence realistic.

The futile attempt to perpetuate the Herbertist model leads to the psychological coping strategy dubbed by Lewis-Anthony 'The Cult of Nice', drawing in particular on the work of Sara Savage (2007) and Yvonne Warren (2002): 'The individual priest ... begins to substitute a "religious performance" for an integrated performance of his personality' (pp. 62–3, quoting Savage, 2006). The long-term impact of this kind of struggle is not infrequently burnout, which Lewis-Anthony deals with in a chapter headed 'a little soft around the edges', a disparaging phrase drawn from a diocesan newsletter in 2002 in which a bishop questioned the stamina and stickability of today's clergy (nowadays I suppose he might have used the word 'snowflakes'). Lewis-Anthony recommends that priests need clarity about roles and responsibilities, enshrined in a personally drawn-up job description, together with a Rule of Life setting times and boundaries for different types of ministerial work and recreation.

Although Lewis-Anthony's practical proposals may help clergy cope more effectively, with less likelihood of doing themselves permanent personal damage, they still work essentially within an unreconstructed fundamental theological understanding of ordination and priesthood. Other contributors delve further than Lewis-Anthony does into the dilemmas and tensions of ministry within this framework.

Embracing humanity, messiness and frustration

An issue that resonates strongly with Owen-Jones's frustrations is whether the demand for 'holiness' can be aligned with the quest for a 'wholeness' that runs with the grain of the minister's humanity, rather than being role-determined. Role and status were once the principal guarantors of social order: 'people needed to submit to their station and role in life in order to function in a traditional, hierarchical and more communal society' (Savage and Boyd-MacMillan, 2007, p. 211). For centuries, 'the Church helped them to do just that', and clergy were as role-dependent as everyone else. But now, 'in order to function in our fluid, invent-it-yourself postmodern society', the model for wholeness for clergy and lay people alike comes not from the artifice of prescribed roles, but the unvarnished truth of the human *reality* of the faith community, typified in the original disciples of Jesus:

> The story of this band of disciples, their disagreements, love, suffering, confrontations of bad behaviour within their midst, their witness and their prayer – all these together empower men and women to take leadership ... This is not simply the back of the canvas, whose messy imperfections are to be kept from public view. (Savage and Boyd-MacMillan, 2007, pp. 225–6)

Perhaps we should have a broader use for the words 'messy church' than what they usually mean today: all church is 'messy church', and that implies 'messy ministry'.

Mark Pryce cautions against trying to smooth and straighten everything out. There needs to be 'a place ... to give room to the struggle, wrestle with and even entertain a little hesitancy about the task and role of the ordained priest' (2013, pp. 79–80), to make room for the disruptive and the angular, the anxious and the discomfited. Pryce looks for inspiration to the work of R. S. Thomas, who sees his ministry in the guise of Pilgrim, Steward, Sentinel, Fugitive and Astronaut (p. 83). The pilgrim's concern is not principally about reaching the final destination as a place where all is resolved, but about the journey itself, the restlessness of travel, the setbacks, obstacles and false roads, where God remains 'dark and inexplicable' (p. 85). As steward of the local church, the priest must be prepared to endure frustration when ministry has to mean working within the congregation's economies of meaning and identity, and not disturbing them (p. 87). As sentinel, the priest keeps watch, sometimes at a distance, at odds with the people among whom s/he is placed (pp. 89–90). As fugitive, Thomas recoils from the role demanded of him as requiring 'an uncritical patriotism and militarism to bolster the self-importance of retired men' (p. 91). In retirement, the priest as astronaut searches the heavens on 'impossible journeys', returning with 'messages I cannot decipher' (p. 94): age does not bring resolution and clarity of vision, but a deepening of the mystery.

The unsettling nature of ministry as conveyed by Thomas is widely remarked upon elsewhere, if more prosaically. In a volume of reflections on the first years of ordained ministry (Ross-McNairn and Barron, eds, 2014), Lincoln Harvey's personal story tells of how, for him, 'the transforming nature of ordination was not as positive' as he might have expected (p. 28). It came as quite a shock to discover that appearing in a dog collar did not always result in a friendly welcome once 'my identity coincided with the public institution' (p. 29). This downside of ministry appears in many of the stories that follow: Lusa Nsenga-Ngoy, a black curate in a Kentish village, was told by a funeral director that the family of an elderly woman did not wish him to take the funeral (chapter 7). Graciously (even *too* graciously?), he recounts what he learned through this incident about helping people to become reconciled with diversity, rather than questioning a Church that was willing to expose him to this situation unprepared.

There are examples in the book of a noble and impressive deployment of a public representative ministry: especially Bruce Goodwin (chapter 8) who was curate in the parish when the vicar, John Suddards, was murdered; and David Smith (chapter 12), who arranged at short notice an unconventional memorial service in the church for a local teenager who died in a road accident. Both of these testify to the need to improvise responses 'on the hoof' in circumstances where 'official' rites and liturgies would not connect with the people involved. Rob Kean (chapter 10) chooses to exercise the 'public representative' function by being in the local pub every Thursday evening. While *he* has to demonstrate 'unconditional acceptance', the landlord brings out every single week the hoary old chestnut about urging the regulars to mind their language because the vicar's in. Kean writes: 'I have found that people have responded to *me being genuinely me*' (p. 58); but there is a risk that the 'vicar in the pub' could itself become a stereotypical role, restricting their judgement about who he 'genuinely is'.

Cultivating resilience and maintaining sanity

Justine Allain-Chapman identifies the three 'building blocks' of struggle, self and relationships for what she calls a 'pastoral theology of resilience':

> The literature identifies the need to embrace struggle and withstand the emotional pain that goes with it. To be resilient people will have a sense of themselves as having worth, control and an inner life resourced by a vision of a future that is better and different. Self-awareness and

discipline go with the self-esteem necessary to face and come through adversity. Relationships with those who support and guide help, not least by fuelling the vision of a different way of life, because they have come through. (2012, p. 35)

In this understanding of the minister, Allain-Chapman acknowledges the influence of Henri Nouwen's well-known model of the 'wounded healer'. However, she indicates the danger that it may facilitate collusion with an unhealthy power dynamic, wherein a virtue is made of the minister's woundedness in order that he or she may then administer healing to the needy. She wishes to reduce the emphasis on the minister's wounds and modify the expectation that the minister's function is always to heal. There can be as much pretence in always presenting as 'wounded' as there is in the opposite, the minister who never owns up to vulnerability. Hence, she prefers the term 'resilient pastor', shifting the focus away from suffering on to the quality of character that deals with it, and the ministry of care for which healing is not always possible.

While Allain-Chapman offers wise counsel for a resilient ministry, Gordon Oliver advises on how to avoid 'madness' (though not in the sense of the 'madness of the impossible' developed in this book). Pondering the life of Christian ministry as a journey, he coins the acronym TRIPS (tasks, resources, identity, purpose and status) to capture the five essentials of finding the ministerial role in a particular context of ministry. He notes this is an intentional pun: a 'trip' can be either a journey or a stumble, and in ministry it is often both. Ministerial tasks are not just givens, dictated by the role; they will vary enormously from place to place and time to time, because the systems, structures and demands of the context are the product of endlessly shifting confluences, alliances and counter-currents of circumstances and people in relationship. Oliver therefore urges 'taking proper time to really join the community we are called to serve and lead' (2012, p. 20). It follows that the minister will need to seek out different, appropriate resources as the priority tasks change.

Regular review of tasks and resources needs to be accompanied by reflection on identity. Given the perpetual change taking place in the ministry context, an identity that is overly dependent on the roles and tasks of the minister can become fragile and contested. There need to be cherished 'personal identifiers' that stay the same and have little to do with 'the job', and that help ministers to clarify the 'value we place on who we are' in ourselves (p. 25). This may be expressed in such things as family relationships, secular employments, personal passions and interests, hobbies, sports, pets, music, travel ... whatever we recognize as intimately bound up with who we are, regardless of any of the outward paraphernalia of religion. Keeping in touch with that unique person the minister *is*, underneath it all, can enhance the sense of purpose and reduce anxiety about status:

> Purpose in ministry ... has to be *discerned, discovered and practised.* True purpose in Christian ministry cannot be adequately described by expressions such as having vision, being knowledgeable and good at projects ... one of the most important qualities in a Christian minister is a habitual sense of curiosity ... which makes us keep asking what is going on, what God is calling for, and how to join in to help it bear fruit that will last. (p. 29)

The relevance of Oliver's reflections on task, purpose and identity is clear among the case studies of six ministers presented by Frances Ward in her work on theological reflection and supervision in ministry (2005, pp. 20–50). It is noteworthy that the two who come across as most balanced, sane and content in their ministries are a Church Army Officer and a Diocesan Rural Adviser, who is also in rural parish ministry. These are ministers with a specialism, offering them a chance to play to their strengths and particular passions. They both share responsibility with others for defined projects that have a sense of progress; they come over as personalities for whom role and person are in harmony. The Rural Adviser is able to combine the focused tasks of her specialism with a community-centred ministry of presence, in which the 'public *persona*' aligns with the real person. By contrast, a Team Rector and a Methodist Superintendent seem wearied and disappointed by the round of meetings and trivial local concerns; they have to grab welcome interludes of recreational time in order to be their 'true self' while all too often 'keeping up appearances' when in ministry mode. As for the Anglican curate in the study, for the sake of his well-being one hopes that he has learned over the years how to handle his role and manage his life. This brings us to the final section, looking at how the churches support ministers in doing just that.

Ministerial support, accountability and review

Some years ago, the Church of England published a set of *Guidelines for the Professional Conduct of the Clergy* (Archbishops' Council of the Church of England, 2003, revised edition 2015). They form a revealing portrait of challenging and sometimes conflicting expectations. There is a welcome reference to clergy ministering 'through their own broken humanity' (13.1; citations are from the 2015 edition), and the need to 'discern and make clear their own limitations of time, competence and skill' (2.3). Alongside these merciful counsels, however, there come the stern admonitions: 'the reputation of the Church in the community depends to a great extent on the integrity and example of its clergy' (9.1) and, starkly, 'the clergy are called to an exemplary standard of moral behaviour' (10.1).

While it is 'important to recognize and affirm lay ministry that already exists and to encourage new ministries, both lay and ordained' (6.3), there is no getting away from the overwhelming sense that, when push comes to shove, the clergy for the most part are 'going it alone'. One revealing item (13.5) requires that both ministerial review and spiritual direction should 'offer the opportunity for the clergy to reflect on whether they are giving sufficient time to family life, friendship, recreation and renewal and to consider any health issues'. While this is no doubt well-intentioned as pastorally supportive, there is an inevitable 'edge' to it that arouses discomfort: there is no 'private life' here, it seems, if ministerial review *and* spiritual direction are to cover all these things as well as the tasks and commitments of ministry itself.

Today, ministers in most communions are expected or required to take part in some form of Ministerial Review as part of the process of accountability. The Church of England (2010) and the Methodist Church (2011, revised edition 2018) have both issued guidelines for such review. In highlighting a few differences between them, I am commenting solely on what the documents say; I do not have evidence on which to judge whether the two churches differ significantly in their actual practice of review. Each document places a scriptural verse on the front page: the Church of England has 'You did not choose me, but I have chosen you and appointed you to go and bear fruit' (John 15.16); the Methodist Church (citations are from the 2011 version), 'as in one body we have many members, and not all the members have the same function, so we, who are many, are one body in Christ, and individually we are members one of another' (Rom. 12.4–5). The one has a more individual emphasis, the other chooses to prioritize the corporate; the first introduces immediately the challenge of producing *results*, while the second begins from the affirmation of *relationships*.

Both sets of guidelines envisage Ministerial Development Review in terms of a process of reflection aimed at learning from experience and, from this, setting goals and identifying developmental needs. The Church of England process expects the review meeting to involve the minister and one reviewer, who may be the bishop. The guidelines state very plainly that 'MDR is episcopally led' (3.1), and 'it is for the bishop to decide who will conduct reviews in his [*sic*] diocese. The bishop will decide whether he wishes to conduct reviews himself' (4.1). There is provision for written feedback to be sought from a 'representative range of others ... including lay representatives' (6.1). By contrast, the Methodist process directs that each review meeting will have three participants: the minister being reviewed, another minister who is above that one in the church hierarchy (e.g. for a circuit minister, the superintendent), and 'a lay person agreed by both' (p. 12). There is also provision to invite written input from others, but all three participants in the forthcoming review meeting are to agree not only on who these should be, but also on what questions they should be asked to offer feedback upon.

The Methodist Church document foregrounds prayer more conspicuously than the Anglican one: 'each component of the Ministerial Development Review process is to be *rooted in prayer and reflection*' (p. 8, emphasis in original; further on, on p. 14, the document prefaces each aim of the process with the words 'prayerfully and reflectively'). The Anglican document only refers to the formation of objectives 'following prayerful reflection before the MDR ...' (5.3), but does not appear to envisage the review meeting itself being conducted in an environment of prayer. The Anglican guidelines (6.3) refer to identifying the minister's particular strengths and gifts with a view to encouraging their wider use within the deanery or the diocese (i.e. for the minister to develop an element of specialism); the Methodist document contains a more worked-out theological statement:

> Ministerial Development Review recognises, embraces and reinforces the mutual respect and accountability – the partnership and interdependence – which is at the heart of Christian discipleship, of Christian learning and of connexionalism ... Ministerial Development Review should truly be a process which enables rather than controls, which empowers, and which releases gifts and skills in the service of the ministry of Christ, in which we all share. (p. 19)

On the whole, it is the Methodist document that enshrines a more holistic approach to review, setting the minister more clearly in the context of colleagues and highlighting the spiritual and pastoral dimensions of the process. The Anglican guidelines seem more concerned to make plain that review is not the same as either pastoral counsel or spiritual direction, with the result that as it stands the process can be read as somewhat task-oriented and impersonal. However, neither version really addresses the issues of role and person we have been exploring.

The Church of England *Guidelines* were published with a 'theological reflection' by Francis Bridger appended, retained in a revised version in 2015, which offers a framework of Christian concepts valuable for ministers wrestling with the challenge of how to practise ministerial roles while retaining integrity as human persons. First, ministry lies within a framework of covenant. 'Covenant partners are bound together not by a set of legal requirements but by the relational nexus of gracious initiative followed by thankful response' (p. 26). Second, ministry is shaped by *agape*. This means that it is governed by gift; it involves faithfulness and constancy; and it is 'always searching for the good of the other' (p. 27). Third, ministry is expressed in virtue: 'the ethics of conduct must be shaped by the ethics of character and the ethics of integrity', drawing on the notion of the 'habits of the heart' that are formative of character and behaviour (p. 30). It is open to question whether the Church has yet fashioned processes for supporting its ministers that adequately model the values commended by Bridger.

Conclusion

Within the various sources examined in the later parts of this chapter, there are concepts and models for ministerial practice that seem well fitted to an adaptive ministry in the context of the uncertain and shifting patterns of postmodernity and post-Christendom. Oliver recognizes the fluidity and diversity of the contexts, communities and relationships in which contemporary ministry roles have to be negotiated. Frances Ward identifies the importance of individual specialisms and passions that help to unite role and person in the commitments of the minister. The Church of England acknowledges 'ministering through a broken humanity', 'encouraging collaborative ministry' and 'learning from experience', and the Methodist Church partnership and interdependence. Bridger commends notions of 'gift', 'relational open-endedness', and 'openness to the possibilities of the other'. These culturally relevant, forward-looking insights about ministry are interspersed with others that reflect a more dated and dangerous set of assumptions. The challenge is for the creatively adaptive values to gain momentum and win the day in transforming both ministry and Church for the emergent future.

It is time now to gather up the argument and proposals of the book as a whole, together with a few suggestions about the way ahead for the churches.

Conclusion

Throughout the last 60 years or so, traditional denominational churches in the former Christendom territories of the West have been troubled by the decline in their congregations and the ebbing away of their social significance. From the 1960s to the 1980s, the churches interpreted their fortunes through the lens of sociological secularization theory: broadly the view that the advances of modernity over the previous 200 years were bringing about a steady erosion of the plausibility of religious beliefs and the claims of religious institutions to occupy a central role in society with authority over morals, public and private life. Some commentators thought that the churches needed to modernize in order to ally themselves more closely with the *zeitgeist*, while others believed that Christianity should reassert its distinctiveness as a challenging alternative to secular modernity. Roughly over the last 30 years, while the churches' declining attendances and increasing social marginalization have continued, the cultural analysis in response to which they have sought to revive their fortunes has shifted from the secularization paradigm to the framework of postmodernity.

The churches have been attracted by those aspects of postmodernity that could be defined as 'post-secular': the renewed salience of religion for many critical issues on the political and public agenda, the increasing popular mistrust of purely 'scientific' accounts of reality and, in particular, the rise of multiple varieties and expressions of 'spirituality'. The Fresh Expressions movement in the Church of England and the Methodist Church combines the evidence of a new interest in spirituality (even when this is often combined with a rejection of 'religion') with the rampant consumerism and ideology of 'choice' within advanced modernity, to create its vision of new forms of church that connect with particular target groups within the 'unchurched' markets of contemporary society. The flourishing of these initiatives, together with other factors such as the vitality of many large churches in the charismatic Evangelical tradition and, by contrast, evidence of increased attendance at cathedral worship (Muskett, 2019) has led the churches to promote a 'good news' narrative of 'turning the corner'. Nevertheless, overall, there is little evidence of a revival in churchgoing, and the churches' diminished social significance has not been reversed. Ominously, among the under-25s, there has been a large increase in the response 'no religion' to survey questions about religious affiliation in the UK.

This is the story that has provided the background for this book. Within this environment, one major theme that has exercised the churches has been the nature, roles, functions and provision of their authorized ministries, lay and ordained. In the Church of England, there has long been a conviction that the 'parson in the parish' model is no longer viable, even if only because of insufficient numbers coming forward for ordination to staff it, let alone the cost of paying their stipends. Ever since the 1960s, proposals for changed structures of ministry have usually involved the pursuit of increased lay ministry and various ways of getting clergy to work together across parish boundaries: group ministries, team ministries, local ministry teams and so on. All of these have quite understandably had to operate within the constraints of inherited ecclesiology and ministerial theology, and whenever a proposal has surfaced that some consider to be 'un-Anglican', such as the 'two-tier' model of the Tiller Report or the introduction of Ordained Local Ministry, there have always been some vocal opponents in the churches' councils and synods. More recently, some of the more radical ideas emanating from the Fresh Expressions constituency have met with a similar reception: a harbinger of trouble ahead if the Church wants to continue its embrace of diversity while maintaining its inherited orders and structures of ministry intact.

This book has argued that the challenges of the cultural climate of late or postmodernity will not be sufficiently met by an appeal to greater consumerist diversity in the provision of ecclesial innovations that leave fundamental ecclesiology and ministerial orders untouched. If postmodernity has to do with 'incredulity towards metanarratives', as Lyotard famously put it, then it likewise expresses profound scepticism towards 'meta-institutions'. The culture shifts in favour of fluid, hybrid and adaptive systems that emerge, mutate, regroup and dissipate according to social need and circumstance: a good example of this is the phenomenon of the 'pop-up' shop, cafe or drop-in centre that appears on the high street (and the 'pop-up church' is starting to join them). Church and ministry need to become much more nimble in adjusting to change, so that the very word 'church' conjures up not so much images of massive institutional solidity and permanence as lightness of touch, innate adaptability and agility in responding to the Spirit who blows where s/he wills.

The long journey of Church history contains numerous crisis moments, when the Church's very future might have seemed imperilled, that have brought forth new departures in ministerial order, or in the adaptation of the established order to new social circumstances. Not infrequently, disputes among the churches have hit home practically in the breakdown of mutual recognition of ministries; sometimes, those on the losing side of the argument have been deemed heretical. The Christianization of the Roman Empire at the decree of Constantine, the ascent of the papacy to unimagined worldly power during the Dark Ages, the cataclysmic upheaval of Reformation and Counter-Reformation, the Evangelical and Wesleyan revivals and the very different Anglo-Catholic and Pentecostal movements of renewal, have all rewritten the ministry text-book in various ways. In recent decades, the smaller and less historically momentous, but still significant, developments of Local Collaborative Ministry and Fresh Expressions have posed their own challenges to established patterns.

For mainstream churches within the Catholic tradition, the threefold order of bishops, priest and deacons has provided a semblance of continuity and consistency through all these disturbances, but closer inspection shows that these have in fact undergone serial mutations in their theological interpretation and their practical expression. This is why some contemporary writers have preferred to refer to 'episcopal, presbyteral and diaconal ministry', an approach that more readily grants validity to the ministries of other churches, but leaves unresolved the question of whether a church like the Church of England could permit alternative ways of expressing these types of ministry to those that have been inherited from the past. Over and beyond the threefold ordering of ministry and other inherited patterns, the more fundamental question of the nature of ordination itself is also raised by the present drive to innovate in response to the new socio-cultural environment.

Although the term 'ordain' has connotations of official appointment to a position, a role and function, that contributes to the 'ordering', or proper organization, of an institutional body, the Church also wants to maintain that those who are ordained are recipients of a calling and a charisma that are sovereignly bestowed by the Spirit. It is easy to insist that both are true: but what is the relationship between them? A related question is whether 'the Church', as an institutional hierarchy, has priority over 'church', as a grass-roots 'people movement'; the nature and tasks of ordained ministry will look very different depending on how this question is answered. A third issue concerns whether the person ordained to ministry is principally outward-facing as a representative 'public Christian' in the world, or oriented to the congregation in oversight, pastoral care, teaching, formation in discipleship and leadership in mission. In what sense is a 'priest' in a city-centre church with little residential population, but multiple points of contact with society at large through community projects that make use of the building, and a tiny Sunday congregation of people who drive in from the suburbs because they like the formal choral worship on offer, essentially the same as a 'priest' in a fresh expression gathering a new congregation from unchurched families on a large modern estate, seeking to nurture them in the infancy of their faith?

Some of the most interesting and productive initiatives in ministry over the last 40 years or so raise these sorts of questions in acute form. Varieties of local collaborative ministry, including ministry teams and Ordained Local Ministry, constitute a direct challenge to the leadership styles of ordained clergy, especially in a Church where the incumbency role is explicitly designated as 'having charge'. Authorized lay ministries such as Reader (or Lay Preacher), Pastoral Minister or Evangelist raise questions about the nature of the clergy/laity line, for example with regard to deacons, and about the levels of training and public authorization that are appropriate. For instance, is the distinction sustainable that whereas the licensing of a Reader is essentially about function, the ordination of a Priest is a profoundly ontological act? Ordained Local Ministry is rejected by some on the grounds that it is 'non-deployable' and therefore not properly apostolic; and yet, if priesthood is an ontological category, by what logic should the priesthood of an Ordained Local Minister be any the less authentic if it is expected that they will exercise it very much in relation to a particular place? Where there is a Local Ministry Team with an Ordained Local Minister, especially in rural churches, what should be the role of an 'incumbent' who is not resident in the parish? If it is 'oversight beyond the level of the local', where does that leave the bishop?

Such questions often present in a slightly different form in denominational churches that have been positively influenced by Pentecostalism via the charismatic movement. The giftings of members of the congregation that seem most appropriate to a church's needs do not necessarily correspond well to the categories on offer from the diocesan or national Church. For example, the gift of preaching may be viewed in a 'prophetic' light in terms of the person who discerns and brings a 'word from the Lord' to the people assembled, relevant to a particular Sunday; the minister may be unconvinced whether training to be a Reader or a Local Preacher is quite what this person needs, but there is no other option on offer. A worship team may include a leader who takes a significant role in setting the mood and guiding the congregation through a sequence of songs interspersed with spontaneous words of praise or encouragement: what training and type of public recognition are required for this, and does the church have to go 'freelance' in order to find it? Christians newly come to faith are keen to be baptized; but it turns out they were christened in infancy. How close to a baptismal rite can an initiation involving water be allowed to come, and who should be permitted to administer it?

Given the fluidity of the present social and cultural circumstances and the challenges they bring to traditional local church-based ministry, it is no accident that recent years have proved particularly hospitable to a revival of interest in chaplaincy, and an expansion of its reach. Chaplaincy is a form of ministry going back at least to medieval times, and probably earlier, at least in the case of the military chaplain. The long-established institutional chaplaincies in 'gated communities' like hospitals, alms-houses, prisons, schools and religious houses could be viewed as the extension of local church (parochial) ministry into residential places less accessible to the parish priest. But the emerging chaplaincies in 'transient communities', such as transport hubs, train stations, airports, leisure centres, shopping malls and town centres (including the 'night-time economy' of clubgoers) are very different, dependent on a strong sense of representative presence, accessibility and the ability to maximize the opportunity of fleeting contact that may never be repeated. The emerging chaplaincies push at all the established ministry boundaries. A massive out of town shopping park or an airport may know that it wants to employ a chaplain, but may neither know nor care whether that chaplain should be a deacon or a priest, ordained or lay, of one denomination or another, even of one particular faith or another, and their role is unlikely to be seen as having much if anything to do with the Church.

The denominational hierarchies, however, tend not to include chaplaincy among their list of ecclesial, ministerial and missional innovations. The radicalism of chaplaincy exists to a large extent under the radar. The churches have chosen to place most of their eggs into the basket of Fresh Expressions, in terms of promotion, resourcing and their general seal of approval. One likely reason for the difference must be that chaplaincy by and large does not operate in a way that has any direct pay-off for the local churches, despite the fact that there are plenty of stories of people whose journey to faith began with an episode of contact with a chaplain. But fresh expressions can only function in a relationship with a sponsoring church, within the life of which they are set up as an experimental innovation in mission and ministry. Because of this, many of those in the regular Sunday congregations of churches sponsoring a fresh expression have expected any success to spill over into the life of the 'parent' church.

At one level, the Fresh Expressions movement has indeed been successful, such that Messy Church, for example, has evolved into a recognized brand, with a kind of franchise model for churches wishing to introduce it. An authorized form of Pioneer Ministry to resource Fresh Expressions, with designated pathways of selection, training and deployment, has been put in place with remarkable speed. Fresh expressions have also been attracting a significant amount of interest for academic research purposes, and this is where the challenge comes: whether, as is often the case with the churches, the hard questions being identified, that will materially affect the ongoing success of the initiatives, will be fully taken on board. I am not convinced that the churches are yet anywhere near to that painful grasping of nettles that will be necessary in order to deal with the issues that arise.

For example, although the official definition of a fresh expression states that it should have the potential to develop into a 'mature' form of church in its own right, many in the sponsoring church congregations still regard it as a 'bridge' into 'real church', into which those who participate in it will transition in due course. If this does not happen, and the relentless demographic means that the 'traditional' congregation continues to decline while the new one flourishes, what then? The old wineskins of inherited ecclesiology and ministerial order may really struggle to contain the new wine of the more effervescent forms of innovation. Already some fresh expressions communities are challenging the status quo on the appropriate way for the new church to celebrate the Lord's Supper with people of no previous church allegiance, whose image of 'church' has been extremely negative. The leaders of the new church do not lack respect for the rich resources of Christian liturgical tradition, but know that they will need a much greater latitude and flexibility than the Church's rules currently allow if they are sensitively and imaginatively to introduce their congregation to some of those resources.

Then there is the issue of who those 'leaders' are: if they are already ordained clergy, then this at one level solves the question of who should preside at the Communion celebration. But what about lay leaders emerging within the new expression of church whose recognition as respected senior figures (i.e. elders) has arisen very much as a grassroots phenomenon? The easy answer is to reiterate the official position against so-called 'lay presidency': either they will need to go forward as candidates for ordination, or an ordained priest who may not normally be present at the fresh expression gathering will have to be drafted in for the occasion. But the rejection of 'lay presidency' begs the question: nobody seriously thinks that just anyone should be able to preside at the Eucharist, for example by setting up a rota or taking it in turns. Rather, anyone who does so should have the endorsement of the whole church community that they are an appropriate person and, from a 'bottom-up' perspective of church, this *ipso facto* amounts to recognizing them as a minister. It is highly questionable whether the existing processes for facilitating the transition from lay to ordained status are what this person needs.

Strategies based on forms of collaborative ministry, charismatic gifting, experimental types of presence as in chaplaincy, and alternative modes of church as in Fresh Expressions, have all contributed to the imaginative renewal of ministry over recent decades. The institutional churches have encouraged these in varying degrees, but innovation regularly comes up against the constraints of inherited ecclesiology and ministerial order. This is problematic from both without and within the churches. From without, social and cultural changes militate strongly against institutional immobility and the enshrining of 'spiritual capital' in strongholds from which it is difficult to extract its potential. Moves towards fluidity, hybridity, emergence and adaptivity are the order of the day, but the denominational churches tend to be associated with the reverse of these values. The pressures are increasingly being felt within the churches as well, as new forms of ministry and ecclesiality put a strain on established patterns, some of which are sanctified by enjoying the status of 'official ecclesiology'. These pressures need to be addressed, first by making a case for *all* ordering and structuring of ministry being always and everywhere provisional, contextual and time-limited, and second, by sketching out a blueprint for an adaptive, deconstructive model that would free up the energies for innovation without the constraints that hold it back.

The ways in which the place of religion and the churches in the societies of the former Christendom has been changing demands a fresh approach to what Christianity brings to the table. It can no longer function in a Durkheimian way as a means of societal cohesion, nor of moral surveillance. Nor can it in any *direct* way employ its liturgies and sacraments to sacralize the general human fears, longings, aspirations and joys associated with critical times of transition like birth, adolescence, marriage and death; most people nowadays below the age of 60 are too far removed from Christian tradition to be able to make the theological links with baptism, confirmation, matrimony and funerals. But the picture of the Church as a distinctive moral and ethical community, typified by the theology of Hauerwas (2001), is also problematic in the context of a fluid and mobile society in which those who *do* find their way into some form of ecclesial practice may well be enormously diverse in their origins, values, previous experience of religion, if any, and level of understanding of inherited Christian teachings.

I have therefore drawn on postmodern thinking to argue for Christian faith performing a social role of signalling, symbolizing and (fitfully and fallibly) practising 'the impossible', a category of which society must be reminded for the sake of its health and humanity. 'The impossible' is taken in the sense in which the philosopher-theologian Caputo attributes it to religion, based on the thought of Derrida: that there are concepts and practices that, when deconstructed, appear to collapse under the weight of rational logic and make no sense at all. Insofar as society is dominated by a secular rationalist instrumentalism, these concepts and practices will be marginalized, overlooked or derided. The role of religion is to keep them 'on the agenda'; and although I am not competent to judge whether this can apply to all 'religion' (I suspect not), I do think it is a very good fit with the basic commitments of Christianity, deriving especially from the teaching, activities and ultimate fate of Jesus of Nazareth.

For the gospel is a nest of impossibilities: that there can be an unconditional gift (that we call grace), that debts can be forgiven, enemies can be loved, sinners welcomed to the table and prodigals worthy of a massive party; that there are no quantifiable measures for human worth, neither of achievement, nor riches, nor power, nor physical attractiveness; that the first can be last, and the last first; that leadership is service, and authority must be given away; that the poor are blessed and it is easier for a camel to pass through the eye of a needle than for a rich man to enter the kingdom of heaven; that the way to life lies through a death, and those who strive to save their life will lose it. There is more than enough here to be going on with if we maintain that Christianity is impossible, and the role of the Church is to remind the world of the mysterious transformative potential of embracing impossibility, to signal it, stand for it and be content to make a hash of actually living it. This is what St Paul knew, doubtless a man often nigh on impossible to live with: 'the message is foolishness to those who are perishing, but to us who are being saved it is the power of God ... for God's foolishness is wiser than human wisdom, and God's weakness is stronger than human strength' (1 Cor. 1.18, 25).

This book has proposed a model of 'ecclesianarchy' as the best hope of responding to the social and cultural changes of the post-Christendom West, and bringing to expression that wrestling with the impossible which will ensure that the churches still have a vital role to play. An ecclesianarchy is not mere chaos, but a maximally fluid, adaptive, non-hierarchical communion in which structural patterns emerge and decay, ebb and flow, evolve and mutate, according to need, across time and space: churches will look very different in different places at the same time, and at different times in the same place. An ecclesianarchy does not require any existing expression of church to be got rid of, unless its lack of social and cultural connectedness causes it simply to wither on the vine; there is great rejoicing to be had in letting a million flowers bloom.

The same is true of ministry. An ecclesianarchy does not have to discard bishops, eject priests or eliminate the diaconate. It need not abandon territorially based ministry, nor the idea of a local church serving a specified area. It has no interest in evicting Anglo-Catholics, ostracizing liberals or stigmatizing old-school conservatives in favour of some kind of shapeless charismatic free-for-all. But what it does do is embrace all possibilities that have traction with the contexts, communities and cultures where church is being expressed. A diaconal minister might be the energizer of a church-based community project, or a hospice chaplain, or a minister for the local retail community on the high street. Priestly ministry might be exercised through something approximating to the traditional 'vicar' role in a large church serving a market town, or a team of local ministers working together across a rural area comprising a dozen small villages, or a teacher who oversees a congregation in a fresh expression and carries out her profession in a local school, drawing out links between school, church and community. A ministry of *episcope* might be a role at national church level, overseeing the delivery of continuing professional development for ministers, or a presiding elder for a group of churches across a particular region, small enough for the *episcope* to be exercised in a personal way, or the leader of a unit charged with the task of creating new pioneering mission opportunities. Any or all of these churches and contexts might embrace multiple styles of worship, without the need for 'tribal' identification or mutual suspicion.

But for all of this to flourish, all sorts of 'red lines' will need to be breached. For example, what an 'ordination' looks like, what is required for someone to be authorized to preside at Holy Communion, what is liturgically permissible in any context, how candidates for different ministries are selected, trained and deployed, and much of the historical system, at least in the Church of England, concerning incumbency, livings, patronage and legally enforceable parish boundaries. Public recognition of ministry will not be artificially constrained by the two major dividers of the 'clergy/lay' line and the 'threefold order'. Thus it becomes possible for someone to be selected, trained and authorized as a preacher/teacher, a pastor, an evangelist, even a prophet (though that one would be rather hard to 'contain' within any structures), without the encumbrance of having to decide whether this is a 'lay' or 'ordained' role, and whether it needs to align with either the diaconate or the priesthood. Instead, in an ecclesianarchy there would be a plurality of means of public recognition and authorization for ministries that would be contextually sensitive.

This levelling of the playing field between ministries currently seen as 'lay' or 'ordained', 'local' or 'deployable', full or part-time, paid or unpaid, would require a menu of mutually compatible and adaptable training units, some more local, others regional or national, including some requiring residence, from which bespoke programmes of ministerial education could be put together. At regional or national level, coordination and oversight of these would be an episcopal responsibility: this is not the same as saying 'a bishop would do it', in the sense of appointing someone who was already a bishop in the familiar sense. Rather, recruitment to the post would specifically identify this as an episcopal ministry, but in principle that would not mean that the successful candidate would have to be in priest's orders.

A similar flexibility would need to be put in place for the ongoing support of ministers, in terms of continuing professional development, ministerial review and personal pastoral care. In an environment where almost all ministry would be experimental, contextual and subject to change, pastoral support would need to be agile, discerning and generous. A ministry devoted to realizing the impossible does not come with any guarantee of success, nor therefore any simple, quantifiable means of measuring it. It does come with risk and insecurity baked in, together with a healthy dose of absurdity and a hint of madness.

The churches urgently need to set up something like 'zones of experimentation' in which it is agreed that inherited ecclesiologies and ministerial order shall not apply, so that innovation is not constrained. They will need to be monitored and reviewed, but by way of appropriately developed processes of their own, not by bishops or inspection teams 'coming in' from the institutional hierarchy. Good news stories emerging from these zones can of course be celebrated, but they also need permission to fail, or to flourish for a time and then be discontinued, without this being seen as evidence that the initiative was ill-judged. They must be recognized in their own right as fully 'church' for the foreseeable future without the expectation of eventual conformity to tradition. They must be laboratories for the nurture and trialling of new ministerial cultures, such that over time they can be recognized as equal partners in a pluralist church. Inherited orders and structures of ministry will endure wherever they continue to relate meaningfully to local contexts and cultures, but multiple modes and patterns of ministry will joyfully coexist with them in an ecclesianarchy of faith, hope, love and mutual celebration of the impossibility of Christian faith.

The most vivid account of this ministry of the impossible is provided by St Paul in several passages in his tempestuous second letter to the Corinthians. It is impossible because it can only create life by being delivered to death:

> We have this treasure in jars of clay to show that this all-surpassing power is from God and not from us. We are hard pressed on every side, but not crushed; perplexed, but not in despair; persecuted, but not

abandoned; struck down, but not destroyed. We always carry around in our body the death of Jesus, so that the life of Jesus may also be revealed in our body. For we who are alive are always being given over to death for Jesus' sake, so that his life may be revealed in our mortal body. (2 Cor. 4.7–12)

It is scarcely surprising that Paul was suspected of not being entirely sane: 'If we are "out of our mind," as some say, it is for God' (5.13). Perhaps his most devastating tour de force about the calamities, contradictions and consolations of ministry comes a little later (6.4–10):

As servants of God we commend ourselves in every way: in great endurance; in troubles, hardships and distresses; in beatings, imprisonments and riots; in hard work, sleepless nights and hunger; in purity, understanding, patience and kindness; in the Holy Spirit and in sincere love; in truthful speech and in the power of God; with weapons of righteousness in the right hand and in the left; through glory and dishonour, bad report and good report; genuine, yet regarded as impostors; known, yet regarded as unknown; dying, and yet we live on; beaten, and yet not killed; sorrowful, yet always rejoicing; poor, yet making many rich; having nothing, and yet possessing everything. (2 Cor. 6.4–10)

Paul's 'madness' is further highlighted when he entreats the Corinthians to 'bear with him in his foolishness', as in a series of ironic boasts he pleads for understanding of what could be called the 'impossibility' of ministry. He is moved to 'compete' with the so-called 'super-apostles' who were dazzling – and therefore spiritually blinding – the Corinthian Christians with their seeming 'success' in ministry and mission, casting himself again as 'out of his mind':

Are they servants of Christ? (I am out of my mind to talk like this.) I am more. I have worked much harder, been in prison more frequently, been flogged more severely, and been exposed to death again and again ... three times I was shipwrecked, I spent a night and a day in the open sea, I have been constantly on the move. I have been in danger from rivers, in danger from bandits, in danger from my fellow Jews, in danger from Gentiles ... I have laboured and toiled and have often gone without sleep; I have known hunger and thirst and have often gone without food; I have been cold and naked. Besides everything else, I face daily the pressure of my concern for all the churches. (2 Cor. 11.23–28)

And of course, it is the final sentence that is the most telling, and the truest.

Bibliography

Adorno, T. W. (2001), *The Culture Industry: Selected Essays on Mass Culture*, London: Routledge.

Advisory Board of Ministry (1993), *GS 1084: Order in Diversity*, London: General Synod.

Advisory Board of Ministry (1998), *Stranger in the Wings: A Report on Local Non-Stipendiary Ministry*, London: Church House Publishing.

Advisory Council for the Church's Ministry (1968), *A Supporting Ministry*, London: Church Information Office.

Advisory Council for the Church's Ministry (1974), *Deacons in the Church*, London: Church Information Office.

Advisory Council for the Church's Ministry (1990), *Deacons Now: The Report of a Church of England Working Party concerned with Women in Ordained Ministry*, London: Church Information Office.

Allain-Chapman, J. (2012), *Resilient Pastors: The Role of Adversity in Healing and Growth*, London: SPCK.

Anderson L. W. and Krathwohl D. R., eds (2001), *A Taxonomy for Learning, Teaching, and Assessing: A Revision of Bloom's Taxonomy of Educational Objectives*, New York: Longman.

Appignanesi, R. and Garratt, C. (2004), *Introducing Postmodernism*, Royston: Icon Books.

Arbuckle, G. (1993), *Refounding the Church: Dissent for Leadership*, London: Geoffrey Chapman.

Arbuckle, G. (1999), 'Chaplaincy, Teams and Ecumenism', in Legood, G., ed., *Chaplaincy: The Church's Sector Ministries*, London: Cassell, pp. 152–63.

Archbishops' Council of the Church of England (2003), *GS 1496: Formation for Ministry within a Learning Church: The Hind Report*, London: Church House Publishing.

Archbishops' Council of the Church of England (2003, revised 2015), *Guidelines for the Professional Conduct of the Clergy*, London: Church House Publishing.

Archbishops' Council of the Church of England (2004), *Mission-shaped Church: Church Planting and Fresh Expressions of Church in a Changing Context*, London: Church House Publishing.

Archbishops' Council of the Church of England (2005), *Guidelines for the Identification, Training and Deployment of Ordained Pioneer Ministers*, London: Church House Publishing.

Archbishops' Council of the Church of England (2006), *Shaping the Future: New Patterns of Training for Lay and Ordained*, London: Church House Publishing.

Archbishops' Council of the Church of England (2010), *Ministerial Development Review Guidance*, London: Church House Publishing.

Archbishops' Council of the Church of England (2015), *GS 1977: Developing Discipleship*, London: Church House Publishing.

Archbishops' Council of the Church of England (2015), *GS 1979: Resourcing Ministerial Education in the Church of England – A Report from the Task Group*, General Synod.

Archbishops' Group on the Episcopate (1990), *Episcopal Ministry*, London: Church House Publishing.

Astley, J. (1996), 'Theology for the Untheological?', in Astley, J. and Francis, L., eds, *Christian Theology and Religious Education: Connections and Contradictions*, London: SPCK, pp. 60–77.

Aston, M. (2003, orig. pub. 1981), 'Popular Religious Movements in the Middle Ages', in Barraclough, G. ed., *The Christian World: A Social and Cultural History of Christianity*, London: Thames & Hudson, pp. 157–70.

Aveyard, I. (2013), 'Growing into Responsibility', in Ling, T., ed., *Moving On in Ministry: Discernment for Times of Transition and Change*, London: Church House Publishing, pp. 31–45.

Avis, P. (2005), *A Ministry Shaped by Mission*, Edinburgh: T & T Clark.

Badham, P., ed. (1989), *Religion, State and Society in Modern Britain*, Lampeter: Edwin Mellen Press.

Baigent, J. (2006), 'Bible, Tradition and Ministry', in Rowdon, H., ed., *Serving God's People: Re-thinking Christian Ministry Today*, Carlisle: Partnership for Paternoster Press, pp. 2–18.

Baker, C. (2009), *The Hybrid Church in the City: Third Space Thinking*, London: SCM Press.

Baker, J. (2010), *Curating Worship*, London: SPCK.

Baker, J. and Ross, C., eds (2014), *The Pioneer Gift: Explorations in Mission*, Norwich: Canterbury Press.

Ballard, P. (2009), 'Locating Chaplaincy: A Theological Note', *Crucible*, July–September, pp. 18–24.

Barnett, R. (1997), *Higher Education: A Critical Business*, Milton Keynes: Open University Press.

Barraclough, G., ed. (2003, orig. pub. 1981), *The Christian World: A Social and Cultural History of Christianity*, London: Thames & Hudson.

Barry, F. R. (1969), *Secular and Supernatural*, London: SCM Press.

Bartley, J. (2006), *Faith and Politics after Christendom: The Church as a Movement for Anarchy*, Milton Keynes: Authentic Media.

Bauman, Z. (2001), *Liquid Modernity*, Cambridge: Polity Press.

Bayes, P. and Sledge, T. (2006), *Mission-shaped Parish: Traditional Church in a Changing Context*, London: Church House Publishing.

Beattie, T. (2007), *The New Atheists: The Twilight of Reason and the War on Religion*, London: Darton, Longman & Todd.

Beckford, J. (1989), *Religion and Advanced Industrial Society*, London: Unwin Hyman.

Beeson, T. (2007), *Round the Church in 50 Years: An Intimate Journey*, London: SCM Press.

Bentley, J. (1978), *Cry God for England*, London: Bowerdean Press.

Berger, P. L. (1967), *The Sacred Canopy: Elements of a Sociological Theory of Religion*, New York: Doubleday.

Bettenson, H. and Maunder, C., eds (1999), *Documents of the Christian Church*, new edition, Oxford: Oxford University Press.

Beville, K. (2016), *The Church Community in Contemporary Culture: Evangelism and Engagement with Postmodern People*, Cambridge, OH: Christian Publishing House.

Billings, A. (2010), *Making God Possible: The Task of Ordained Ministry Present and Future*, London: SPCK.

Billings, A. (2013), *Lost Church: Why We Must Find it Again*, London: SPCK.

Billings, A. (2015), 'The Place of Chaplaincy in Public Life', in Swift, C., Cobb, M. and Todd, A., eds, *A Handbook of Chaplaincy Studies: Understanding Spiritual Care in Public Places*, Aldershot: Ashgate, pp. 31–46.

Bloom, B. S. (1956), *Taxonomy of Educational Objectives*, Boston, MA: Allyn and Bacon.

Borgeson, J. and Wilson, L., eds (1990), *Reshaping Ministry: Essays in Memory of Wesley Frensdorff*, Arvada, CO: Jethro Publications.

Bosch, D. (1992), *Transforming Mission: Paradigm Shifts in the Theology of Mission*, New York: Orbis Books.

Boulard, F. (1960), *An Introduction to Religious Sociology*, London: Darton, Longman & Todd.

Bowden, A. (2003), *Ministry in the Countryside: A Model for the Future*, London: Continuum.

Bowden, A. and West, M. (2000), *Dynamic Local Ministry*, London: Geoffrey Chapman.

Bowden, A., Francis, L. J., Jordan, E. and Simon, O., eds (2011), *Ordained Local Ministry in the Church of England*, London: Continuum.

Bowden, J., ed. (1993), *Thirty Years of Honesty: 'Honest to God' Then and Now*, London: SCM Press.

Bowler, K. (2013), *Blessed: A History of the American Prosperity Gospel*, Oxford: Oxford University Press.

Bradley, I. (2003, 2nd edn, orig. pub. 1993), *The Celtic Way*, London: Darton, Longman & Todd.

Bradley, I. (2018), *Following the Celtic Way: A New Assessment of Celtic Christianity*, London: Darton, Longman & Todd.

Brewin, K. (2000), *Other: Loving God, Self and Neighbour in a World of Fractures*, London: Hodder & Stoughton.

Brown, A. and Woodhead, L. (2016), *That Was the Church That Was: How the Church of England Lost the English People*, London: Bloomsbury.

Brown, C. (2001), *The Death of Christian Britain*, London: Routledge.

Brown, C. and Lynch, G. (2012), 'Cultural Perspectives', in Woodhead, L. and Catto, R., eds, *Religion and Change in Modern Britain*, Abingdon: Routledge, pp. 329–51.

Bruce, S. (2011), *Secularization*, Oxford: Oxford University Press.

Buck, J. (2016), *Reframing the House: Constructive Feminist Global Ecclesiology for the Western Evangelical Church*, Eugene, OR: Pickwick Publications.

Buckley, A. (2013), 'From Parish to Chaplaincy', in Ling, T., ed., *Moving on in Ministry: Discernment for Times of Transition and Change*, London: Church House Publishing, pp. 114–27.

Burkhard, J. J. (2004), *Apostolicity Then and Now: An Ecumenical Church in a Postmodern World*, Collegeville, MN: Liturgical Press.

Buschart, W. David and Eilers, Kent D. (2015), *Theology as Retrieval: Receiving the Past, Renewing the Church*, Downers Grove, IL: InterVarsity Press.

Caperon J. (2015), *A Vital Ministry: Chaplaincy in Schools in the Post-Christian Era*, London: SCM Press.

Caperon, J. (2018), 'Chaplaincy and Traditional Structures', in Caperon, J., Todd, A. and Walters, J., eds, *A Christian Theology of Chaplaincy*, London: Jessica Kingsley, pp. 119–42.

Caperon, J., Todd, A. and Walters, J., eds (2018), *A Christian Theology of Chaplaincy*, London: Jessica Kingsley.

Caputo, J. D., ed. (1996), *Deconstruction in a Nutshell: A Conversation with Jacques Derrida*, New York: Fordham University Press.

Caputo, J. D. (1997), *The Prayers and Tears of Jacques Derrida: Religion without Religion*, Bloomington, IN: Indiana University Press.

Caputo, J. D. (2001), *On Religion*, Abingdon: Routledge.

Caputo, J. D. (2006), *The Weakness of God: A Theology of the Event*, Bloomington, IN: Indiana University Press.

Caputo, J. D. (2007), *What Would Jesus Deconstruct? The Good News of Postmodernism for the Church*, Grand Rapids, MI: Baker Academic.

Caputo, J. D. (2013), *The Insistence of God: A Theology of Perhaps*, Bloomington, IN: Indiana University Press.

Caputo, J. D. (2015), *Hoping Against Hope: Confessions of a Postmodern Pilgrim*, Minneapolis, MN: Fortress Press.

Caputo, J. D. (2016), *The Folly of God: A Theology of the Unconditional*, Salem, OR: Polebridge Press.

Carr, W. (1992), *Say One for Me: The Church of England in the Next Decade*, London: SPCK.

Carrette, J. and King, R. (2005), *Selling Spirituality: The Silent Takeover of Religion*, Abingdon: Routledge.

Central Advisory Council for the Ministry (1967), *Partners in Ministry (The Morley Report)*, London: Church Information Office.

Chasan, M. (2014), 'Situationally Adaptive Organizations for 21st Century Transformation and Thriving', www.huffpost.com/entry/situationally-adaptive-organizations-for-21st-century-thriving, accessed 16.02.20.

Chopp, R. (1995), *Saving Work-Feminist Practices of Theological Education*, New York: Westminster John Knox Press.

Christoyannopoulos, A. (2010), *Christian Anarchism: A Political Commentary on the Gospel*, Exeter: Imprint Academic.

Clark, J. (undated), 'David du Plessis, Smith Wigglesworth, and Charismatic Movement', www.jonasclark.com/david-du-plessis-mr-pentecost/, accessed 23.09.2019.

Clark, P. (1984), 'Snakes and Ladders: Reflections on Hierarchy and the Fall', in Furlong, M., ed., *Feminine in the Church*, London: SPCK, pp. 178–94.

Clements, K. (1988), *Lovers of Discord: Twentieth Century Theological Controversies in England*, London: SPCK.

Clitherow, A. (2004), *Renewing Faith in Ordained Ministry: New Hope for Tired Clergy*, London: SPCK.

Cocksworth, C. (2008), *Holding Together: Gospel, Church and Spirit – The Essentials of Christian Identity*, Norwich: Canterbury Press.

Cocksworth, C. and Brown, R. (2006), *Being a Priest Today*, Norwich: Canterbury Press.

Collins, J. (2002), *Deacons and the Church: Making Connections between Old and New*, Leominster: Gracewing.

Countryman, L. W. (2012), *Calling on the Spirit in Unsettling Times: Discerning God's Future for the Church*, Norwich: Canterbury Press.

Cray, G. (2010), 'For the Parish by Andrew Davison and Alison Milbank – a Response', *Anvil*, 27.1, available at https://churchmissionsociety.org/resources/anvil-archives/, accessed 25.02.2020.

Cray, G., Kennedy, A. and Mobsby, I., eds (2012), *Fresh Expressions of Church and the Kingdom of God*, Norwich: Canterbury Press.

Crevani, L., Lindgren, M. and Packendorff, J. (2007), 'Shared Leadership: A Postheroic Perspective on Leadership as a Collective Construction', *International Journal of Leadership Studies*, Vol. 3.1, pp. 40–67.

Croft, S. (1999 and 2008), *Ministry in Three Dimensions: Ordination and Leadership in the Local Church*, London: Darton, Longman & Todd.

Croft, S. (2002), *Transforming Communities: Re-imagining the Church for the 21st Century*, London: Darton, Longman & Todd.

Croft, S., ed. (2006), *The Future of the Parish System: Shaping the Church of England for the 21st Century*, London: Church House Publishing.

Croft, S., ed. (2008a), *Mission-Shaped Questions: Defining Issues for Today's Church*, London: Church House Publishing.

Croft, S. (2008b), 'What Counts as a Fresh Expression of Church and who Decides?', in Nelstrop, L. and Percy, M., eds, *Evaluating Fresh Expressions*, Norwich: Canterbury Press, pp. 3–14.

Cunningham, A. (1990), 'Elements for a Theology of Priesthood in the Teaching of the Fathers of the Church', in Wister, R., ed., *Priests: Identity and Ministry*, Wilmington, DE: Michael Glazier, chapter 2.

Cupitt, D. (1989), *Radicals and the Future of the Church*, London: SCM Press.

Davie, G. (2002), *Europe: The Exceptional Case. Parameters of Faith in the Modern World*, London: Darton, Longman & Todd.

Davie, G. (2015), *Religion in Britain: A Persistent Paradox*, Chichester: Wiley Blackwell.

Davies, M. (2019), 'Synod Will be Asked whether it "Gladly Bears" Eucharistic Presidency by Methodist Presbyters as "Temporary Anomaly"', *Church Times*, 14 June at www.churchtimes.co.uk/articles/2019/21-june/news/uk/, accessed 12.09.19.

Davis, C. (1967), *A Question of Conscience*, London: Hodder & Stoughton.

Davison, A. and Milbank, A. (2010), *For the Parish: A Critique of Fresh Expressions*, London: SCM Press.

Dormor, D., McDonald, J. and Caddick, J., eds (2003), *Anglicanism: The Answer to Modernity*, London: Continuum.

Duin, J. (2009), *Days of Fire and Glory: The Rise and Fall of a Charismatic Community*, Baltimore, MD: Crossland Press.

Dunn, J. D. G. (2006, 3rd edn, orig. pub. 1977), *Unity and Diversity in the New Testament: An Inquiry into the Character of Earliest Christianity*, London: SCM Press.

Durkheim, E. (2001, orig. pub. 1915), *The Elementary Forms of the Religious Life*, Oxford: Oxford University Press.

Earey, M. (2013), *Beyond Common Worship: Anglican Identity and Liturgical Diversity*, London: SCM Press.

Edmondson, C. (2002), *Fit to Lead: Sustaining Effective Ministry in a Changing World*, London: Darton, Longman & Todd.

Ellul, J. (2011), *Anarchism and Christianity*, Eugene, OR: Wipf and Stock.

Evans, G. (2008), *The History of Christian Europe*, Oxford: Lion Hudson.

Farley, E. (1983), *Theologia: The Fragmentation and Unity of Theological Knowledge*, Philadelphia, PA: Fortress Press.

Farley, E. (1988), *The Fragility of Knowledge: Theological Education in the Church and the University*, Philadelphia, PA: Fortress Press.

Farley, E. (2003), *Practicing Gospel: Unconventional Thoughts on the Church's Ministry*, Louisville, KT: Westminster John Knox Press.

Ferris, P. (1964), *The Church of England*, Harmondsworth: Penguin Books.

Flanagan, K. and Jupp, P., eds (2007), *A Sociology of Spirituality*, Aldershot: Ashgate.

Forder, C. R. (1959), *The Parish Priest at Work: An Introduction to Systematic Pastoralia*, London: SPCK.

Francis, L., ed. (1989), *The Country Parson*, Leominster: Gracewing Fowler Wright.

Frend, W. H. C. (2003, orig. pub. 1981), 'Christianity in the Roman Empire', in Barraclough, G., ed., *The Christian World: A Social and Cultural History of Christianity*, London: Thames & Hudson, pp. 45–60.

Freston, P. (2000), 'The Road to Damascus: Global Dimensions of Religious Conversion Today', in Percy, M., ed., *Previous Convictions: Conversion in the Present Day*, London: SPCK, pp. 77–92.

Furlong, M., ed. (1984), *Feminine in the Church*, London: SPCK.

Furlong, M. (2000), *C of E: The State It's In*, London: Hodder & Stoughton.

Gamble, R. (2006), 'Doing Traditional Church Really Well', in Croft, S., ed., *The Future of the Parish System: Shaping the Church of England for the 21st Century*, London: Church House Publishing, pp. 93–109.

Gay, D. (2011), *Remixing the Church: Towards an Emerging Ecclesiology*, London: SCM Press.

Gay, D. (2014), 'Prospective Practitioners: A Pilgrim's Progress', in Baker, J. and Ross, C., eds, *The Pioneer Gift: Explorations in Mission*, Norwich: Canterbury Press, pp. 39–54.

Gaze, S. (2006), *Mission-Shaped and Rural: Growing Churches in the Countryside*, London: Church House Publishing.

Gehrz, C., ed. (2015), *The Pietist Vision of Christian Higher Education*, Downers Grove, IL: InterVarsity Press.

General Synod of the Church of England (1978), *GS 374: The Future of the Ministry. A Report Containing Thirteen Resolutions of the House of Bishops*, London: Church Information Office.

General Synod of the Church of England (1988), *GS 802: Deacons in the Ministry of the Church*, London: Church House Publishing.

General Synod of the Church of England (2001), *GS 1407: For Such a Time as This: A Renewed Diaconate in the Church of England*, London: Church House Publishing.

General Synod of the Church of England (2012), *GS 1025: Pursuing the Three Quinquennial Goals*, London: Church House Publishing.

Gibbs, E. and Bolger, R. (2006), *Emerging Churches: Creating Christian Community in Postmodern Cultures*, London: SPCK.

Gibbs, E. and Coffey, I. (2001), *Church Next: Quantum Changes in Christian Ministry*, Leicester: IVP.

Gill, R. (2012), *Theology Shaped by Society: Sociological Theology Vol. 2*, Aldershot: Ashgate.

Gittoes, J., Green, B. and Heard, J., eds (2013), *Generous Ecclesiology: Church, World and the Kingdom of God*, London: SCM Press.

Goodhew, D., ed. (2012), *Church Growth in Britain, 1980 to the Present*, Aldershot: Ashgate.

Goodhew, D., Roberts, A. and Volland, M. (2012), *Fresh! An Introduction to Fresh Expressions of Church and Pioneer Ministry*, London: SCM Press.

Graham, E. (1996), *Transforming Practice*, London: Mowbray.

Green, A. (2009), *A Theology of Women's Priesthood*, London: SPCK.

Greenacre, R. and Podmore, C. (2014), *Part of the One Church? The Ordination of Women and Anglican Identity*, Norwich: Canterbury Press.

Greenwood, R. (1994), *Transforming Priesthood: A New Theology, Mission and Ministry*, London: SPCK.

Greenwood, R. (2002), *Transforming Church: Liberating Structures for Ministry*, London: SPCK.

Greenwood, R. (2009), *Parish Priests for the Sake of the Kingdom*, London: SPCK.

Greenwood, R. and Pascoe, C., eds (2006), *Local Ministry: Story, Process and Meaning*, London: SPCK.

Grenz, S. (1996), *A Primer on Postmodernism*, Grand Rapids, MI: Eerdmans.

Grey, M. (1989), *Redeeming the Dream: Feminism, Redemption and the Christian Tradition*, London: SPCK.

Grundy, M. (2011), *Leadership and Oversight: New Models for Episcopal Ministry*, London: Mowbray.

Grundy, M. (2015), *Multi-Congregation Ministry: Theology and Practice in a Changing Church*, Norwich: Canterbury Press.

Guérin, D., ed. (2005), *No Gods, No Masters: An Anthology of Anarchism*, Edinburgh: AK Press.

Guest, M. (2007), 'In Search of Spiritual Capital: The Spiritual as a Cultural Resource', in Flanagan, K. and Jupp, P., eds, *A Sociology of Spirituality*, Aldershot: Ashgate, pp. 181–200.

Gunton, C. and Hardy, D., eds (1989), *On Being the Church: Essays on the Christian Community*, Edinburgh: T & T Clark.

Hall, C., ed. (1991), *The Deacon's Ministry*, Leominster: Gracewing.

Hardy, D. (2006), 'Afterword: Evaluating Local Ministry for the Future of the Church', in Greenwood, R. and Pascoe, C., eds, *Local Ministry: Story, Process and Meaning*, London: SPCK, pp. 131–50.

Harper, M. (1973), *New Way of Living: How the Church of the Redeemer, Houston, Found a New Life Style*, London: Hodder & Stoughton.

Harper, M. (1988), *Let My People Grow*, London: Hodder & Stoughton.

Harris, J. (2000), *Chocolat*, London: Black Swan.

Hartshorne, K. (2014), 'The Upper Room', in Baker, J. and Ross, C., eds, *The Pioneer Gift: Explorations in Mission*, Norwich: Canterbury Press, pp. 216–37.

Harvey, D. (1990), *The Condition of Postmodernity*, Oxford: Blackwell.

Hastings, A. (1992), 'All Change: The Presence of the Past in British Christianity', in Willmer, H., ed., *20/20 Visions: The Futures of Christianity in Britain*, London: SPCK, pp. 13–29.

Hauerwas, S. (1981), *A Community of Character: Towards a Constructive Christian Social Ethic*, Notre Dame, IN: University of Notre Dame Press.

Hauerwas, S. (2004), *Performing the Faith: Bonhoeffer and the Practice of Nonviolence*, London: SPCK.

Hawkins, T. (1997), *The Learning Congregation: A New Vision of Leadership*, Louisville, KY: Westminster John Knox Press.

Heard, J. (2013), 'Inculturation – Faithful to the Past: Open to the Future', in Gittoes, J., Green, B. and Heard, J., eds, *Generous Ecclesiology: Church, World and the Kingdom of God*, London: SCM Press, pp. 61–77.

Heelas, P. (2008), *Spiritualities of Life: New Age Romanticism and Consumptive Capitalism*, Oxford: Blackwell.

Heelas, P. and Woodhead, L. (2005), *The Spiritual Revolution: Why Religion is Giving Way to Spirituality*, Oxford: Blackwell.

Heywood, D. (2011), *Reimagining Ministry*, London: SCM Press.

Heywood, D. (2017), *Kingdom Learning: Experiential and Reflective Approaches to Christian Formation*, London: SCM Press.

Hoad, A. (1984), 'Crumbs from the Table: Towards a Whole Priesthood', in Furlong, M., ed., *Feminine in the Church*, London: SPCK, pp. 100–18.

Hocken, P. (1986), *Streams of Renewal: The Origins and Early Development of the Charismatic Movement in Great Britain*, Carlisle: Paternoster Press.

Hollenweger, W. (1976), *The Pentecostals*, London: SCM Press.

Hollenweger, W. (1986), 'Pentecostal Spirituality', in Jones, C., Wainwright, G. and Yarnold, E., eds, *The Study of Spirituality*, London: SPCK, pp. 551–2.

Holloway, R. (1972), *Let God Arise*, Oxford: Mowbray.

Holloway, R. (1997), *Dancing on the Edge: Faith in a Post-Christian Age*, London: HarperCollins.

Hornby, N. (2001), *How to be Good*, London: Penguin Books.

Howatch, S. (1987), *Glittering Images*, London: HarperCollins.

Howatch, S. (1988), *Glamorous Powers*, London: HarperCollins.

Hoyle, D. (2016), *The Pattern of our Calling: Ministry Yesterday, Today and Tomorrow*, London: SCM Press.

Hoyle, L. (2003), *Over the Circumstances*, Bradford-on-Avon: Terra Nova Publications.

Hunt, S. (2004), *The Alpha Enterprise: Evangelism in a Post-Christian Era*, Aldershot: Ashgate.

Ison, D., ed. (2005), *The Vicar's Guide: Life and Ministry in the Parish*, London: Church House Publishing.

James, E. (1987), *A Life of Bishop John A. T. Robinson: Scholar, Pastor, Prophet*, London: Collins.

Jamieson, P. (1997), *Living at the Edge: Sacrament and Solidarity in Leadership*, London: Mowbray.

Jeanrond, W. (1999), 'Community and Authority', in Gunton, C. and Hardy, D., eds, *On Being the Church: Essays on the Christian Community*, Edinburgh: T & T Clark, pp. 81–109.

Jenkins, T. (2003), 'Anglicanism: The Only Answer to Modernity', in Dormor, D., McDonald, J. and Caddick, J., eds, *Anglicanism: The Answer to Modernity*, London: Continuum, pp. 186–202.

Jenkins, T. (2006), *An Experiment in Providence: How Faith Engages with the World*, London: SPCK.

Kay, W. K. and Dyer, A. E., eds (2004), *Pentecostal and Charismatic Studies: A Reader*, London: SCM Press.

Kee, A. (1982), *Constantine Versus Christ*, London: SCM Press.

Keith, B. (2014), 'To Pluck Up and to Pull Down, to Build and to Plant', in Baker, J. and Ross, C., eds, *The Pioneer Gift: Explorations in Mission*, Norwich: Canterbury Press, pp. 117–40.

Kelsey, D. (1993), *Between Athens and Berlin: The Theological Education Debate*, Grand Rapids, MI: Eerdmans.

Kim, S. and Kollontai, P., eds (2007), *Community Identity: Dynamics of Religion in Context*, London: T & T Clark.

Kuhrt, G., ed. (2001), *Ministry Issues for the Church of England: Mapping the Trends*, London: Church House Publishing.

Lamdin, K. (1999), 'Professional Issues', in Legood, G., ed., *Chaplaincy: The Church's Sector Ministries*, London: Cassell, pp. 143–51.

Lartey, E. (2013), *Postcolonializing God: An African Practical Theology*, London: SCM Press.

Leach, J. (1997), *Visionary Leadership in the Local Church*, Nottingham: Grove Books.

Lees, J. (2018), *Self-Supporting Ministry: A Practical Guide*, London: SPCK.

Legood, G. (1999), *Chaplaincy: The Church's Sector Ministries*, London: Cassell.

Legood, G. (2000), 'Liberal Theology and Church Structures', in Jobling, J. and Markham, I., eds, *Theological Liberalism: Creative and Critical*, London: SPCK, pp. 126–41.

Lewis-Anthony, J. (2009), *If You Meet George Herbert on the Road, Kill Him: Radically Re-thinking Priestly Ministry*, London: Mowbray.

Lindberg, C. (2010), *The European Reformations*, Chichester: Wiley Blackwell.

Ling, T., ed. (2013), *Moving On in Ministry: Discernment for Times of Transition and Change*, London: Church House Publishing.

Lomax, T. (2015), *Creating Missional Worship: Fusing Context and Tradition*, London: Church House Publishing.

Lynch, G. (2002), *After Religion: 'Generation X' and the Search for Meaning*, London: Darton, Longman & Todd.

Lynch, G. (2005), *Understanding Theology and Popular Culture*, Oxford: Blackwell.

Lyon, D. (2000), *Jesus in Disneyland: Religion in Postmodern Times*, Cambridge: Polity Press.

Lyotard, J. (1984, orig. pub. 1979), *The Postmodern Condition: A Report on Knowledge*, Manchester: Manchester University Press.

MacCulloch, D. (2010), *A History of Christianity*, London: Penguin Books.

MacLaren, D. (2004), *Mission Implausible: Restoring Credibility to the Church*, Milton Keynes: Paternoster Press.

MacRobert, I. (1989), 'The New Black-led Churches in Britain', in Badham, P., ed., *Religion, State and Society in Modern Britain*, Lampeter: Edwin Mellen Press, pp. 119–44.

Maltby, J. (2005), '"Aaron's Drest"; Priestly Formation in the Church of England, 16th to 19th Centuries', in Sangalli, M., ed., *Pastori Pope Preti Rabbini*, Rome: Carocci Editore, pp. 207–23.

Marti, G. and Ganiel, G. (2014), *The Deconstructed Church: Understanding Emerging Christianity*, Oxford: Oxford University Press.

Martin, D. (1967), *A Sociology of English Religion*, London: Heinemann.

Martin, D. (1980), *The Breaking of the Image: A Sociology of Christian Theory and Practice*, Oxford: Blackwell.

Martin, D. (1996), *Reflections on Sociology and Theology*, Oxford: Oxford University Press.

Martin, D. (2005), *On Secularization: Towards a Revised General Theory*, Aldershot: Ashgate.

Martin, D. (2011), *The Future of Christianity: Reflections on Violence and Democracy, Religion and Secularization*, Aldershot: Ashgate.

Martin, J. and Coakley, S., eds (2016), *For God's Sake: Re-imagining Priesthood and Prayer in a Changing Church*, Norwich: Canterbury Press.

Mascall, E. L. (1965), *The Secularization of Christianity*, London: Darton, Longman & Todd.

Mason, K. (2002, orig. pub. 1992), *Priesthood and Society*, Norwich: Canterbury Press.

Maxtone Graham, Y. (1993), *The Church Hesitant: A Portrait of the Church of England Today*, London: Hodder & Stoughton.

McCord Adams, M. (2010), 'The Episcopacy of All Believers', *Modern Believing*, 51, no. 4, pp. 9–28.

McGrath, A. (2007), *The Christian Theology Reader*, Oxford: Blackwell.

McGuire, M. (2008), *Lived Religion: Faith and Practice in Everyday Life*, New York and Oxford: Oxford University Press.

McIntosh, M. (2008), *Divine Teaching: An Introduction to Christian Theology*, Oxford: Blackwell.

McLeod, H. (1995), 'The Privatisation of Religion in Modern England', in Young, F., ed., *Dare We Speak of God in Public?*, London: Mowbray, pp. 4–21.

Mehta, V. (1965), *The New Theologian*, London: Weidenfeld and Nicolson.

Melinsky, M. A. H. (1992), *The Shape of the Ministry*, Norwich: Canterbury Press.

Methodist Church (2011, revd edn 2018), *A Guide to Ministerial Development Review*, London: Methodist Church House.

Ministry Co-ordinating Group of the Church of England (1980), *GS 459: The Church's Ministry: A Survey*, London: Church Information Office.

Ministry Co-ordinating Group of the Church of England (1988), *GS 858: The Ordained Ministry: Numbers, Cost and Deployment*, London: General Synod.

Ministry Division of the Church of England (2013), 'Archbishop Issues Call for Church Revolution', www.churchofengland.org/more/media-centre/news/archbishop-issues-call-church-revolution, accessed 1.08.2018.

Mitchell, R. H. (2011), *Church, Gospel and Empire: How the Politics of Sovereignty Impregnated the West*, Eugene, OR: Wipf and Stock.

Mitchell, R. H. (2013), *The Fall of the Church*, Eugene, OR: Wipf and Stock.

Moberly, R. C. (2012, orig. pub. 1897), *Ministerial Priesthood*, Berkeley, CA: Apocryphile Press.

Mobsby, I. (2007), *Emerging and Fresh Expressions of Church: How Are They Authentically Church and Anglican?*, London: Moot Community Publishing.

Mobsby, I. (2012), *God Unknown: The Trinity in Contemporary Spirituality and Mission*, Norwich: Canterbury Press.

Mobsby, I. and Berry, M. (2014), *A New Monastic Handbook: From Vision to Practice*, Norwich: Canterbury Press.

Moltmann, J. (1997), *The Source of Life*, London: SCM Press.

Moody, C., ed. (1999), 'Spirituality and Sector Ministry', in Legood, G., *Chaplaincy: The Church's Sector Ministries*, London: Cassell, pp. 15–24.

Moody, K. S. (2015), *Radical Theology and Emerging Christianity: Deconstruction, Materialism and Religious Practices*, Abingdon: Routledge.

Moreton, C. (2010), 'The Church of Everywhere', *Third Way*, April, pp. 22–6.

Morisy, A. (2004), *Journeying Out: A New Approach to Christian Mission*, London: Continuum.

Morisy, A. (2009), *Bothered and Bewildered: Enacting Hope in Troubled Times*, London: Continuum.

Morley, J. (1988), 'Liturgy and Danger', in Furlong, M., ed., *Mirror to the Church: Reflections on Sexism*, London: SPCK.

Morris, C. (2003, orig. pub. 1981), 'Medieval Christendom', in Barraclough, G., ed., *The Christian World: A Social and Cultural History of Christianity*, London: Thames & Hudson, pp. 133–46.

Morris, H. D. (2019), *Flexible Church: Being the Church in the Contemporary World*, London: SCM Press.

Moynagh, M. (2006), 'Good Practice is not what it Used to Be: Accumulating Wisdom for Fresh Expressions of Church', in Croft, S., ed., *The Future of the Parish System: Shaping the Church of England for the 21st Century*, London: Church House Publishing, pp. 110–24.

Moynagh, M. with Harrold, P. (2012), *Church for Every Context: An Introduction to Theology and Practice*, London: SCM Press.

Moynagh, M. (2017), *Church in Life: Innovation, Mission and Ecclesiology*, London: SCM Press.

Murray, S. (2004, 2nd edn 2018), *Post-Christendom: Church and Mission in a Strange New World*, Carlisle: Paternoster Press.

Muskett, J. (2019), *Shop Window, Flagship, Common Ground: Metaphor in Cathedral and Congregation Studies*, London: SCM Press.

Nelstrop, L. (2008), 'Mixed Economy or Ecclesial Reciprocity: Which does the Church of England really Want to Promote?', in Nelstrop, L. and Percy, M., eds, *Evaluating Fresh Expressions*, Norwich: Canterbury Press, pp. 187–203.

Nelstrop, L. and Percy, M., eds (2008), *Evaluating Fresh Expressions: Explorations in Emerging Church*, Norwich: Canterbury Press.

Nevins, K. (2015), 'Calling for Pietist Community: *Pia Desideria* in the Classroom', in Gehrz, C., ed., *The Pietist Vision of Christian Higher Education*, Downers Grove, IL: InterVarsity Press, pp. 52–66.

Norman, E. (2002), *Secularization*, London: Continuum.

O'Donnell, K. (2003), *Postmodernism*, Oxford: Lion Publishing.

Oliver, G. (2012), *Ministry without Madness*, London: SPCK.

Owen-Jones, P. (1996), *Bed of Nails: An Advertising Executive's Journey through Theological College*, Oxford: Lion Publishing.

Page, R. (2000), *God With Us: Synergy in the Church*, London: SCM Press.

Palmer, P. (1998), *The Courage to Teach: Exploring the Inner Landscape of a Teacher's Life*, San Francisco, CA: Jossey-Bass.

Pattison, S. (2015), 'Situating Chaplaincy in the United Kingdom: The Acceptable Face of "Religion"?', in Swift, C., Cobb, M. and Todd, A., eds, *A Handbook of Chaplaincy Studies: Understanding Spiritual Care in Public Places*, Aldershot: Ashgate, pp. 13–30.

Paul, L. (1964), *The Deployment and Payment of the Clergy*, London: Church Information Office.

Paul, L. (1968), *The Death and Resurrection of the Church*, London: Hodder & Stoughton.

Percy, E. (2018), *Mothering as a Metaphor for Ministry*, Abingdon: Routledge.

Percy, M. (1996), *The Toronto Blessing*, Oxford: Latimer House.

Percy, M. (1998), *Power and the Church: Ecclesiology in an Age of Transition*, London: Cassell.

Percy, M. (2001), *The Salt of the Earth: Religious Resilience in a Secular Age*, London: Sheffield Academic Press.

Percy, M. (2005), *Engaging with Contemporary Culture: Christianity, Theology and the Concrete Church*, Aldershot: Ashgate.

Percy, M. (2008), 'Old Tricks for New Dogs? A Critique of Fresh Expressions', in Nelstrop, L. and Percy, M., eds, *Evaluating Fresh Expressions*, Norwich: Canterbury Press, pp. 27–39.

Percy, M. (2017), *The Future Shapes of Anglicanism: Currents, Contours, Charts*, Abingdon: Routledge.

Perham, M. (2002), 'How Distinctive should Anglican Worship be?', *Anvil*, Vol. 19, no. 1, pp. 33–44.

Pickard, S. (2009), *Theological Foundations for Collaborative Ministry*, Aldershot: Ashgate.

Pierson, M. (2012), *The Art of Curating Worship: Reshaping the Role of Worship Leader*, Norwich: Canterbury Press.

Pinnock, J. M. (1991), 'The History of the Diaconate', in Hall, C., ed., *The Deacon's Ministry*, Leominster: Gracewing, chapter 3.

Platten, S. (2007), *Rebuilding Jerusalem: The Church's Hold on Hearts and Minds*, London: SPCK.

Podmore, C. (2008), *The Governance of the Church of England and the Anglican Communion* (GS Misc 910), London: Church House Publishing.

Podmore, C., ed. (2015), *Fathers in God? Resources for Reflection on Women in the Episcopate*, Norwich: Canterbury Press.

Postman, N. (1985), *Amusing Ourselves to Death: Public Discourse in the Age of Show Business*, Harmondsworth: Penguin Books.

Pryce, M. (2013), 'A Pilgrimage to My Own Self? R. S. Thomas and the Poetic Character of Reflective Ministry', in Ling, T., ed., *Moving On in Ministry: Discernment for Times of Transition and Change*, London: Church House Publishing, pp. 79–97.

Pulkingham, G. (1972), *Gathered for Power*, New York: Morehouse Barlow.

Rahner, K. (1977), *The Shape of the Church to Come*, London: SPCK/Catholic Book Club.

Ramsey, A. M. (1990, orig. pub. 1963), *The Gospel and the Catholic Church*, London: SCM Press.

Rees, C. and Percy, M., eds (2010), *Apostolic Women, Apostolic Authority: Transfiguring Leadership in Today's Church*, Norwich: Canterbury Press.

Reiss, R. (2013), *The Testing of Vocation: 100 Years of Ministry Selection in the Church of England*, London: Church House Publishing.

Richardson, A. (1966), *Religion in Contemporary Debate*, London: SCM Press.

Riddell, M. (1998), *Threshold of the Future: Reforming the Church in the Post-Christian West*, London: SPCK.

Roberts, R. (1989), 'Lord, Bondsman and Churchman', in Gunton, C. and Hardy, D., eds, *On Being the Church*, Edinburgh: T & T Clark, pp. 156–224.

Roberts, R. H. (2002), *Religion, Theology and the Human Sciences*, Cambridge: Cambridge University Press.

Robertson, D. (2007), *Collaborative Ministry: What it Is, How it Works and Why*, Oxford: Bible Reading Fellowship.

Robinson, J. A. T. (1960), *On Being the Church in the World*, London: SCM Press.

Robinson, J. A. T. (1963), *Honest to God*, London: SCM Press.

Robinson, J. A. T. (1965), *The New Reformation*, London: SCM Press.

Rock, H. (2014), *God Needs Salvation: A New Vision of God for the Twenty First Century*, Alresford: Christian Alternative Books.

Roderick, P. (2008), 'Dynamic Tradition: Fuelling the Fire', in Nelstrop, L. and Percy, M., eds, *Evaluating Fresh Expressions: Explorations in Emerging Church*, Norwich: Canterbury Press, pp. 135–47.

Rollins, P. (2006), *How (Not) to Speak of God*, London: SPCK.

Rollins, P. (2008a), *The Fidelity of Betrayal: Towards a Church Beyond Belief*, London: SPCK.

Rollins, P. (2008b), 'Biting the Hand that Feeds: An Apology for Encouraging Tension between the Established Church and Emerging Collectives', in Nelstrop, L. and Percy, M., eds, *Evaluating Fresh Expressions*, Norwich: Canterbury Press, pp. 71–84.

Rorem, P. (1990), 'Mission and Ministry in the Early Church: Bishop, Presbyters and Deacons, but ...', *Currents in Theology and Mission*, 17, no. 1, pp. 15–22.

Ross, M. (1994), 'The Seven Devils of Women's Ordination', in Walrond-Skinner, S., ed., *Crossing the Boundary: What Will Women Priests Mean?* London: Mowbray, pp. 93–131.

Ross-McNairn, J. and Barron, S. (2014), *Being a Curate: Stories of What it's Really Like*, London: SPCK.

Rowdon, H. H. (1971), 'Theological Education in Historical Perspective', *Vox Evangelica*, 7, pp. 75–87.

Rumsey, A. (2017), *Parish: An Anglican Theology of Place*, London: SCM Press.

Ryan, B. (2015), *A Very Modern Ministry: Chaplaincy in the UK*, London: Theos.

Sadgrove, M. (2008), *Wisdom & Ministry: The Call to Leadership*, London: SPCK.

de Saussure, F. (1959, orig. pub. 1916), *Course in General Linguistics*, New York: Philosophical Library.

Savage, S. (2006), 'On the Analyst's Couch', in Croft, S., ed., *The Future of the Parish System: Shaping the Church of England for the 21st Century*, London: Church House Publishing, pp. 16–32.

Savage, S. and Boyd-MacMillan, E. (2007), *The Human Face of Church*, Norwich: Canterbury Press.

Schillebeeckx, E. (2000), *Church: The Human Story of God*, London: SCM Press.

Selby, P. (1991), *Belonging: Challenge to a Tribal Church*, London: SPCK.

Senior, D. (1990), 'Biblical Foundations', in Wister, R., ed., *Priests: Identity and Ministry*, Wilmington, DE: Michael Glazier, chapter 1.

Shaw, J., ed. (2010), 'Women and Leadership: What's the Difference?', in Rees, C. and Percy, M., *Apostolic Women, Apostolic Authority: Transfiguring Leadership in Today's Church*, Norwich: Canterbury Press, pp. 86–96.

Shier-Jones, A. (2009), *Pioneer Ministry and Fresh Expressions of Church*, London: SPCK.

Slater, V. (2015), *Chaplaincy Ministry and the Mission of the Church*, London: SCM Press.

Smith, A. (2008), *God-shaped Mission*, Norwich: Canterbury Press.

Smith, J. K. A. (2006), *Who's Afraid of Postmodernism? Taking Derrida, Lyotard and Foucault to Church*, Grand Rapids, MI: Baker Academic.

Smith, M. (2014), *Steel Angels: The Personal Qualities of a Priest*, London: SPCK.

Soskice, J. M. (2007), *The Kindness of God*, Oxford: Oxford University Press.

Spencer, S. (2007), *SCM Studyguide to Christian Mission*, London: SCM Press.

Stacey, N. (1971), *Who Cares? The Autobiography of an Impatient Parson*, London: Hodder & Stoughton.

Stamp, G. (2004), *Strategic Thinking and its Impact on Leadership*, Swindon: Christian Research.

Standing, R. et al. (2013), *As a Fire by Burning: Mission in the Life of the Local Congregation*, London: SCM Press.

Stanford, P. (2011), 'History Overturned as Anglican Bishops are Ordained as Catholic Priests', *Guardian*, www.theguardian.com/world/2011/jan/15/anglican-bishops-ordained-catholic-priests, accessed 24.04.19.

Starkey, M. (2011), *Ministry Rediscovered: Shaping a New and Creative Church*, Abingdon: Bible Reading Fellowship.

Steele, H. (2017), *New World, New Church? The Theology of the Emerging Church Movement*, London: SCM Press.

Stevenson, J., revised Frend, W. H. C. (1987), *A New Eusebius: Documents Illustrating the History of the Church to AD337*, London: SPCK.

Stewart-Darling, F. (2017), *Multifaith Chaplaincy in the Workplace: How Chaplains Can Support Organizations and Their Employees*, London: Jessica Kingsley.

Sturges, J. (2013), 'Understanding and Enabling Clergy Careers', in Ling, T., ed., *Moving On in Ministry: Discernment for Times of Transition and Change*, London: Church House Publishing, pp. 46–61.

Summerton, N. (2006), 'Staff Leaders and Other Leaders', in Rowdon, H., ed., *Serving God's People: Re-thinking Christian Ministry Today*, Carlisle: Partnership for Paternoster Press, pp. 36–48.

Sutcliffe, S. (2014), 'Located and Rooted: Contextual Theology and Pioneer Ministry', in Baker, J. and Ross, C., eds, *The Pioneer Gift: Explorations in Mission*, Norwich: Canterbury Press, pp. 158–77.

Suurmond, J.-J. (1994), *Word and Spirit at Play: Towards a Charismatic Theology*, London: SCM Press.

Swift, C. (2009, 2nd edn 2014), *Hospital Chaplaincy in the Twenty-first Century: The Crisis of Spiritual Care on the NHS*, Aldershot: Ashgate.

Swift, C., Cobb, M. and Todd, A., eds (2015), *A Handbook of Chaplaincy Studies: Understanding Spiritual Care in Public Places*, Aldershot: Ashgate.

Tanner, K. (1997), *Theories of Culture: A New Agenda for Theology*, New York: Fortress Press.

Tartaglia, P. (2017), 'Holy Priests are Set Apart, as the Church is from Culture', www.catholicculture.org/culture/library/view.cfm?recnum=11635#, accessed 7.11.2019.

Taylor, S. (2019), *First Expressions: Innovation and the Mission of God*, London: SCM Press.

Thiemann, R. (1991), *Constructing a Public Theology: The Church in a Pluralistic Culture*, Louisville, KY: Westminster John Knox Press.

Thomas, K. (1971), *Religion and the Decline of Magic*, London: Weidenfeld and Nicolson.

Thompson, J. and Thompson, R. (2012), *Mindful Ministry: Creative, Theological and Practical Perspectives*, London: SCM Press.

Threlfall-Holmes, M. (2011), 'Exploring Models of Chaplaincy', in Threlfall-Holmes, M. and Newitt, M., eds, *Being a Chaplain*, London: SPCK, pp. 116–226.

Threlfall-Holmes, M. and Newitt, M., eds (2011), *Being a Chaplain*, London: SPCK.

Tickle, P. (2012), 'Changes and a Changeless Faith', in Cray, G., Kennedy, A. and Mobsby, I., eds, *Fresh Expressions of Church and the Kingdom of God*, Norwich: Canterbury Press, pp. 59–76.

Tiller, J. (1983), *A Strategy for the Church's Ministry*, London: Church Information Office.

Todd, A. (2018), 'A Theology of the World', in Caperon, J., Todd, A. and Walters, J., eds, *A Christian Theology of Chaplaincy*, London: Jessica Kingsley, pp. 21–42.

Todd, A. (2018), 'Conclusion: An Invitation to Theology', in Caperon, J., Todd, A. and Walters, J., eds, *A Christian Theology of Chaplaincy*, London: Jessica Kingsley, pp. 159–68.

Todd, A., Slater, V. and Dunlop, S. (2014), *The Church of England's Involvement in Chaplaincy*, The Cardiff Centre for Chaplaincy Studies (CCCS) and The Oxford Centre for Ecclesiology & Practical Theology (OxCEPT), Cuddesdon.

Torry, M., ed. (2007), *Regeneration and Renewal: The Church in New and Changing Communities*, Norwich: Canterbury Press.

Torry, M. (2010), *Bridgebuilders: Workplace Chaplaincy – a History*, Norwich: Canterbury Press.

Torry, M. and Heskins, J., eds (2006), *Ordained Local Ministry: A New Shape for Ministry in the Church of England*, Norwich: Canterbury Press.

Toulmin, S. (1996), 'Theology in the Context of the University', in Astley, J., Francis, L. and Crowder, C., eds, *Theological Perspectives on Christian Formation*, Leominster: Gracewing, pp. 393–405.

Troxell, T. P. (2012), 'The Subversive Kernel: Anarchism and the Politics of Jesus in Postsecular Theology', unpublished PhD Thesis, Michigan State University.

Tyndale, W. (1525), Doctrinal Treatises, http://archive.churchsociety.org/publications/tracts/ CAT232_PriestinPrayerBook.pdf, accessed 11.09.2019.

Van der Ven, J. (1998), *Education for Reflective Ministry*, Louvain: Peeters Press.

Veblen, T. (2009, orig. pub. 1899), *The Theory of the Leisure Class*, Oxford: Oxford University Press.

Vincent, J. (1992), 'People's Church: Christianity as a Movement of the Poor', in Willmer, H., ed., *20/20 Visions: The Futures of Christianity in Britain*, London: SPCK, pp. 65–81.

Viola, F. (2008), *Reimagining Church: Pursuing the Dream of Organic Christianity*, Colorado Springs, CO: David C. Cook.

Voas, B. and Bruce, S. (2007), 'The Spiritual Revolution: Another False Dawn for the Sacred', in Flanagan, K. and Jupp, P., eds, *A Sociology of Spirituality*, Aldershot: Ashgate, pp. 43–62.

Volf, M. (1998), *After Our Likeness: The Church as the Image of the Trinity*, Grand Rapids, MI: Eerdmans.

Wakefield, G. (2007), *Alexander Boddy: Pentecostal Anglican Pioneer*, Milton Keynes: Paternoster Press.

Walrond-Skinner, S., ed. (1994), *Crossing the Boundary: What Will Women Priests Mean?*, London: Mowbray.

Ward, F. (2005), *Lifelong Learning: Theological Education and Supervision*, London: SCM Press.

Ward, G., ed. (2005), *The Blackwell Companion to Postmodern Theology*, Oxford: Blackwell.

Ward, G. (2006), 'The Future of Religion', *Journal of the American Academy of Religion*, 74:1, pp. 179–86.

Ward, G. (2009), *The Politics of Discipleship: Becoming Postmaterial Citizens*, London: SCM Press.

Ward, P. (2002), *Liquid Church*, Carlisle: Paternoster Press.

Ward, P. (2008), *Participation and Mediation: A Practical Theology for the Liquid Church*, London: SCM Press.

Ward, P. (2011), *Gods Behaving Badly: Media, Religion and Celebrity Culture*, London: SCM Press.

Ward, P. (2017), *Liquid Ecclesiology: The Gospel and the Church*, Leiden: Brill.

Warner, R. (2007), 'York's Evangelicals and Charismatics: An Emergent Free Market in Voluntarist Religious Identities', in Kim, S. and Kollontai, P., eds, *Community Identity: Dynamics of Religion in Context*, London: T & T Clark, pp. 183–202.

Warner, R. (2010), *Secularization and Its Discontents*, London: Continuum.

Warren, Y. (2002), *The Cracked Pot: The State of Today's Anglican Parish Clergy*, Stowmarket: Kevin Mayhew.

Watson, N. (2002), *Introducing Feminist Ecclesiology*, Sheffield Academic Press; Cleveland, OH: Pilgrim Press.

Wells, S. and Coakley, S., eds (2008), *Praying for England: Priestly Presence in Contemporary Culture*, London: Continuum.

Wenger, E. (1998), *Communities of Practice*, Cambridge: Cambridge University Press.

Williams, D. (2015), 'Pietism and Faith-Learning Integration in the Evangelical University', in Gehrz, C., ed., *The Pietist Vision of Christian Higher Education*, Downers Grove IL: InterVarsity Press, pp. 35–51.

Williams, J. A. (1986), 'Church, Religion and Secularization in the Theology of Christian Radicalism, 1960-69: Critical Perspectives from the Sociology of Religion', unpublished PhD thesis, University of Durham.

Williams, J. A. (1998), 'Towards Diversity: Renewing the Church's Ministry', *Anvil*, Vol. 15, no. 1, pp. 41–51.

Williams, J. A. (2000), 'Set Apart?', *Ministry*, Vol. 2, Edition 4.

Williams, J. A. (2002), 'Local Ministry: Subversion or Solution?', *Ministry*, Vol. 2, Edition 10, pp. 7–8.

Williams, J. A. (2004), 'Towards a People's Church', *Modern Believing*, Vol. 45.2, pp. 27–46.

Williams, J. A. (2010), 'Ministry and Praxis', *Discourse*, Vol. 9, no. 2, pp. 183–92.

Williams, J. A. (2011), '21st Century Shapes of the Church?', *Theology*, Vol. 114, no. 2, pp. 108–19.

Williams, J. A. (2013), 'Conflicting Paradigms in Theological Education for Public Ministry in the Church of England: Issues for Church and Academy', *International Journal of Public Theology*, Vol. 7.3, pp. 275–96.

Williams, J. A. (2015), 'Ecclesial Reconstruction, Theological Conservation: The Strange Exclusion of Critical Theological Reflection from Popular Strategies for the Renewal of the Church in Britain', *Ecclesiology*, Vol. 11, pp. 289–305.

Williams, J. A. (2016), 'In Search of "Fresh Expressions of Believing" for a Mission-shaped Church', *Ecclesiology*, Vol. 12, pp. 279–97.

Williams, J. A. (2018), 'Ecclesianarchy: Excursions into Deconstructive Church', *Ecclesial Practices*, Vol. 5, pp. 121–37.

Williams, R. (1984), 'Women and the Ministry: A Case for Theological Seriousness', in Furlong, M., ed., *Feminine in the Church*, London: SPCK, pp. 11–27.

Williams, R. C. (2018), *A Theology for Chaplaincy: Singing Songs in a Strange Land*, Cambridge: Grove Books.

Willmer, H., ed. (1992), *20/20 Visions: The Futures of Christianity in Britain*, London: SPCK.

Wilson, B. (1966), *Religion in Secular Society: A Sociological Comment*, Harmondsworth: Penguin Books.

Wister, R., ed. (1990), *Priests: Identity and Ministry*, Wilmington, DE: Michael Glazier.

Woods, T. (2009), *Beginning Postmodernism*, Manchester: Manchester University Press.

Worthen, J. (2012), *Responding to God's Call: Christian Formation Today*, Norwich: Canterbury Press.

Youngs, J. W. T. (2003, orig. pub. 1981), 'The Social Impact of Puritanism', in Barraclough, G., ed. (1981), *The Christian World: A Social and Cultural History of Christianity*, London: Thames & Hudson, pp. 201–14.

Zahl, D. (2019), *Seculosity: How Career, Parenting, Technology, Food, Politics, and Romance Became Our New Religion and What to Do about It*, Minneapolis, MN: Fortress Press.

Zizioulas, J. D. (1985), *Being as Communion: Studies in Personhood and the Church*, New York: St Vladimir's Seminary Press.

Index of Names and Subjects